MANILA JOHN

★ ★ ★

THE LIFE AND COMBAT ACTIONS OF
MARINE GUNNERY SERGEANT JOHN BASILONE
HERO OF GUADALCANAL AND IWO JIMA

by Joseph A. Grasso

RoseDog ✿ Books

PITTSBURGH, PENNSYLVANIA 15222

ISBN: 978-1-4349-9946-7

Printed in the United States of America

First Printing

For information or to order additional books, please write:
RoseDog Books
701 Smithfield St.
Pittsburgh, PA 15222
U.S.A.
1-800-834-1803
www.rosedogbookstore.com

ENDORSEMENTS

Joe Grasso has given us a splendid combat biography of an iconic American hero, Gunnery Sergeant John Basilone. In it, there is a fine quote from former New York City Mayor Jimmy Walker made after John came home from Guadalcanal: "We can learn from him what a precious privilege you and I have to be citizens of this great country." "Manila John" had three great loves which literally were his life: Sergeant Lena Mae Riggi, who became his wife in July 1944; his wonderful family from Raritan, New Jersey, who raised a tough, humble, religious and very fine man; and his Marines, who he inspired and who also inspired him. Marines will always remember Manila John, who refused to stay home after the terrific combat that resulted in his Medal of Honor. Manila John's third love was his Marines, who were his calling to teach and to lead, to train them for war and take care of them in battle. When the going got tough on Guadalcanal and again on Iwo Jima, Manila John literally stood up and this tough Marine got his men going."

General Robert Magnus
Assistant Commandant,
United States Marine Corps

★   ★   ★

Finally! After so many years—Gunnery Sergeant John Basilone's story. His heroism was instrumental to turning the tide of war at Guadalcanal thus becoming a Marine Corps Medal of Honor icon. As the legendary Chesty Puller before him, Basilone walked fearlessly on that beach at Iwo Jima among his young Marines who were held captive and prone, pinned down by Japanese fire. He called to them to move forward, off the beach thus sending them to safety. Grasso's carefully written narrative gives us Basilone's poignant story in all its depth.

James Kallstrom
Marine Corps Captain, Vietnam Era

Cofounder and Chairman, Marine Corps
Law Enforcement Foundation (MCLEF.org))

Assistant Director in Charge, FBI,
New York Division

Director of Public Security,
State of New York

Counter-Terrorism Planning Director,
State of New York, Point of Contact
with White House Office of Homeland Security

Senior Advisor for Counter-Terrorism to the Governor, New York State

★   ★   ★

John Basilone's story—a Marine Corps legend. He was one of our nation's first real hero of World War II. Here is his story with all its glory and pain. The reader will truly come to know of Basilone's instinctive courage. But, more than that, he will come to know John Basilone as one of those restless young American children of the depression years who answered his country's call to service. It is the story of a Marine who truly contributed decisively to turn the tide of battle in the Solomon Islands and, hence, the war in the Pacific. Joe Grasso has achieved even more. He presents Basilone's story as definition of the Marine Corps-bravery, fidelity and death before dishonor.

Harvey C. "Barney" Barnum, Col.. USMC (Ret.)
Deputy Assistant Secretary of the Navy
Medal of Honor Recipient, Vietnam

DEDICATION

The Marine Corps was his vocation. Some are destined to it. Before there was time, before there was life, before there was John, when John became John, touched by heaven before his birth, he was to be with them. The yearning desperate force within him transcended time. As Moses clasped the Tablet, he reached out for his destiny. He was to be with them always.

To the Corps

Eighty-one Marines won Medals of Honor
during World War II. John Basilone was the
only one to win it, then return
to war and die in battle.

Basilone is the only enlisted Marine to have been
awarded both the Medal of Honor and Navy Cross in World War II.

John Basilone is the only Medal of Honor winner for
whom a parade is held each year.

★　　　★　　　★

"Roosevelt and Churchill had years to change
history—Basilone did it in one day."

- From Charles Herbek's *A Marine's Marine*

[The Marine] "who turned the tide of the war."

- Look Magazine

"John Basilone is a one-man army."

- Douglas MacArthur

"One of the truly epic stories of the South Pacific campaign, the story of a New
Jersey tailor's son who held a strategic machine post for three days and three
nights without rest or food against a Japanese regiment"

- Associated Press

ACKNOWLEDGEMENTS

Very special thanks must go to businessman, and Raritan, New Jersey friend, Ed Danberry, for his Marine Corps liaison work that led to making this book a reality, and for his manuscript reviews and untiring, on-going, willingness to assist in every way possible.

My sincere thanks to:

General Robert Magnus, Assistant Commandant of the United States Marine Corps.

Former Marine Corps Captain and Newark FBI Office Director James Kallstrom.

Marine Corps Colonel (Ret.), Deputy Assistant Secretary of the Navy and Medal of Honor recipient Harvey C. "Barney" Barnum,

Former Marine and author Chuck Tatum for kindly opening his files to me, without which, this book would not have been possible.

For their endorsements of this book

Annette Amerman at the Marine Corps Museum for her assistance during my research there.

Master Sergeant Jack Giancaspro, USAF (Ret.), Sergeant Howard M. Stark, USMC (Ret.), and Susan Danberry for kindly reviewing the manuscript and making necessary corrections.

Mr. Craig Turpin, Executive Editor, The Reporter (The Somerset Messenger Gazette) for allowing the re-printing of much of John's narrative and for photos from the Messenger Gazette library.

Barbara Garner, Lena Basilone's dearest friend, for kindly providing letters from John's buddies, news clippings and information regarding the Basilone Freeway in California.

Mr. and Mrs. Grady Peek, friends of Lena Basilone, for providing photos and copies of John's letters to Lena during that critical interval of time between their marriage and John's landing at Iwo Jima .

Mr. Phil Hernandez and Richard Greer, John's Marine Corps buddies for providing invaluable input.

Bill Keegan, author of *Closure: The Untold Story of the Ground Zero Recovery Mission* for his very kind assistance in acquiring the publication of this book

Joseph Monti, award-winning history teacher, broadcaster and well-known New Jersey historian for his dedication to John's memory.

To my wife, Karen, for her kind urging during times of discouragement.

A NOTE FROM THE AUTHOR

Some psychologists have said that if heroes truly knew that their heroic acts would lead to death, they would be repulsed into inaction. One might wonder though whether this is really just an academic question. By dismissing their self-sacrifice so easily, perhaps the conscience is eased of another question. Would we have had their courage? Admittedly, then, we may not allow ourselves to believe that there are those who will lay down their lives for their brothers.

Actions of heroism are numerous. For example, did those servicemen—and there were many—that did thrust themselves down onto live grenades to protect their buddies do so instinctively? Surely they must have known, even in that microsecond of time, after so much training and combat experience that death would be the consequence of their action.

But then there are those who are possessed by an intense restlessness, that yearning to go beyond themselves that can never be explained completely. It drives them beyond even their own comprehension. Perhaps it is this internal strife which defines the zenith, the ideal manifestation of heroism as embraced by the American character. Faith, absolute self-confidence, and total immersion in the moment consistently fire them forward. From author, Joanna Russ:

> Faith is not, contrary to the usual ideas, something that turns out to be right or wrong, like a gambler's bet; it's an act, an intention, a project, something that makes you, leaping into the future, go so far, far, far ahead that you shoot clean out of time and right into Eternity, which is not the end of time or a whole lot of time, but timelessness, that old Eternal Now.

Here is where we find John Basilone. He is that blend of Italian-American ethnic pride, love of home, family, country and American idealism and resourcefulness. It is hoped that the reader will gain some understanding—and *feeling*, if you will, of that unexplainable unknowable soul of the hero. For it is within John Basilone that we find that indefinable quality of resolve and courage that epitomizes the American soldier. One can perhaps even say that he was *born* to be one, and maybe, just maybe, he was just supposed to be where he found himself—on Guadalcanal and Iwo Jima.

As he was a son to those who nurtured him, John was a son of the Corps, guided by the present moment as duty and honor dictated. And that moment for him was *embodied* in the Corps. John was first and always, a Marine. Always the Corps.

Semper Fi, John.

INTRODUCTION

In conjunction with the John Basilone Parade held each year in Raritan, New Jersey, John's hometown, one will usually find local news articles outlining John's combat actions. Through the years there have been stories written about John in various periodicals and, of course, the Marine Corps publications. Authors such as Eric Hammel in his very fine book, *Guadalcanal, Starvation Island*, and Richard Frank in his finely detailed *Guadalcanal, the Definitive Account of the Landmark Battle*, do mention Basilone's significant contribution to the decisive winning battle for Henderson Field. Charles "Chuck" Tatum, in his *Red Blood Black Sand*, a first hand graphic account of the Marine Corps' bloody sacrifices on Iwo Jima, speaks of John's heroic actions there as no other has, or perhaps, can. Indeed, Tatum, who was mentored by Basilone in machine gun operation, can and does speak with authority regarding John's expertise and ability to teach young marines thoroughly in the operation of the 30-caliber light machine gun. But he further speaks of John's respect and genuine caring for the young men learning and fighting under his leadership. Tatum's insightful A & E documentary on Basilone gives us a real sense of who John Basilone really was. He is Tatum's genuine "Soldier of the Sea." Most of the combat action at Iwo Jima herein contained is quoted directly from his *Red Blood Black Sand* with permission. The most recent book by Jim Prosner, *I'm Staying With My Boys, The Heroic Life of Sgt. John Basilone, USMC*, does grandly capture John's personality through first–person narrative style and is certainly a work to be read by anyone desiring to know John Basilone more intimately.

With the above considered it was this author's desire to at last have the most complete story of John Basilone's life and heroism placed between the covers of one book. John and our country, especially our youth, are entitled to that effort.

Herein are presented for the first time excerpts from John's letters to Lena following their marriage when John was at Camp Pendleton and onboard his transport on the way to Iwo Jima. These are, then, his last known writings.

While doing research at the Marine Corps Historical Center, Washington, DC, the author discovered "The John Basilone Story," by Phyllis Basilone Cutter, John's now-deceased sister. This is a running narrative from Basilone's letters to his family compiled by Phyllis Basilone and presented in episode format beginning in November1962 by the Somerset Messenger Gazzette, a weekly news publication headquartered in Somerville, New Jersey, only a mile from John's hometown. Certainly Phyllis did not transcribe the letters totally verbatim, but did edit to allow the narrative to flow.

With permission I have excerpted much of John's narrative placing it in chapter format within the Pacific War scene thereby offering some setting if you will. John's narrative ends just before the beginning of the Iwo Jima conflict. Although it is not within the scope of this work to immerse the reader in the totality of the Pacific Islands campaign, it is believed that a true understanding of Basilone's contribution can be achieved only by placing his combat actions within some historical context.

It should be mentioned at the outset that the machine gunner's lot is a lonely and dangerous one, perhaps the most dangerous during any firefight. His position is the most threatening to any well-trained enemy army so to knock him out is key to advancement. Indeed, the machine gun is the firepower heart of the defensive infantry platoon. At night the machine gunner is especially vulnerable. His position is the first observed by the enemy; every fifth round in the belt is a tracer round clearly displaying the muzzle flash. He fires at 500 to 600 roounds per minute creating an almost straight-line pathway back from the enemy's advance. Johnnie M. Clark a machine gunner in Vietnam, in his book Gunner's Glory, speaks from first-hand experience,

> "….the machine gunner is not only the one visible target but the most important. You know that truth every single time you pull the trigger. You know every enemy soldier will see your posiiton the instant you open fire. The gunner knows that the enemy will throw everything they have at him—mortars, rockets, artillery, grenades, satchel charges, rifle and machine gunfire. I served as a gunner with the famed 5th Marine Regiment.
> During my tour with the 5th Marines, I knew of no machine gunner in the regiment who was not killed or wounded. Many were wounded more than once. It was the same for every Marine gunner no matter which war they were fighting.

Basilone's heroic combat action on that October 24th night on Guadalcanal has been described by many in various publications. I have endeavored to get to John's real movements that night by first examining his running narrative that, we must remember, was put together after his death from his letters, by his sister Phyllis. There follows, in comparison, some inconsistencies when one reads later narratives both from various publications, and from John himself.

It should be said at the outset that contrary to much writing about John having been the first enlisted Marine to receive the Medal of Honor in World II, he was not. He was the second. The first was Sergeant Clyde Tomanson for his heroic combat actions on Makin Island on August 17, 1942 during the Marine Raiders' raid there. His medal was awarded posthumously. Basilone was the first enlisted man to receive the Medal of Honor and, after receiving it, return to combat. Following immediately after Basilone, Marine 1st Lieutenant George Cannon received the Medal of Honor at Midway on December 7, 1942. More significantly, as this book will evidence, John Basilone was America's first nationally recognized hero of World War II.

In 2004 Basilone was included among perhaps the three most "Distinguished Marines," in all of history, for whom, a US Postal Stamp was issued.* There, on that same sheet of stamps, appears John Basilone with those other Marines of such great stature—Lejeune, "Chesty" Puller and Dan Daly.

Some have commented on, wondered about, and, in some cases, even caustically criticized John's decision to return to battle after receiving the Medal of Honor and after being recognized by a grateful nation as a true hero of the time. We must consider that John Basilone had, as other servicemen and women, taken an oath to serve and protect the United States as induction into the armed services dictated. "To serve and protect" had intense meaning to John Basilone. He was a Marine. When he said to the commandant, "Sir, I want the fleet," thereby requesting a return to combat in 1944, he was declaring that he was duty bound to do the job he was trained to do. It was really that simple to him. He confided to his new wife that he knew "those kids" landing on the beaches of the South Pacific would need his leadership in order to survive the battle to take place there.

Prosner fixes a scene for us. Basilone has arrived at Long Beach, California, after receiving his medal. He looked about him as he rode to his next assignment at Terminal Island and gazed at the wartime industry booming at the port area. Prosner quotes him as saying:

> As long as these cranes and ships were working, that was the important thing, and my face being in the papers was all tied up with that now. It wouldn't help the new Carolina or Pennsylvania boys in the 1/7 to know what a Jap Nambu machine gun sounded like when it jammed so they could move safely, or remind them that Japs sometimes used firecrackers to draw their fire and reveal their position, or that the Japs threw smoke grenades and then yelled, "Gas attack!" which was all bullshit, or teach them a thousand other tricks to keep them from getting their asses shot off....

Ernie Pyle, correspondent, who "went back" and lost his life, said after leaving the European Theater of Operations, "I have had it. If I hear one more shot, or see one more dead man, I'll go off my nut." But he was drawn to it; it pulled him in and before he knew it he was in the Pacific. He said then,

> Of course I am very sick of war and would like to leave it, and yet I know I can't. I've been part of the misery and tragedy of it so long that I've come to feel a responsibility to it or something. I don't quite know how to put it into words, but I feel if I left it now it would be like a soldier deserting....I have known all the time I was going back. I have got to go, and I hate it.

---

* See "A Grateful Nation Remembers" at end of book.

He *had* to be with them— those who had been ordinary American citizens, but now were soldiers. And they, in a sense, needed him, too. Ernie Pyle's dilemma was John Basilone's dilemma.

Charles Tatum recalls:

> It hardly seems very long ago, when in January, 1944, I was the first Marine to enter the empty barracks of the Fifth Division, B Company, 1st Battalion, 27th Marines, at Camp Pendleton, California, where our new unit would be formed. John Basilone was the first NCO to arrive and we made up the whole company for several days. From the day I met him, I was a confirmed John Basilone watcher.

Perhaps Chuck Tatum says it all: "I discovered in these long years of research, I was not alone in my adoration. Millions once revered him as a glittering example of a wartime hero, but those who knew him on a personal basis revere him as a man and a Marine—not because he was a worthy recipient of the Medal of Honor."

So it is hoped that the heroic combat actions of this lone figure in our nation's history will be seen as contributing decisively to winning the war in the Pacific. It is without question that John's combat actions did save countless lives of those who fought at, and would come after, the Battle for Henderson Field, and of those who would have remained trapped on the beach at Iwo Jima. So even after these many years I, too, am a "confirmed John Basilone watcher," and as his buddy, Nash Phillips said, "I'll never forget him. He'll never be dead in my mind."

PROLOGUE

The ball arced high and long, but too wide to the right as it plunged to earth far short of the green. The eighteen-year-old caddie smiled to himself as the Japanese businessman cursed. His partner laughed openly as the three progressed down the fairway. The caddie knew the Raritan Valley Country Club course like the back of his hand and had inwardly predicted the drive's direction after studying the man's follow-through from the first tee. The caddie was quite an accomplished golfer himself.

He listened with increasing curiosity as the pair talked together in their foreign tongue. They had previously played the course, but he had not caddied for them until today. Now, up close, he studied them. They were on his turf, here in Raritan, New Jersey, and they were strange to him. In a town of predominantly Italian-Americans sprinkled with Irish, Polish, Slovak and a few Jewish families he could not help but wonder about them. He remembered the world maps at St. Bernard's grammar school that the sisters had forced him to study and had pictured their country somewhere on the other side of the world with shores on the Pacific Ocean.

He had no reason to dislike his two patrons as they chatted to each other amiably and, in sorry struggle with the English language, even attempted to include him in conversation. The two jovial sportsmen exuded oriental charm and humility as they allowed other more practiced golfers to play through. And the huge tips they offered during these post-depression days were very much appreciated. Our young caddie, always concerned about his family's financial well being, looked forward to carrying their bags and the extra cash it would bring.

He was proud of his little hometown and loved the people there. He believed that these men liked the area too as they gestured to him with arms outstretched toward the beautiful countryside. To the south the white steeple of the First Reformed Church was plainly visible. Further south the historic Raritan River meandered with its Tom Sawyer-like fascination where mules once towed barges there along the towpath that ran between the river and canal. The scenic river area had been home to tobacco baron and Duke University founder, James Buchanan Duke. Before 1925, the year of his death, 2000 acres surrounding the Raritan River had been named Duke Farm where he created a literal fairy tale land of lakes, fountains and gardens. Visitors from around the country traveled there to ride the beautifully placed roadways that wove through this magnificent estate. Following his death Buchanan's daughter, Doris, inherited the estate and further enhanced its beauty.

So the caddie could not have been suspicious as one of his golfers snapped pictures of the panoramic view before them. And that view was very interest-ing to them indeed—especially to the south. There, now, as they gazed in that direction, the steam trail and whistling of the east bound racing locomotive betrayed the afternoon serenity. The Central Jersey Rail Road system carried freight from points west through the Central Jersey corridor link to the Newark Bay area. There, PT Boats and landing craft would soon be built, and from there ocean-going vessels would carry precious cargoes across the Atlantic to America's allies.

But this was the autumn of 1935 and the young caddie was becoming bored. Restlessness stirred within him as the leaves began to fall, and a yearning for adventure gnawed at him. Having been a rather poor student, school was not even considered an option.

Now, as the trio approached the last hole he was becoming fatigued. No doubt it was the heat and the heavy weight of the golf bags that caused trickles of sweat to course down his back. But there was something more. As he fought the increasing weakness, he began to pick up an undertone to the periodically quieted conversation his two golfers were having. Their gestures toward town were now strangely more concentrated. Down deep within his being there was something about these men that caused his stomach to tighten. Were they *too* accommodating? Was there something disingenuous in their eyes?

Was this to be the genesis of an acute instinctive awareness about others like them? But here and now there flashed through him a twinge of eeriness. Within him, as he stood on the edge of that enormous expanse of the cultural divide between him and them, there was a fleeting ominous anxiety that chilled him to the bone. Then it was gone.

Understand folks, I had no idea that I would ever be up for the Congressional Medal of Honor. All I did was to follow out orders, "Hold until you are killed." Well, we held, thanks to my buddies.

CHAPTER 1

Salvatore Basilone was born in Benevento, Italy, a short distance from Naples, on December 24, 1884 and came to the United States in 1903 at the age of 19. As with most other Italian immigrants of the day he came to America with the skills of a trade and an intense desire to find greater success in a new land. Living in Raritan, New Jersey, he was to meet Theodora Bengivenga, born in the United States on February 20, 1889 in Raritan, the daughter of Naples-born mill worker Carlo Bengivenga and his wife Catrina.

Salvatore, working as a tailor's assistant was able to save some money, so the couple married after three years of dating and moved into the Bengivenga family home, a spacious Victorian built in 1858 at 113 First Avenue and purchased by them in 1901. There, "Dora" gave birth to five children, Phyllis, Angelo, Catherine, Mary and Carlo during those earlier years of their marriage. Sadly, their first son, Angelo, was to die at age one during a dysentery epidemic. As was the custom in those days the name of the deceased male child was given to the next male child born. So there followed, Phyllis, Angelo, Catherine, Mary, Carlo and John Francis, who was born on November 4, 1916.

Salvatore remained, however, in generally poor health during these years and he was finding it difficult to make a good living in Raritan during that time, so he moved his family to Buffalo, New York, with a desire to own his own business. He became an American citizen there and was finally able to open a tailor shop on the U.S. side of Niagara Falls.

After John's birth the family returned to Raritan and lived on Anderson Street* for a while, but soon they moved back into the Bengivenga family home, which had now become a two-family house, and remained there for the rest of their married lives. After some time Salvatore's health miraculous improved and he was able to open a tailor shop in Somerville at 10 East Main Street, about a mile or so away. Dora soon gave birth to Alphonse, George, Dolores and Donald. By this time Salvatore had moved his business a short distance to 13 South Bridge Street in Somerville.

Eventually Dora's parents moved to another home in Raritan and Dora's brother John and wife Josephine moved into the added half of the family home.

As most immigrant sons of the day, Salvatore believed deeply in America and instilled that love of country into his children. He called the United States the "greatest country in the world." He was a quiet man who worked hard during those Great Depression days and tried to give his children a better life than his own.

---

* The home located not far from the author's.

1

Wanting their son to have a religious education, the Basilones sent John to St. Bernard's school in Raritan, not far from their home.

Normally shy and quiet, John would infrequently have a bad temper. If one looked deeply within though, the view would reveal a blend of cheerfulness and intense determination. But always present was the smile mated with an incessant gleam in his eye disclosing the tempered tempest within. Raging deep inside was a perpetual windstorm, warmed with sunshine that would consistently propel him. At seven years of age John decided to challenge the basic instincts of a bull which roamed a local pasture. Surely the bull could be tamed, he thought. With planned approach he crept cautiously toward the animal. Although the bull's fearsome size became more apparent as the young man came nearer he continued on. Finally, when the bull's tolerance of the boy's impudence diminished, he moved slowly, but steadily forward and threw young John a good distance. The young man was thereby cured of his obsession to tame the bull.

John's happy-go-lucky youth was filled with baseball and swimming. The little town of Raritan with its meandering river and surrounding wooded paths presented a Tom Sawyer world to John and his friends. It was the ideal place for Salvatore and Dora Basilone to raise their ten children. In those days a young Raritan boy dared not stray far from proper attitudes and behavior, for if his parents were not aware of his foolishness neighbors and parents of peers would be, and the harsh word of reprimand would soon take hold. When he was ten there came a day when his friend was jumped by two local toughs guys. Young John finished the fight very easily.

John was not a serious student at St. Bernard's School, even with the prodding of Sister Mary Cordula. But there was something about John that attracted her. He was different. His quiet, shy, respectful manner was ever present, even with the mischief. There was a sweetness about him. Many years later, after Guadalcanal, she would write to him and remind him of those days at St. Bernard's school. That letter will appear later in this book.

At his eighth grade graduation in 1932, the school's mimeographed "Year Book" would say of John, "the most talkative boy in his class." But his classmates would say, "He has quite a winning way." For misconduct the students at St. Bernard's, in addition to having their knuckles rapped, would have "ten points" deducted from their school grade for the week. This did not concern John at all. He would simply say, "Take them all off."

But as a boy John preferred more adventurous days, days of stealing apples with his gang at the local orchards, swimming in the Raritan River and running through the Duke Estate. When Dora heard of John's apple stealing, she said years later, "I slapped him good." But this was to no avail. John loved the excitement of the game so he would soon be back with his friends executing further raids at the orchards. He became very good at planning the operations involving the posting of lookouts and fast getaways. Soon, by hitchhiking, the attack plan was carried miles away to orchards far from home.

When not plundering for apples during the mid-1920's, John and his boyhood friends could be seen at the local movie theater hissing, catcalling and stomping their feet during the silent Tom Mix cowboy films and serials at the *Empire Theater* just a half-mile from John's home. The *Empire Theater* closed later on in the 1930's, but it was opened again in the early 1940's re-named *The Raritan Playhouse.* The 10 cents admission in those days was beyond some of the boys so that problem was solved by opening the side doors from the inside after one of the crew got inside. The fun popcorn throwing started and poor Miss Traynor, the piano player, was right in the middle of it.

He loved to slip out of the house and run down to the Raritan River to go skinny-dipping with Carmine Corona and the rest of his buddies at "Bare Ass Beach." Other places at the river were named, like "The Ropes," where the boys would swing out into the water from ropes strung from trees, and further up-stream the "New Dam." The police, in most cases, did not bother the boys, knowing that they did not cause harm to anyone. John's father would become distressed, however, when John "borrowed" his gun and went out hunting or shooting cans in the woods.

Carlo, John's older brother, told that he and John would play baseball in a field that was located across the street from their home. John liked playing golf, too, and it became a favorite pastime for him as the years went by.

His sister Phyllis recalls:

> *From the very first Johnny was different. He could not seem to buckle down to even ordinary study and by the time he had reached the eighth grade he had made up his mind that high school was not for him. He was to regret this later on. However, at the time no one could convince him to enter high school. My parents were very much upset over his attitude. No amount of pleading could change Johnny's mind. In the end we had to give in, much as we knew how difficult it would be for him to obtain work with only a grammar school education.*

CHAPTER 2

He stared through the Pullman car window transfixed by the dizzying scene. Chicago's busy rail interchange had long since faded away and he sat comfortably on the West Coast Limited. The telephone poles flashing by seemed to frame the images-houses, farms, the countryside, all of what he always knew was there around him. But now it all took on a new significance. A new realization of its beauty took hold of him, and now he felt the smallness of his being within the scene. How much there was to care about—home, family.

His mind wandered into a hypnotic listlessness. "Johnny, you're crazy, you're only a kid. There's no war. Why do you want to join the Army?" Papa had said. It was unusual for him, and his sister Phyllis had sensed that something was wrong. They all knew he was unhappy. And that he had been looking for work, but caddying, at least, seemed to have subdued his restlessness. Those days of caddying and poker and the Raritan Valley Country Club rolled through his mind. There, in that old root cellar that had once been a part of an old farmhouse, but now the club house, young John Basilone, like his brother Carlo, played cards. And he played cards endlessly. If he wasn't caddying, it was pinocle or poker. As he said many times later, card playing at the caddyshack would be prep for those many games played later in the Army and Marine Corps.

From Jim Prosner's *The Heroic Life of Sgt. John Basilone, USMC*:

> *The math of cards taught me. That's the only way I can explain it. I could figure the odds and read people a whole lot better than I could read a textbook. If they had made a way to teach lessons with card games I would have done a lot better in school. I wasn't much of a talker anyway, so cards suited me. I could sit quietly for a long time in the company of the caddies, some young and some old duffers, who had been through a lot in their own ways. I could slip in questions that got them to talk about how they figured out what they were supposed to do in life. Mostly, it was a lot of baloney because, after all, they'd wound up sitting in this root cellar with me all day.*
>
> *…We put in a potbelly stove and had our very own gentlemen's card club, complete with an ice box, a sink, garden tools, a few hundred-pound bags of fertilizer for the putting greens. We feathered our gambler's nest with a cast off couch and a reading lamp. We were planning to keep the game going until spring, and I believe many of the original members made it. I didn't.*

5

But this Army thing, it came right out of the blue. The whole family was stunned.

"Papa, the depression has been rough. There aren't any jobs out there, " he responded, "maybe when I get out things will be better."

The thought of him leaving the family at such a young age frightened them so they all took a hand at trying to convince him that he was wrong and that he should reconsider. So the days following John's announcement were somber ones at the Basilone home. Dora prayed for something to happen which would change his mind. But it was no use. He became even more determined. He had made up his mind.

"O, solo mio," John sang in a mellow tone as he entered the kitchen. Dora could not laugh as she usually did. She only shook her head as she wiped her eyes with the bottom of her apron. He knew she was hurting so he sang all the more as he wrapped his arms around her.

"Mama, don't worry. Everything will be okay," he assured her. He was compelled to his decision. A new life was calling him, and he yearned for the adventure and excitement he instinctively felt would be waiting for him. So finally, after a few days Salvatore signed the enlistment papers for his seventeen-year-old son.

Now it seemed like ages ago. He was headed for San Diego and basic training. But he was still sad remembering how Dora had cried when he left the house that morning.

Again, from Phyllis:

> *It seemed only a short time when Johnny left heading for the railroad station and the trip to Newark. He had insisted on saying good-by at home. All this time Mama had prayed that something might happen to change things. When Johnny kissed her* good-by *she realized he was actually leaving. All her pent up emotion gave way and she broke down completely. Seeing Mama break down tore at our hearts and Johnny leapt from the porch and headed down First Avenue. I know he was crying as he hardly turned when he waved good-by. We waved until he crossed the rise at the railroad tracks and disappeared from view. Going back into the house, which seemed empty already, we all had a good cry.*

CHAPTER 3

n February 5, 1936 John Basilone enlisted in the United States Army. He was off to seek the adventure that the recruiting posters promised.

Well, sis, I'm on my way. I wonder if this is really what I want; everybody's advice is still ringing in my ears. Do you remember Pop bidding me good-by on the porch? He stood erect and proud and said, "Johnny, I let you go. I tell you only one thing. You do what the Army tells you. You do good. Remember, Basilone is a good name with much honor in the old country. Keep our name high."

Sis, how is Mom? Tell her I love her and miss her very much, and oh yes, sometime when you're alone with Pop, tell him for me that he'll never regret giving me his consent. Tell him no matter what, the Basilone name will always be held high.

Gosh, the swearing-in ceremony was short and to the point. I'm in the Army now. The group of us were herded into buses for the quick trip to Pennsylvania Station in New York. Arriving at this tremendous station, our sergeant for the trip counted noses as we filed out of the buses and stood at attention on the sidewalk. To the curious onlookers we must have presented quite a sight as we marched through the station, down the steps to the lower level where our train lay waiting.

I was anxious for a window seat as I had never traveled much before and did not want to miss the view. Approaching the vestibule of the Pullman car, I broke and ran for a window seat, which, fortunately, I got. In a few minutes I heard the conductor's "all aboard," the "peep-peep" of the signal cord and we were on our destined ways.

Gliding silently we entered the the long tunnel under 33rd Street into the blackness that was the hole under the North River, once more to emerge into daylight. I looked around at the vast swampy meadows of Secaucus rushing past my window. To my right, standing aloof, was Snake Hill. Jersey City swept by and it seemed only minutes before we were breaking into the station at Newark.

The passengers boarding the train at Newark seemed disappointed that they could not enter our Pullman, not knowing that the Army had taken over.

Leaving Newark, our porter unlocked the doors. I did not want to leave my window seat for fear of losing it. I sat and watched as the towns slid by. Some of the boys had a poker game going. I would have liked to join them but was short on money. In the lounge room I heard there was a big crap game rolling; evidently all the boys were not as broke as I was.

Hours dragged on and I decided that by now the window seat was mine. I could chance leaving it to stretch my legs and give the balance of the train a once-over. I had sampled the food in the diner, it was good, the service was excellent, but it was not enough. I kept my eyes open for a vendor passing through the cars. Catching one, I bought some chocolate bars and my favorite peanut brittle. Heading back for our Pullman I got into my seat, hunched back and munched on the goodies. So far so good.

Reaching Chicago, Illinois, we passed over a maze of tracks and had a tiresome three-hour lay-over waiting for the West Coast Limited. Finally we were made a part of this supertrain and headed westward. Looking back, the huge buildings and skyscrapers of Chicago faded into the distance as our train picked up speed.

As I watched the countryside passing by, milepost after milepost, I was amazed and felt small indeed as the vast panorama spread itself before my eyes. I had never been on such a long trip. I soaked up the ever-changing landscape like a dry sponge, for which, during the dark and anxious days still to come, I thanked God, because it gave me strength when I needed it most. Just to feel that I was a tiny part of a vast country that we all more or less take for granted, until we sense the danger of losing it, was the spark that kept us going in the face of odds that seemed insurmountable.

So, you see, folks, we young-uns do think seriously on occasions. I'll admit not too often, but we do.

The arrival at San Diego, California was quiet. After a few days of getting settled and outfitted, we started our basic training. The next few days gave us our first real taste of Army life. It was one continuous round of training, marching, drilling, so dog-tired at night we had just enough strength to tumble into our bunks. We were growing, filling out, and, before we knew it, basic was over.

It is well known that for Basilone, unlike the other recruits, basic training was an experience at which he excelled. He was determined to be the best he could be. But there was more to it. The determination was a seeking of that unknown direction to his life. He had come to the Army with that desire. What, he wondered, could propel him to a place where his restlessness could be calmed. Was this it? He would be the best he could be and he would find the answer. But in the Army, at least, he felt for the first time that sense of belonging.

After basic training Basilone was assigned to Company D, 16th Infantry Regiment and served at Fort Jay on Governor's Island, New York. Fort Jay was the first fortification built on Governors Island in New York City and is the oldest structure on the island, having been built to defend Upper New York Bay. The first series of earthen forts on the island were built in 1776 and 1794. The Americans abandoned the fort in 1776 when the British occupied New York. The fort's barracks date back to 1834, and the three 10" and one 15" Rodman cannons still in place date back to about 1861. The guns had an accurate range of about one mile.

The fort was named for one of the United States' founding fathers, John Jay, who became the first Supreme Court Justice, appointed by George Washington in 1789. It was renamed Fort Columbus at the completion of construction in 1808 since John Jay was not appreciated for assisting in the draft of the peace treaty with Great Britain. However, in 1904 the installation was again renamed Fort Jay.

The thick, low-walled structure of brick and granite situated on beautiful grounds included a small golf course where John spent time sharpening up his game. And Manhattan was right across the bay where women and good times were plentiful. It is a sure thing that John spent many a weekend furlough there, for it can't be denied that John Basilone loved the ladies. With the fort's 35-mile proximity to Raritan, John was often home to see the family on a two or three-day pass and frequently stopped to play some golf and see his caddying comrades.

At Fort Jay Basilone discovered, to his delight, the Browning 1917A water-cooled 30- caliber machine gun. It suited him right out of the gate. He could become a part of it—and he did just that. From his sergeant's first-day introduction he loved it and soaked up every word of instruction. He was amazed at its accuracy—right on the money at 150 yards. He wanted to know all that the weapon could do and how to care for it and instinctively became highly proficient in tear down and re-assembly blindfolded. One of his buddies from New Jersey would shill for him as they hustled other machine gunners. They paid off as John completed the re-assembly a good ten seconds ahead of all of them. At Fort Jay, Basilone was the undisputed 30-caliber machine gun master.

Combat operations fascinated him. He studied the weapon's trajectory and set-up for interlocking fields of fire. Off its tripod, muscular Basilone could cradle the 36-pound gun as if it were designed for him, almost like one would carry a Browning Automatic Rifle (BAR). He would find a way to hold the sizzling hot barrel with his left hand so as not to be confined to the tripod. He would turn the gun into what he believed to be the perfect personal weapon. He knew the weapon and its power. In the knowing he believed nothing could harm him, for it would protect him.

John's initial Army enlistment came to an end on May 10, 1937. At the time the Army had a "short-term enlistment program" in effect and, for their convenience, discharges were effective after the first fifteen months. John re-enlisted for another three-year hitch the next day.

After re-enlisting John was stationed in the Philippines, assigned to Company D, 31st Infantry. The Philippines was considered great duty so the assignment was an exciting one for young, handsome dark-haired Basilone. John's sister, Mary, had said that sending money home to the family was a major concern to John. America was still recovering from the depression in those days so $21.00 per month, Pvt.'s pay, was an additional attraction to him. In the Philippines, "Pearl of the Orient," he would become a kind of movie star personality.

We were shifted over to the staging area, where we received our shots and awaited the USS Republic that was to transport us to the Philippines. We were the fortunate ones that had drawn garrison duty in the Philippines. All the old-

timers passing through the staging area on their way home had told us many tales about the islands. We were anxious to get going and see for ourselves.

CHAPTER 4

That night as I lay on my bunk, I thought of my family so far away and a wave of homesickness engulfed me. As I thought of the thousands of miles separating us, I cried, yes, I actually broke down and cried. Trying to get hold of myself I turned off the light and picked up my machine gun. Working it in the dark by the feel of my fingers, I took it apart and reassembled it. Time and again I broke the gun down and reset the parts, thinking how it felt so natural.

As a matter of fact, all during my basic our sergeant was always bringing me a machine gun that was jammed. In no time at all I'd have it working again. Maybe I thought as I kept taking the gun apart and assembling it, maybe I'll get a job as a mechanic when I get out. No, better yet, I'll buy my own place and have men working for me. With that part of my future neatly disposed of, I dropped off into a sound sleep.

The next morning right after chow our "CO" had us assemble on the parade grounds where we were subjected to one of his rare speeches. He gave us a lot of "bull" as to how we were to conduct ourselves in the Islands so as to make Uncle Sam proud of us. I remember that part particularly, because you could hear the boys snicker. Politics we knew from nothing and at that stage of the game cared less. However, he got rousing cheers when he broke the news that we would be sailing with the flood tide that night.

All leaves were cancelled and we were restricted to the base. Many of the boys took the opportunity to catch up on their mail, which I'm sorry to say most of us neglected

At eight that night we were all assembled outside our barracks with full pack and gear. With the company band striking out a military march, we briskly and bursting with pride took off for the pier where the USS Republic was berthed. As we marched up the gangplank the music grew fainter. Looking back I could see the lights of San Diego flicking on until the sky seemed to glow.

Facing the ship once more, the decks seemed to be alive with dark, shadowy figures. I found out later they were staking out their claims for the best sleeping spots. The accommodations on these military transports at best were only fair, so that sleeping below deck and heading for the tropics could make for a very uncomfortable trip.

I found that out the first night. I felt stifled and could not sleep. Slipping out of my bunk I edged to the upper deck. After considerable looking and being the target of some well-rounded cursing, I was lucky enough to find a vacant spot near the stern. Making myself as comfortable as was possible I stretched out. Looking up I could see the sky with its thousands of stars blinking, so close you felt you could reach up and touch them. Well, I thought this is better. Outside of

11

one rainy night that was my bedroom for the remainder of the trip.

Days passed and outside of one morning drill and setting-up exercises (which our dear old sergeants said were good for us), the trip was uneventful and a bit on the dull side.

Suddenly one beautiful clear Sunday morning right after mass the ship began to hum and buzz with expectancy. Scuttlebutt had it that before nightfall we would be in Manila Bay. However, on account of our late arrival we would not debark until the following morning. Just as dusk was falling the lights of Manila appeared on the horizon. The ship resounded with loud cheers as we realized the long trip was over. The vision of lithe, brown-skinned natives welcoming us ashore gave us a lift. The old pros in the outfit really laid the bull out, so that there was little sleep to be had that night.

We raised anchor with the rising of the sun over the bay and slowly steamed towards Manila. Past the Mariveles Mountains which I found out later were still the home of the pygmy Negritos. Maintaining a steady pace we slid by Corregidor, grim island fortress with its guns guarding the harbor. Corregidor at that moment was just a name. How were we to know that in a short time it would become famous for its stubborn, courageous, resistance in the face of superhuman odds?

Upon the low coast that stretches away to the distant mountains the white docks and buildings of Manila slowly took form.

By now we were gliding by the Bataan peninsula. Cavite, the big American naval base, went by our bow. Names only, but names that were to become a mark of honor and courage, written on the pages of history with the blood shed by our boys. All this was to come, but now in the dawn everything was peaceful. We were anxious to feel good old mother earth under our feet once more.

We docked early in the morning, a little disappointed at our reception. No bands or fanfare, just a few early risers. Boarding our trucks lined up on the long pier, we sped quickly to camp and were assigned to what was to be our home for the next three years.

To a youngster like me it was a good life. At least my restlessness was somewhat curbed. I know each night I discovered new muscles. Getting to sleep was no problem. I was so tired it was merely a matter of hitting the sack.

CHAPTER 5

The Spanish had ruled the Philippines since the sixteenth century having been named after King Phillip of Spain. But after America's war with Spain in 1898, the Philippine Islands became a United States protectorate. It was in that same year that Brigadier General Arthur MacArthur, father of Douglas MacArthur, was sent to the Philippines as a volunteer officer reporting to the peace keeping contingent there. With independence from Spain came rebellion and war between Spain and the United States. With the progression of the Spanish campaign, Arthur MacArthur became, shortly after February 1901, the military governor of the Philippines.

Following in his father's footsteps, Douglas MacArthur was sent to the Philippines upon graduation from West Point in June of 1903, and served there until October of 1904. It was with Filipino leader, Manuel Quezon, that MacArthur had early discussions regarding the growing threat which Japan posed in that area of the Pacific. Henry Stimson, who some years later would serve Franklin Roosevelt as Secretary of War, was, in those early days, the Governor General there.

To Arthur MacArthur the archipelego

> ...was the finest group of islands in the world. Its strategic position unexcelled by that of any other position on the globe. The China Sea, which separates it something like 750 miles from the continent, is nothing more or less than a safety moat. It lies on the flank of what might be called a position of several thousand miles of coast line; it is in the center of that position. It is therefore relatively better placed than Japan, which is on a flank, and therefore remote from the other extremity; likewise, India, on another flank. The Philippines are in the center of that position. It affords a means of protecting American interests which with the very least output of physical power, has the effect of a commanding position in itself to retard hostile action.*

Young Lieutenant Douglas MacArthur in 1906 would say, after an Asian tour which included Japan, "...It was crystal clear to me that the future and, indeed, the very existence of America, were irrevocably entwined with Asia and its island outposts." Both father and son observed first hand the deep strength

* William Manchester, *American Ceasar*

that epitomized the Japanese military character. In the mid-1920's MacArthur was to realize the potential Japanese threat to the islands as Japanese immigration throughout the islands increased. MacArthur's personal adoption of the islands was its only defense in those early days, as America had, at the time, considered the islands indefensible.

After service in the United States, MacArthur found himself placed in the Philippines in 1935 with the assigned task of establishing a Philippine defense structure. The United States Army would be the backbone of that defensive force. The Philippino Constabulary policed the islands with leadership provided by American Army officers. American Army participation lasted right into the beginning of World War II. In 1934 Manuel Quezon requested MacArthur's assistance in planning for the defense of the Philippines. Planning for the islands'defense went forth with U. S. Army presence continuing. And it is on this stage that John Basilone finds himself during his Army days in the Philippines.

Threat From the Rising Sun

Japan had indeed come a long way. The ancient years of feudalism, introversion and the strictly codified internal order were in the past. It had succumbed to the industrial age and had achieved by the 1920's a modern manufacturing base second to none in the world. Also, she had fought and won two wars with her neighbors Russia and China. But the winds of discontent blew ominously through the Japan of the 1920's as she sought to gain the national respect she deemed owed her following the first world conflict. Inherent to that socio-political struggle, was her military's fierce compulsion to racial nationalism.

Following World War I, as a reward to her participation in the war on their side, the nations of the west ceded to Japan those German island colonies in the Pacific that were to become so strategically invaluable to her. Japan's powerful Navy would soon prowl those islands seeking the food and raw materials required to sustain her and to further elevate her dominance in the Pacific. Japanese conquests in China since 1931 rankled America's feathers, and the seeds of the Pacific War to come had, by those actions, already been planted.

After taking all of Manchuria in 1931, she enjoyed the occupation of practically all of China in 1936. She skirmished with the Russians at the China / Mongolia border. The "Manchurian Incident" aroused American anger especially, since America had assumed a protective role with regard to China. The seeds of distrust between the two countries were thus planted and the conflict beginning to brew between them is heightened when Japan harassed American and British Navy units along the Yangtse and Yellow Rivers.

Japan's aggression toward China, however, is rooted much deeper. She had lost all respect for China at a much earlier date, at least back to 1912, when China's stability both economically and politically descended to a state of warlord turmoil. And Japan was deeply resentful of China's subservience to the "imperial transgressions" of the West.

The Japan of 1936 was in a state of political turmoil though, and her army had gained increasing governmental power after the assassination of the Grand Chamberlain, among others, in February 1936. The die was thus cast for extreme nationalists to take control of Japan's destiny.

Although there was some controversy in American circles as to whether Japan would attack the Philippines, it remained clear that the archipelago was on the flank of Japan's sea lanes to the Dutch East Indies where raw materials were plentiful. And Japan needed oil, rubber and tin to be sure. For some time Japanese residents, workers, tourists among others in the Philippines were constantly sending information regarding the islands' defenses to their home country. It was true, as Douglas MacArthur said, that whoever holds the Philippines holds "the key that unlocks the door to the Pacific."

CHAPTER 6

By now my natural aptitude with machine guns had become known throughout the base and I was assigned to various units to show them how to take the guns apart and reassemble them. This continual handling of the machine guns gradually became automatic and it became quite a game. The sergeant would blindfold me and I would, with no hesitation or fumbling, go through the ritual of repairing and assembling the machine guns much to the amazement of my buddies.

We had acclimated ourselves to Manila and prided ourselves on knowing our way around, even condescending to showing the gobs* on shore leave the best spots in town. Of course we rode free on the gobs. We felt we were showing them the short cuts and were entitled to what we could finagle from them. It got so whenever one of our boats docked in Manila harbor, we could actually smell the steaks at the Army and Navy Club. They served the thickest charcoal broiled filet mignons, the best French fries, plus tomato with Roquefort dressing, in the Islands.

You could make a bet that "Manila John," the nickname the gobs hung on me, would be showing them the Army and Navy Club as soon as they docked.

All in all Army life appealed to me and I enjoyed every minute with exception of the destructive typhoons sweeping in from June to October.

It was during one of the storms that spring up so suddenly that I met Lolita. I had taken refuge in a native club to escape the driving rain and wind. Being thrown together by the elements it only seemed natural that we talked. Taking her home I had a good look. What I saw I liked. She was beautiful in a breathtaking way. Fairly tall, lithe, with big black eyes and just enough of the oriental to make here stand out from other brunettes.

During the days that followed, I spent every free moment with her, seeing Manila through her eyes, the Manila that hides itself from tourists. Like the day we came upon the ramparts of the historic walled section of the city, and turned a picturesque corner of old Europe invaded by the changing Orient.

We walked through a maze of narrow streets with Spanish names. The houses joined side by side, with barred windows, overhanging second stories and stone-flagged courtyards. Among them were many churches, monasteries, government bureaus, colleges, hospitals, stores and restaurants.

Rubbing elbows one could see the monks in their lengthy cassocks, with huge crosses and rosaries. We crossed over a bridge spanning the Pasig River into the older part of Manila. A short block beyond the Escolta (a main busi-

---

* Marine-speak for "Sailors"

ness street) were the honeycomb of streets and alleyways where the great mass of the city's Chinese and Filipinos work and live.

The best part was getting back to camp and watching my buddies' eyes pop as I rehashed my experiences of the day. By now I let drop some native terms, just for kicks. Like the morning I told the boys, "So long suckers, I'm off to the Barrio," leaving them bug-eyed. They had no idea that a Barrio was a native village made up of nipa huts, built among coconut palms and other trees.

The hut itself was merely a single room with thatched sides and roof, up off the ground four or five feet on bamboo stilts. Under it the natives keep their pigs and chickens. The floor is split bamboo and never tight. In one corner is a sandbox upon which they build a fire for cooking. There is no chimney. The smoke just goes out of the windows or through the floor cracks.

In turn, I showed Lolita the harbor and surrounding coves. Like the morning we went down to the waterfront, rented a native boat and told the boy we wanted to see the "Pearl of the Orient."

He took us down Manila Bay, pointing out the big Cavite base on the lower side of the base about half way between Manila and the harbor's mouth. Past the Bataan Peninsula and Batangas, with the "Rock" (Corregidor) between the two of them and, just opposite Corregidor on Bataan, the naval base in Mariveles harbor. Rounding the coast from Mariveles we put into Sisiman Cove for a native dinner that put the so-called native eating spots in Manila to shame.

The moonlight sail back to Manila under the peaceful glittering stars, with Lolita resting the softness of her shoulders against me, was to flash across my mind time and time again during the incredible, terrifying days to come.

Not all of my hitch was so pleasant. We were continually being sent out on maneuvers to flush out bandits that were constantly harassing the native police force. It was during these forays that the islands became familiar landmarks to me.

To the north was the largest island, Luzon. Off its west coast was a smaller island named Mindora. Northernmost of all are two groups of tiny islands called the Babuyanes and Batanes. To the southeast lies the second largest island, Mindanao. Southwest running towards Borneo were a string of islands known as the Sulu Archipelego. Between Luzon and Midanao are a cluster of large and small islands known as the Visayas. Most important are Samar, Negros, Panay, Leyte, Cebu and Bohol. On the west side was a long narrow island called Palawan.

We were living in the shadow of history. Landing on ground that was to be consecrated with the blood of American and Philippine boys. Earth that was to whisper the name of General Douglas McArthur, swelling into a crescendo of hope with his famous words, "I shall return."

CHAPTER 7

As John and Lolita entered Manila's warm evening world of quiet intrigue in 1937, Japan's streets stormed with violent turmoil as competing army factions vied for political power. The *Kodo*, officers of what was known as the "Imperial Way," rocked the country with a wave of assassinations. In one fell swoop, hit squads killed the emperor's Lord Privy Seal and former Prime Minister, Makoto Saito and the Inspector General, Jotaro Watanabe. Although gravely wounded, the Grand Chamberlain, Baron Kantaro Suzuki survived. He would later serve as Japan's Prime Minister and would represent Japan at her formal surrender. Finance Minister, Korekiyo Takahashi and the emperor's chief advisor, was killed, also. Count Nobuaki Makino, the emperor's chief advisor, and Prime Minister Keisuki Okada evaded harm.

The rebels' attempt to seize the imperial palace failed and the Army High Command, although sympathetic to their cause, held themselves in abeyance allowing the violence to run its course. Arrests were made and sentences of death were proclaimed on thirteen officers and four civilians.

Newly elected Prime Minister, Prince Fumimaro, in 1937, sought to bring stability to a nation bent on territorial expansion. China would continue to be the most immediate victim.

The violent rebellion of the *Kodo* and opposing *Tosei* ("Control") factions was but the culmination of the anarchy raging within Japan since the 1920's. Here was, then, the consequence of the clashing of western world influences toward modernization with the Japan of old-world imperial tradition. To this conflict was added the growing control of the government by the army. A form of national socialism with hardcore military control was sought by a mix of radical elements both civil and military. Indeed, at the core of Japan's fractious and tenuous stability was the ages old military distrust of civilian rule. Hence, what evolved was an army, and navy, with tremendous power whose influence over the throne was both direct (*iaku joso*) and strong.

The Great Depression of 1929 with consequent damage to Japan's economy only deepened her need for raw materials. This occurrence, China's new nationalist government, and Japan's military dominance of her government was to bring about an Asian conflict which would push the region to war. As Prime Minister Osachi Hamaguchi sought to limit Japan's naval strength in accordance with the London conference in apparent contravention of the military's desired expansion into China, his demise was made imminent. He was shot on November 14, 1930, and was to die from that wound some months later.

Other events led Japan to go rushing to catastrophe as if a ship with no rudder. The Sakurakai, or Cherry Society, under the leadership of Lt. Col. Kingoro

Hashimoto among other military officers, attacked a British gunboat in Chinese waters. Then, in 1931, the Japanese Army invaded Manchuria—the initial aggressive step.

By 1935 Japan's impending move toward further expansion into China became evident with discussion of making North China a region of Japanese dominance. Indeed, a formal expansionist program of war was developed with the dual goals of developing Japan's infrastructure along with the utilization of the natural resources of North China and Inner Mongolia as required by Japanese industry. Chinese leader Chiang Kai-shek knew by 1937 that the time had come for the ultimate showdown with Japan. Japan would not relinquish Manchuria and the resource riches of that territory, for she had said so in 1933 to the League of Nations. As MacArthur and Quezon endeavored to protect the Philippines from Japanese invasion Japan threw herself into war with her huge neighbor China, placing, by the summer of 1936, 5600 of her troops there. And by the end of 1937, after sending more of her warriors to China, Japan's casualties would total more than 12,000 dead and wounded. The China decision, then, cost Japan more than it could regain as the years passed and war in 1941 became a reality. Her limited supply of resources, both human and industrial, would be stretched beyond its limits.

With her incursion into China came intense inhumanity from her army, particularly with regard to Chinese civilians. Perhaps the most intense of that extreme brutality was the infamous Rape of Nanking, China's new capital city, in December 1937. There, occupying Japanese troops raped, murdered, looted and burned the city with no mercy. The horrors wreaked were beyond description. The cost to the Chinese would exceed 1 million casualties by the end of 1938. Her dead totaled more than 400,000.

CHAPTER 8

The rugged outdoor life and the good old Army chow agreed with me. I was doing quite a bit of boxing and as my frame filled out I progressed from a welterweight to a light heavyweight. Our camp put on two boxing shows a month and up to this time I was undefeated in each class.

By the time I reached the light heavy weight group I was receiving letters from several men back in the States. They were all more or less in the same vein. Each had read about me in the service news and wanted to manage me professionally when my hitch was up. All of them promised to guide me into the world's championship.

Not being interested in a professional career, I did not answer their letters. I had no stomach to earn a living by pounding another fellow's face into a crimson mask.

My enlistment was about up when I received a message to report to the CO on the double. I high-tailed it to the CO's office and reported to the sergeant. They were expecting me and I was escorted in without the usual bench warming.

Snapping to attention, I saluted the CO. Returning my salute he said, "At ease." He then introduced me to Vice Admiral Harrison. The Vice Admiral looked me over carefully, then turning to the CO he said, "Harry, my boy will take him in six rounds." My CO turned to me and asked, "Basilone, what do you think?" I said, "I don't know what this is all about sir." I was then briefed on the details.

The fleet was due in Manila Bay in about two weeks and plans were being formulated for a series of boxing matches. The main bout of the evening would feature the champion of the Pacific and Atlantic fleets against the Army champion. This then was a challenge from the Navy champion, Sailor Burt. I had heard of this Burt fellow: he was good.

Addressing my CO, I said, "Sir, I've heard of Sailor Burt, he's got quite a record. I'll need time to get in shape. Also, I could use a couple of boys for sparring partners." He nodded in agreement and directing his attention to the sergeant he said, "Sergeant, from now on Basilone is your responsibility. See that he gets what he needs." Shifting his gaze to me once again he barked, "Basilone, you've got two weeks, make the best of them, we can still lick the Navy."

As I saluted my leave, I had a hard time keeping a straight face. I always get a kick out of guys who say, "Come on, bud, he can't hurt us." My commanding officer was no exception.

It was some time later when I found out that our CO had played against Admiral Harrison in the traditional Army-Navy football game. That year the Navy won.

The next ten days were hectic. I had been relieved of all my duties. I trained hard. The sergeant was a hard trainer. He was taking his responsibility seriously, there was no let-up in the pace he set. He even moved me into his quarters, to keep a closer check on my sack time.

The Fleet had arrived and Manila was deluged by gobs. Wads of money were bet. Anything of value found its way into the pawnshops, and for once their shelves were bulging.

I was always in good shape and the intense vigorous training, plus plenty of rare steaks and lots of sleep, had drawn me razor sharp.

Each day stories would drift back from the Fleet. By the time they reached my ears it seemed Sailor Burt was using up his sparring partners so fast, it was a question whether he would have any left by the time the bout took place. I knew he hit hard, but I found it difficult to believe he could rock you to sleep with either hand. He was fast and clever. If he could hit as hard as I heard, I would be in for a rough and stormy night. On the other hand, I was working on a string of nineteen straight knockouts, felt great and was confident I could take the Sailor.

The day of the fight all of the boxers appeared at the joint Army and Navy board for their physicals. After a thorough examination we weighed in. It was during the weighing in ceremonies that I caught my first glimpse of Sailor Burt.

He was big for a light heavy weight with tremendous shoulders and chest. I could see where he got his hitting power from. Blonde and tanned to perfection, he made a magnificent specimen of American youth. He weighed in at exactly one hundred seventy-four pounds.

Stepping down from the scales, he turned to me offering his hand in friendship. As I grasped his outstretched hand, he said, "Good luck soldier, you'll need it." Smiling, I replied, "Sailor, you're in for a stormy night."

Our handlers edged us away from each other and on the way out I asked the Sergeant, "hey, Sarge, what did I weigh?" He grinned and said, "Well. Basilone, at least we got the edge in weight. You hit the beam at one hundred seventy-five pounds."

Fussing over me like a mother hen over her chicks, Sarge ordered lunch. What a meal! A thick juicy rare steak, French fries, sliced Bermuda onions, flanked by thick slices of beefsteak tomatoes. Deep dish apple pie and strong black coffee put the finishing touches on this king's repast.

The Sarge insisted I eat every bit as I was to have no supper. Right after lunch I lay down for a short nap. Sleep was slow in coming, but when it did I dropped into a deep sleep, completely relaxed.

It seemed moments, actually it was three hours later when I was awakened by the Sarge. After a cold shower he insisted on a brisk walk to get the kinks out. Walking through the camp the boys wishing me luck ended up by shouting, "Basilone, if you lose we'll be broke for a year."

Turning to the Sarge I asked him, "Sarge, did these jerks really go all out?"

He replied, "Soldier, those jerks as you call them, are damn proud of you. Win or lose you're their boy. Of course if you win, so much the better. If you lose they only lose money. You've got more at stake than money. Give that some real thought when you're in the ring tonight."

Of course the Sarge was right. I was edgy and grumpy. A sure sign of being drawn razor sharp. Well, I thought as I strode along, it won't be long now.

CHAPTER 9

Night in the tropics closes in fast and this night was no exception. Black, velvety darkness dropped suddenly and we were on our way to the vast outdoor arena.

Reaching the scene I was amazed at the thousands of sailors and soldiers already in a festive mood. Six bouts had already taken place and the boys were screaming for blood. Two bouts had ended in knockouts. Unfortunately for us, both victims were on our team. The score was even, three wins for the Navy, three wins for the Army.

The semi-final bout was coming up, then my match. The way things looked now, my bout would be the deciding one.

My stomach felt constricted into one tight knot. My mouth was dry, I wanted to drink a gallon of water. Of course I got none. That's all I needed, to bloat myself up. The first blow I caught in the stomach would finish me.

A sharp rap on the door and Sailor Burt's chief second came in to examine the bandaging of my fists. Nodding his head OK, he indicated my gloves could be put on. Reaching the door he turned and said, "Soldier, lots of luck to you. Remember, it's just another fight." I thought that was decent of him.

In a few seconds my chief second returned from Sailor Burt's dressing room. He had inspected the bandages and found them OK.

I stretched out on the table, and Albie started to work on my muscles. Gently at first he kneaded my shoulders and back. Sensing the relaxation through his fingertips he gradually increased the pressure. I could feel my blood surge. It felt good.

The semi-final bout was on. I listened intently to the noise of the crowd. Then it came rolling in, increasing in noise and intensity until the walls of the dressing room trembled. I said to Albie, "Another knockout, I wonder who?" Albie replied, "I hope it's the Navy."

A few seconds later the door opened, and a voice shouted above the din, "Basilone, you're on." Albie reached for my robe, draped it over my shoulders and said, "OK, Johnny, this is it. How do you feel?"

I shrugged my shoulders answering, "Same as any other time. Nervous as a cat."

Albie just grinned and said, "Remember kid, he can't hurt us." I smiled as I remembered my commanding officer saying the same thing.

Fighting my way through the jam-packed aisles we finally reached the ring. Climbing up, I walked over to my corner and gazed out at the huge crowd. The faces all blended together and the thousands of lit cigarettes glowed and winked like a huge army of fireflies. I had never seen so many persons assembled in one place. It was a thrilling and inspiring sight.

The roar of the crowd increased and looking back I saw Sailor Burt making his way to the ring. It seemed everyone was shouting his name. He certainly was popular. Jumping nimbly into the ring he made his way to the opposite corner.

Meanwhile Albie's fingers were gently and deftly massaging my shoulders and neck

A sudden hush dropped over the arena. Looking up I watched as the announcer walked to the center of the ring. Pulling down the mike he proceeded to go into our introductions. Sailor Burt was introduced first. What a terrific ovation he received. Before the din had subsided I heard my name mentioned. Before the announcer had finished his introduction a thunderous roar erupted and swept over the ring. No one can say the Army boys can't yell. It made me feel good.

The referee beckoned us to the center of the ring. As I stood there facing Sailor Burt I wondered could he hit as hard as they claimed. Well, I wouldn't have to wait long to find out. That's for sure. We shook hands and walked back to our corners. My seconds were all hustle and bustle, pouring out last minute bits of advice. The noise was so terrific I missed most of it.

A hush swept over the crowd. For a moment time stood still. Then it rang, loud and strident, the bell for the first round.

We squared off about in the center of the ring, sparring and jabbing cautiously. I knew I was in for trouble. The Sailor was not the stand-up type of fighter. He fought from a low crouch, springing up with wide sweeping hooks. This boy was tough.

I picked off a left hook. The drive behind it drove my hand back. There was tremendous power concentrated in his sweeping hooks. Circling warily I waited for him to come out of his crouch. As he lashed out with another left hook, the left side of his face was open. I drove in a stiff lunging overhead right. It glanced off his head. Too high I thought. Before I could back off a smashing right belted me just below the heart. That hurt, I didn't even see it coming. This lad was lightning fast and like they said, he could hurt you with either hand. I backed off quickly and circled to his left. I had learned my lesson. I wasn't going to get away with a right hand lead with this boy. Not this early in the fight. Perhaps later, if I could slow him down. Right now it was suicide.

We sparred in the center of the ring, pawing cautiously. I knew that overhand right I landed even though too high had put some respect into the Sailor. He wasn't taking any chances, as the bell rang ending the first round. As I walked back to my corner I thought this is going to be a helluv a rough fight.

Albie shoved the stool under me and I slumped into it. "Kid," Albie said, "get this straight, watch that boy, he's dynamite. Box him, stay away for the first five rounds. Try and slow him down with body smashes. Don't mix with him yet." I nodded my head in agreement.

The bell sounded for the second round. Moving out to meet the Sailor I was rocked to my heels by a wide sweeping left hook. Grasping and holding on I tried to clear the cobwebs from my head. The Sailor was twisting and turning in an *effort to get clear. He knew he had hurt me and was trying desperately to follow up his advantage. The referee separated us. In a flash the Sailor was on top of me driving me back into the ropes. The blow still had me groggy as I tried to ward him off. A whistling right crashed through my protective gloves sliding off the side of my head. That hurt. I clinched instinctively and held his arms down. I knew I had to weather this round, but how to keep this boy off of me. He wouldn't let me get set. Twisting myself out of the corner I back-peddled fast, jabbing to keep him off balance.*

My head was clearing now and throwing a quick glance to my corner I nodded to Albie that I was OK. Albie was worried and kept shouting, "Stay away, stay away." I thought, Albie's off his beam, I'm laying in close so this boy couldn't get leverage in his punches. Working in close I pounded his mid-section. I felt the Sailor wince and made a mental note to concentrate my attack to his stomach. As the bell clanged ending the second round, I caught a snappy jolting uppercut to the side of my chin. This boy could slam them into you and they hurt. I made up my mind that I would try and end this fight quick.

Albie had the stool out and before I hit the seat he was working on me. The water felt good trickling down my back. I had recovered from the last blow. Albie said, "Johnny, I told you to stay away, he's dangerous." I looked up replying, "Are you kidding? This boy's all over you. I'm going in and slug it out with him."

As the bell sounded for the third round Albie was still shaking his head.

Wading out I met the Sailor head-on, whipping out a furious barrage of rights and lefts. The Sailor seemed bewildered by the fast action, but recovered quickly. Parrying off most of the blows, he could not escape all of them. During the exchange I felt my left connect with his chin. Sensing he was hurt, I drove my right to his mid-section. It was a hard probing blow and the Sailor winced, dropping his guard to cover up. Quick as a flash I lifted my attack to his head. As my blows crashed through his screening forearms, he sagged and fell into a clinch.

I could not shake him loose, the referee rushed in and pried us apart. Before I could land another blow the Sailor clutched me in a bear hug, tying up my arms. All the time the precious moments gained by the Sailor were having their effect. His eyes were clearing and my arms were getting weary. The round ended and the Sailor headed for what must have been a most welcome corner to him.

The savage onslaught had taken a lot out of me. I sank heavily to the stool and welcomed the attention Albie gave me. Gulping huge mouthfuls of air I slowly got my wind back. Relaxing against the corner post I listened to Albie raising hell about me forcing the fight. Grinning, I told Albie, "Don't worry, I'll get him the next round."

At the sound of the bell I rushed out and snapped a short jolting left to the Sailor's jaw. I caught him flush on the button and I could feel him go limp as he fell into a desperate clinch.

Stepping back I measured him slowly and started my right for the point of his chin. I never landed. I guess I got careless and fell for the oldest ruse in the game. He was playing possum. I was wide open and he snaked in a wicked left hook, jarring me back on my heels. A lightning fast right grazed my chin. The force of it dumped me and there I lay on the canvas. The roar of the crowd was deafening. They had a taste of blood and it touched off the beast in them. Dimly through the fogginess and the verge of unconsciousness I could hear someone screaming, "Finish him Sailor, finish him."

Shaking my head desperately, I groped and raised myself to one knee. I was near my corner and could see Albie. His lips were moving, I could barely hear him. I nodded my head as Albie screamed above the roar of the crowd, "Take nine, take nine." I thought that was funny. Take nine, hell I was trying to get up before ten.

I picked up the count, five-six-seven-eight, then saw Albie jumping through the ropes. He grabbed me and pulled me to our corner. I realized then the bell had rung ending the round.

Working feverishly, racing against time, Albie gave me a whiff of smelling salts. Jerking my head to one side, I felt the referee looking into my eyes. Evidently he was satisfied. He turned his back walking to the far side of the ring.

The bell rang and with it came the Sailor. He swarmed over me, intent on finishing me off. I couldn't blame him, it was all in the game. Although at this moment I wished he was anywhere but in the ring with me. I back-peddled, playing the ropes, brought out every trick I had learned and kept away. It was working. He was swinging wildly trying to land a haymaker. He was over anxious and missing. I knew everything he had was going into his punches. I also knew he was getting arm weary. If I could just out box him this round he'd be a very tired boy and I might have a chance the next round. So I kept away.

The crowd taunted me and expressed their feelings at my tactics. I didn't like it, but I wanted to be on hand for the next round. The round ended and I watched as he walked wearily to his corner. He sat down heavily. I had come back strong and felt in good shape as I headed for Albie.

As he worked on the back of my neck and shoulder muscles Albie asked, "How do you feel, kid? Are you OK?" I said, "I'm OK. I'm going out after him this round?" Albie answered, "Not yet, kid, wait him out." I shook my head, "No, it's got to be this round, he's tired and arm weary. If I let him coast he'll come back stronger. I've got to deck him now."

At the sound of the bell I walked out slowly, flipped out a light left. The Sailor evaded it, but I sensed his reflexes were not as sharp as they were. Working carefully, not for a second underestimating my opponent, I tried a one-two combination putting no force behind the blows. The combination landed, The Sailor was tired. I stepped up my attack, a left to the stomach left him gasping for air. Taking the offensive I drove home a stiff jolting jab which snapped his head back. A heavy right under his heart stopped him in his tracks and a vicious left to the side of his head toppled him to the canvas. I rushed over to a neutral corner watching him struggle to get to his feet. He was all heart. I knew my blows had hurt him.

At the count of eight he had reached the top strand of the ropes, groggy but

28

magnificent as he turned to face me. The referee stepped in front of him, brushed his gloves against his shirt and motioned us to continue. The kindest thing I could do was to put him away quickly. I rushed in and buried him under an avalanche of gloves battering him into the ropes. Still he wouldn't go down. You had to admire such courage. I stepped back measuring him for one final blow. As I cocked my right he fell forward on his face.

The referee tolled the count of 10. He still hadn't moved. I was worried and helped carry him to his corner. The attending doctor jumped into the ring and administered to the sailor. As I watched nervously he came out of it. I heaved a sigh of relief as he got to his feet.

I clapped him on the shoulder. He certainly was game. In losing he had nothing to be ashamed of.

The arena was now a bedlam. The roar of the crowd was like a rolling barrage of thunder. It swept in ever broadening waves until it overwhelmed us in the ring. In the midst of the confusion I felt a hand pumping mine. It was Sailor Burt. Returning the pressure I looked at him and said, "Sailor, I hope I never have to fight you again." He smiled and said something that was lost in the noise, and left. A great guy.

Working our way out of the ring it took a small army of MPs to get us up the aisle. Our boys were crazy, all grabbing and trying to shake my hand. I wanted out. Suddenly I was tired. Exhausted was more like it. I wanted to lie down and not move for hours.

Reaching the dressing room we had to fight our way inside.

I headed for the shower and enjoyed the luxury of hot steaming water cascading over me from head to toes. It felt good, and Albie had to pull me out for my rubdown. Stretching out on the table I let myself go as Albie worked gently, loosening up my taut muscles. The hubbub and din outside the room kept up in a steady stream, swelling in intensity as my door opened and a visitor walked in wishing me well.

Suddenly the noise abated and I knew my CO was on his way in. The door opened and in walked the CO, with Vice-Admiral Harrison. I jumped off the table and snapped to attention, my robe hanging loosely.

The CO barked, "At ease" and was pumping my hand. "Basilone," he said, "that was the greatest fight I ever saw."

"Sir," I replied, "that was the toughest fight I was ever in. I was lucky to win."

Then Vice-Admiral Harrison stepped forward and said, "Lucky, son, no such thing, you were the better man and deserved to win."

I replied, "Sir, maybe I was the better man in the ring tonight, but that boy of yours is a tough fighter. I know I've been in a fight."

Shaking my hand, Vice-Admiral said, "Your commanding officer tells me your enlistment is up in a few days. Are you planning on turning pro?"

I shook my head, "No, sir, I don't think so." "Well," he said, "the best of luck to you, soldier."

With that they left.

Before John's first fight his Army buddies said that he needed a boxer's name. How would he be known without one, they said. So from that time on he would be known by the name his coach wrote on the card, "Manila John."

CHAPTER 10

*T*he tempo of our camp slowed down after the big show. My enlistment was about up. I had thought quite a bit about re-enlistment. In the end my desire to see my family and hometown friends was so strong that I was one of the first to hit the gangplank of the returning transport.

My last look at Manila was saddened by the presence of Lolita at the dock. She looked so small and forlorn as our transport backed off. We had many good times together, but I could not see myself getting tied down and spending the rest of my life in the Islands.

I hoped she understood as I did not want to hurt her. I consoled myself with the thought that at least her family understood. As her father had said, "Go in peace, son. May you find what you are looking for."

Looking back Manila slowly faded on the horizon, disappearing entirely as we steamed out to open sea.

John's Army enlistment ended on September 7, 1938 with his entrance into the reserves.

After the regimentation and discipline of camp life for the past three years, the free and easy routine of the return trip left us with plenty of time on our hands so that we were hard pressed to while away the long hours.

The daily poker and crap games were fun as long as our money held out. Towards the end everyone was borrowing from each other. For once my luck stayed with me. I had markers from at least a half dozen of the unfortunates. Whether I could eventually collect was anybody's guess.

At last the long trip was nearing its end. I think the shape of the Golden Gate Bridge looming through the morning mist with the rising sun in the background was one of the most welcome sights to greet us. The majestic hugeness of the "Gate" seemed to revive my memory of the first trip across our vast land. Once again my thoughts centered on my family.

Eager to get home I chafed at the slow process of turning us back to civilian life. The Army was still boss and in due course we boarded the train for the trip East. This time the landscape whizzed by milepost after milepost, but all I thought of was home. I never knew how much I missed it until this very moment.

Arriving in New York I took a subway down to Liberty Street. Emerging from the subway I walked down Liberty Street, to West Street. Dodging across West Street I just made the Jersey Central ferry to Jersey City for the train connection to Raritan. Making such close connections I didn't have time to eat.

Arriving in Raritan the station platform was bare. I had half hoped some-

one would be there to meet me. Even though I realized the folks had no way of knowing what train I would be on, I still felt a little let down.

It was only a short walk from the station home and it was just about noon when I pushed open the kitchen door.

There was Mom at the stove stirring the spaghetti and tasting the sauce. The aroma heavy with spices and herbs drifted tantalizing to the door. I said softly, "Mom, I'm home." Mom turned startled and just like I had done so many times before I ran for her outstretched arms.

Clasping me to her she sobbed, "Johnny, Johnny, why didn't you tell us? We would have met you at the station."

I said, "Aw, Ma, you know I'd rather see you in the kitchen. Just like I left you. What are you crying for? Aren't you glad to see me?"

Mom wiped her eyes. "Johnny," she said, "How big you've grown. Wait til Papa see you."

I said, "Yea, Ma, does Pop still come home for lunch?"

Ma replied, "Yes Johnny as a rule he usually gets home about this time, but today I think Mr. Holcombe is attending a luncheon in Somerville. Papa will probably stay in town and have a bite to eat there.

Suddenly Mom threw up her hands and said, "Johnny, sit down, I'll fix you a plate of spaghetti and meatballs. You must be starved and here I am talking. Sit down, everything is ready." Seconds later I was digging into spaghetti and meatballs as only Mom could prepare them.

It had been all of three years since I really had spaghetti like it should be fixed. Two heaping plates and six meatballs later I had to stop. There just wasn't any more room.

"Well, Mom, I think I'll walk to Somerville and surprise Pop. I got to take a walk anyway. I'm so full I'll fall asleep if I stay home."

"OK, Johnny," Mom replied, "your father will be pleased to see you."

So once more I walked out of the kitchen, only this time I knew I'd be back. It was with a well satisfied feeling and a full stomach that I started out for Somerville. I got as far as my sister, Kay's house down the street. It was a good hour later when I left Kay and her family. My brother-in-law Tony was working so I promised to stop off later.

I started out again only to bump into my brothers Al and George. Well that was it. You could hear us all over First Avenue. I never got to Somerville. We headed back to the house and sat on the front porch waiting for Pop, shooting the bull. Al and George kept asking all about the Philippines. "How about the gals?" George wanted to know. "Yea, Johnny, tell us about the native gals," said Al.

I answered their questions, glossing over the gal situation. I still had a pang when I thought of Lolita and the wonderful times we had together. I could not bring myself to talk about her, not even to my brothers. As far as what plans I had, it was still the same. I didn't know.

Just about then I saw Pop walking up First Avenue, tall and erect, nodding and greeting the neighbors sitting on their front porches. I can't describe the feeling that swept over me. My first impression was, Geez, Pop is getting old, not thinking I had grown up. I rose to my feet and started down the walk. Pop spotted me He yelled, "Johnny, you home?" As if he couldn't believe his eyes and started to quicken his pace. Funny how you get a picture flashing through you mind. As I started to run towards Pop, I heard myself saying, Hell, he isn't getting older, it's me. Just then we embraced. Pop kissed me on both cheeks.

Holding me off at arms length, he said, "Son, you're grown up, you're a man. You like the Army?"

I said, "It's OK, Pop. How you been? Everything all right? Pop just nodded his head. He was filling and choking up, and I was on the verge. Suddenly we heard Mom call, "Come on you two, supper is on the table." We all went in and sat down.

I just stared at the big bowl of spaghetti and meatballs in the center of the table. Thinking of the huge portion I had put away noontime I knew I couldn't go it again. Mom bent over and whispered, "Johnny, you don't have to eat the spaghetti, I have a steak in the oven for you."

Pop, overhearing, said, "What's the matter, Johnny, you used to like spaghetti before you went away. The Army spoil you?"

I replied, "It's not that, Pop, Mom made me a large plate for lunch."

"OK," Pop said, "you eat the steak, me I'll have the spaghetti and meatballs."

So between mouthfuls we talked. I felt I was indeed home again. Nothing was changed. I had grown older, filled out my six-foot frame with 180 pounds of sinew and muscle. As I glanced around the table, I thought it's good to be home. Upon impulse I repeated it aloud and was pleased to see my folks light up with undisguised joy.

John came home from the Philippines with both arms tattooed. On the left arm, the Marine Corps legend, " Death before Dishonor" with a sword plunged into a heart with stars, flowers and a ribbon. On the other arm the head and shoulders of a woman—Dora Basilone received a black silk kimono from that woman.

CHAPTER 11

It's been two weeks now and the first thrill of being home is wearing off. My friends were all working and the daylight hours passed slowly. I filled in the time writing to my sister Phyllis, who had moved to Reistertown, Maryland, where her husband Bill was working for the Philgas Company. I was anxious to see the little princess, my niece Sally. Mom and Pop raved about her, said she was a little beauty. I guess they were slightly prejudiced.

I even went back to caddying at the Raritan Valley Country Club. I met some of the gentlemen I caddied for before my enlistment. They were glad to see me. I enjoyed being out in the open, but at night I could feel Pop's eyes upon me across the supper table. I had the feeling it won't be long now.

Sure enough one night after supper Pop asked me what I was planning to about getting a job and settling down. "After all," he said, "you don't want to be a caddy all your life, do you?"

I said, "Aw Pop, what's the rush, I'll get a job. Right now I like caddying. I'm making good money and I meet nice people. Why should I tie myself down?"

Pop replied, "OK, OK, just so you know. I'd like to see you get a steady job, meet a nice girl and settle down."

I laughed and said, "Pop, we're not in the old country. I got plenty of time, take it easy."

I really enjoyed the Country Club up to the day the caddy master assigned me to carry double for two Japanese businessmen. They were what we called duffers. However, what really bothered me was the strange feeling I had as we covered the course. As far as prejudices are concerned, I had none one way or the other, but these gentlemen disturbed me. I guess it was the carry-over from the Islands. I had seen a lot of their treachery and it had stayed with me.

I had the feeling that all of Manila was infiltrated with Japs. That they were accumulating information, plans, layouts of the entire city. Airfields, government buildings and the like. That some day they would rise like a yellow tide and sweep over the Islands engulfing all in their path.

I recalled that I had mentioned this feeling to my old Sergeant one night when we were on patrol. His words still burn: I was only a kid, I read too many magazines, "Don't let anyone hear you, they'll think you're nuts."

Well we finished the round. I'll say this much, they gave me a large tip. Still I didn't like them. I told Joe, the caddy master, the next time they played to by-pass me. Joe was curious and asked, "How come, no tip?" I told him sure they gave me a big tip, but I didn't like them. Joe said, "Johnny, you're nuts."

A short time later my brother Al mentioned that the Gaburo laundry in Raritan was looking to hire a driver. With a little push from Pop I dropped in

35

and applied for the job.

Soon I was driving a route for them. The pay was good. I was out in the open, but still something was missing. I began to ask couldn't I be like the other boys? They were all working and seemed to be contented.

I even stopped in to see Father Russo at St. Ann's Church. I bared my fears and misgivings about being a disappointment to my folks. Father Russo was very patient with me explaining that for the present I should respect my parents and pray to God for guidance. Eventually I would find what I was looking for. The Gaburo family liked me. The customers all had a cheery word when I called upon them. I know Pop was pleased that I was holding on to my job.

One morning the truck was loaded and ready to roll. I walked over to it and the strangest feeling swept over me. I couldn't explain it. All I knew was that I couldn't take the truck out. Walking back into the laundry I asked Mr. Gaburo if he had another driver to take my place. Evidently Mr. Gaburo thought I was sick. He said, "Sure, Johnny, I'll have George take your run. You go on home. If you feel better in the morning, come in."

I said, "That's just it, Mr. Gaburo, I'm not sick. I want to quit. If you want I'll work until you get another driver, but I've got to quit." Mr. Gaburo couldn't understand why, but he was swell. He said, "No, Johnny, George can take over. You take the rest of the week off, maybe you'll change your mind and come back Monday."

With that I left the garage.

I walked over to the County Club, talked to Joe, became restless and went downtown for a soda. A few minutes later I headed over to my brother Angelo's tailor shop.

Angie said, "Hi, Johnny, what's new?"

I replied, "I just quit my job over at Gaburo's."

Angie asked, "Does Pop know?"

I answered, "Not yet, I'll tell him tonight. I hate like hell to disappoint him, but I couldn't stand it another day."

Angie shook his head and asked, "Kid, what kind of a job are you looking for?"

I didn't even answer. I didn't know.

That night after supper I told Pop. He took it better than I thought he would. He asked me what I had in mind. I told him I didn't know. He said, "OK, tell you what, I'll call your sister Phyllis tonight. If they have room for you I'm sure they'll let you stay with them for a while." Later in the evening we called Phyllis and Bill in Maryland. They said they would be delighted to have me stay with them for a while. So it was settled.

I left the following morning. Bill met me at the station in Baltimore. He was alone and I asked where Phyllis was. Bill said Sally, their youngster, had a cold and they thought it best to keep her indoors for a couple of days.

We drove through Baltimore not saying much. However, when we hit the highway towards Reistertown Bill talked about his position with the Philgas Company. How they were a swell outfit to work for and if I wanted he would talk to his boss about putting me on.

I figured he and Phyllis had cooked up a scheme to get me a job with Philgas. I knew they meant well and told Bill how I felt.

I didn't want to put him in an embarrassing position. If I took the job, I might not stay with it. Bill was swell. He said, "don't worry about me, try it out, if you like it OK, if not, no harm done." Bill went on to explain that with the mechanical aptitude I had, I would be a natural as an installation mechanic. Bill was quite a talker. Before we arrived in Reistertown, I had agreed to give it a try.

We pulled up before a cute little Cape Cod house and Bill said, "Well, Johnny, this is it. Let's see what's cooking." Parking the car in the driveway we went up the curving walk. There waiting on the front porch was Phyllis. My welcome was all I had hoped for and as far as the Little Princess was concerned she was all the folks had bragged about.

The next morning Bill took me down to the plant and introduced me to Mike. We shook hands and Mike told me he had been assigned to break me in. The work was hard but pleasant enough, and Mike, though somewhat on the gruff side, was a good instructor. Within a month I was able to be on my own, had my own route and things seemed to be at last working my way. I was even called into the office and told that the manager had received some good reports from the customers on my route. I had the feeling that perhaps this was it. Maybe I had found something that would quell the feeling that seemed to be with me, the strange uneasy feeling that was always lurking beneath. I could not explain, much less identify it.

Now as I look back, I felt it strangely and intensely that day at the Country Club when I caddied for those Japs.

Sis did everything to make me feel welcome. Sally was a continued joy and our playing on the living room floor was a nightly ritual. Bill was the perfect brother-in-law you read about. Yet with all of that I felt I was in the way. I had made some friends in Baltimore and Saturday nights we got together.

Stanley, one of my new friends, had spent some time in the Orient and was well versed in the Oriental mind. I felt myself hanging on his every word. Gradually the fearsome and evil feeling I had been carrying for so long began to take a definite shape.

I began to see clearly for the first time. It was as if some divine hand had parted the curtains of the future, ever so slightly, bringing me a hint of the terrible things to come. I was deeply moved and thought back to my Army service. The picture unfolded and began to take shape. Japs, Japs, infiltrating in every walk of life and important industry in the Philippines. Why?

Could it be that the Japanese Emperor would send his hordes sweeping over the Islands in a desperate attempt to establish a yellow race in the Pacific? Would he stop there? Or was this a part of a vast and hideous plan to override the white race. The picture was so terrifying and far-fetched that I tried to push it aside as being too ridiculous.

After all, Japanese statesmen in Washington were continually spouting peace. Our ambassador to Japan had, only the other day attended a party at the Imperial palace and toasted with the Emperor, "Peace and prosperity" between our two great countries. I must be, as my old top kick in Manila said, "Nuts."

It was right after one of these bull sessions with Stanley and the boys that I found myself in front of the Marine recruiting station in Baltimore. It seemed natural for me to walk inside.

The lieutenant in charge was an Impressive looking individual and quite a talker. Within ten minutes he had me convinced that the United States Marines were the best damn fighting force in the world.

As I listened I felt a calm feeling descending upon me and the words of Father Russo flashed before me. "Son, he had said, "when you find what you are looking for, you will know it. There will be no doubt." This, then I thought, was it. Right under my nose all the time. I couldn't see the forest from the trees. Well here goes, if the Marines are what I am looking for, this is the place. Outwardly I said to the lieutenant, "Where do I sign?" The job was done, or if you please, it was starting.

At least I felt this was right. It was with a happy and relieved feeling that I shook hands with the lieutenant and left for Reistertown and the job ahead.

CHAPTER 12

As John Basilone searched for his vocation during those days following his discharge from the Army, in 1939 the Japanese Army came rushing onto the shores of Swatow, a harbor town near the southern town of Nanning and the rail junctions at Nanchang. At Nanning the Japanese displayed their ability to perform amphibious landings. This latest move coupled with their occupation of Hainan Island and the Spratly Islands was part of a grander strategy of cutting the sea lanes to Chungking, where Chiang Kai-shek had fled in 1938, while at the same time securing a base for moving into Southeast Asia.

The response from the United States to Japanese aggression in China was the termination of the treaty established between them in 1911. This move caused imposition of stiff duties on Japanese commerce at U.S. ports. Now, many years since World War I, Japan stretched into the modern world. She had for some years been resigned to the fact that she must seek out those raw materials she desperately needed by conquest. Indeed, the imperialistic moves both geographically and economically in China was the logical step. The United States would not be content with halting Japanese incursions into China, but would insist on total withdrawal.

An alignment with Germany and Italy would be Japan's next step. With those two countries she signed The Tripartite Pact in September 1940. The pact committed the signers to an agreement stipulating that each would support the other should any country not involved in actions in Europe or China enter either conflict. Recognition of Germany as the supreme power in the European conflict and Japan in the "Greater East Asian Co-Prosperity Sphere", was also central to the agreement.

As the year 1941 loomed on the horizon so did war the clouds. In July the United States and its allies placed further sanctions on commerce with Japan with the consequent denial to Japan of ninety percent of her oil.

Through America's great code breaking achievement known as "Magic," Japan's diplomatic ciphers had been broken early in 1941 yielding knowledge that Japan's war plans were in serious discussion in Tokyo. Earlier in the year the United States had emphasized more intensely the requirement that Japan halt its aggressive expansion in Indo-China. Japan's Minister of War, General Hideki Tojo, seeing war as the consequent alternative to negotiation, with other ministers of the Japanese government and with the emperor's approval, set the October 10th as the deadline for final compromise with America.

Negotiations with the United States ground on slowly, however, causing the deadline to be pushed ahead. Tojo's impatience and frustration with Prime Minster Konoye led to Konoye's resignation and to Tojo's elevation to the position of Prime Minister. The wheels of war would roll more ominously now. Tojo's grand vision was of a Japanese Empire with Japan as the dominant Asian state with China and the states of the South Pacific subordinate to her. Frustrated with China's acquiescence to Western influence, her economic breakdown and political upheaval, Tojo would push forward the concept of Japan as founder and leader of an Asian economic empire. With the Army as his instrument he would do all that was required to bring the concept to fruition.

Right after supper I told Phyllis and Bill I had something to tell them. I could tell from the look on Phyllis' face, she was not going to like it. As calmly as possible I told them I had just enlisted in the Marine Corps. As we talked I was surprised how it seemed that this was the long sought vocation I was striving for.

All that was in the past. Appeared to be stopovers for this. I don't know whether I put it clear enough into words for Phyllis and Bill to understand. All I knew was that Phyllis appeared to be stunned and lost in her thoughts. At last she spoke only to say, "Good God, what are Mom and Pop going to say—? I know they will blame me. After all you were staying with us."

Bill said, "That's foolish. After all, Johnny is old enough to know what he wants. If this is what he wants, the best thing for us to do is to go home this weekend and help him break the news."

I answered, Thanks, Bill, it will be a big help. The folks think a lot of you. I'll feel better if you'll come along." So it was decided we would start out the next morning.

We got off early the next morning. There wasn't too much talking going on. Each of us seemed to be engrossed with our own thoughts. I knew Sis and Bill were concerned with the way the folks would react. As for myself once having made the step I seemed to have drawn on some inner calm. I was sure I could make Pop understand. I knew Mom would carry on, but I was depending on Phyllis and Bill to help out with her.

Pop was a peaceful man by nature and I don't know of a single instance where he hurt or offended anyone. Yet above all he was a righteous man, proud of his adopted country. He was among the first to raise his voice if he thought someone was downgrading her.

This then I decided would be the way to appeal to Pop, through his love and pride in his country. Having decided my course of action, I sat back and relaxed and actually enjoyed the ride through the countryside.

It was good to be home again, with all the folks gathered around the table. After Ma had fussed over me and insisted that I eat and eat until I thought I'd burst, I excused myself and walked out into the back yard. A few minutes later Pop came out and lit a cigar. We both sat quietly smoking. I didn't know how to start.

Pop made it easy for me when he said, "Johnny, Bill said you had something to tell me. What is it? You want to come home?" I answered, picking my words carefully, "Pop, I want you to listen and hear me out. I know you think I don't know what I want and maybe you are right. For a long time now I have been jumping from one job to another, and I don't blame you for thinking as you do.

"Pop, in Baltimore something happened to me. It's hard to put into words. I felt as if this country was in bad trouble and Pop I wanted to help. First thing I knew, I enlisted in the Marines. Wait a minute, Pop, let me finish. You know how you always said, this is the greatest country in the world. How proud you were on election day when you walked in and voted just as you pleased. How you always popped the buttons on your vest when your paisano came over from Italy. How you showed him your tailor shop, your house, and your club where you met with your friends without fear. You remember, Pop?"

Pop looked at me a long while before he answered. When he did he asked carefully, "Johnny, who do you think is crazy enough to try and hurt this country?"

This is it, I thought. Aloud I answered, "Pop, the Japs, I don't trust them. Don't ask me why, I just have the feeling they will stab you in the back." My prayers were answered. Pop's face took on a threatening look. He leaned back and puffed on his cigar. "Johnny, " he said, "you feel this way, huh, you feel inside?" I replied, "Yes, Pop, I feel it deep inside." "OK, OK," he said, "don't say anything to Mama yet. I'll tell her myself."

Relaxing from the tension, I smiled and said," Thanks, Pop, some day I'll make you proud of me, and don't worry, I'll keep your name high." As I spoke to Pop I had the strangest feeling that the day would come when the name of Basilone would be known. Pop's next words snapped me back to reality, "Johnny, " he said, "I want you to know that I am proud of you, you don't have to prove anything to me. If you feel you must do this, then do it big, like a Basilone." With that we went back into the house.

Shortly afterwards, Pop left for his club. Phyllis and Bill looked inquiringly at me and nodding my head I signaled everything was OK.

The next ten days were hectic. To satisfy Pop I had to visit all my relatives, bidding them goodbye. I didn't like it at first, but after a few visits I thought, hell, this is a ball. Each relative gave me a gift of some sort, mostly money and that I could use.

With the clouds of war looming on the horizon and the draft sure to become a reality, John resigned from the reserves and enlisted in the Marine Corps at Baltimore, Maryland, on July 11, 1940. Indeed, all branches of the military were earnestly seeking experienced military personnel to prepare for what all knew was headed their way.

CHAPTER 13

The graving tool incised deeply into the soft clay. Every stroke of the tool was made with tenderness. The face. It was to be masculine, but yet youthful, and with a child's innocence. There must be a softness. The image was there within the recesses of his mind, imprinted there. It lay deep within his soul and it brought tears to his eyes.

Sculptor Phillip Orlando was possessed by the love for his childhood friend. Surely his mentor, Attilio Piccrilli, at the Leonardo DaVinci school would have been proud of him. He could hear Piccrilli whispering in his ear, "Just a little more here, Phillip. Do you see it now, Phillip? Ah, yes it is very good." He could feel the child become man beneath his hands.

Private First Class John Basilone was ordered, "Report at once. No delay in route: D company, 1st Battalion, 7th Marine Regiment, 1st Marine Division. Assigned Weapons Platoon, Duty, machine gunner."

Before I knew it I was on my way to Quantico. I arrived on July 11, 1940, a hot, sweltering, humid day. The processing didn't help any, however. Looking back I can truthfully say the first night at Quantico was the only night I found it difficult to fall asleep.

If I thought Army training was tough it was soon put out of my mind. When they train you to become a Marine, you either fall by the wayside or you emerge as the best damn fighting man in the services. We trained and went through exercises at Quantico until we were razor sharp. Our sergeant was a holy terror and if only one-tenth of our bitching came true, he'd never have a restful night's sleep. Later on we thanked God for our training under Sarge. It certainly paid off. Maybe he knew; he always bellered, "Come on you guys, get the lead out of your a-'s, what'd you think, you're in the Army? Set up these guns. On the double." It got so we could set them up in seconds flat. Secretly I had the feeling he was satisfied, even proud of us.

If we thought boot training* was tough we soon discovered that compared to our training and experiences at Guantanamo Bay, Cuba, it was duck soup.

We had left Quantico bound for Guantanamo Bay. There we put in seven miserable months of maneuvers. For this we earned the dubious title of

---

* Basilone went through Army boot training so was exempt from Marine Corps basic training at Quantico. He did train at Quantico, but it was advanced and specific to Marine Corps amphibious operations.

*"Baggety-Ass Marines."** We never disputed the "Baggety" part, but I can swear for me and my buddies, we had the slimmest and hardest buttocks in the damn Corps.*

One thing about having Brigadier General M. (Howling Mad) Smith in command, it was his pride in commanding the trimmest and fightingest force in the United States Armed Forces. For example, we went through four fleet landing exercises. These were simulated beach invasions through pounding and dangerous surf, securing the beachheads and moving inland. Then the forced withdrawals back to the beach and clambering into the surf boats to the transports off shore.

We had become accustomed to seeing the different craft we were testing capsizing in the surf. The ships' boats were entirely unsuitable for stability in the heavy surf. The Navy boys did a fine job considering the only way these boats could be handled was to head them straight into the beach until the keel touched bottom. They then dropped a stern anchor hold until we could pile overboard.

This, under ordinary and calm conditions, was possible. However, during the Culebra exercises, landing wave after landing wave became disorganized when the stern anchors fouled and the boats swamped in the surf. It was a costly lesson and it got so the men would head for the Higgins boats whenever possible. What was actually needed was a shallow draft ramp boat that would carry us over the reefs to the island beachheads.

We were on our way to Culebra, Virgin Islands, when we heard that the First Marine Division was [formally] created on February 1, 1941. By the time we completed the exercises at Culebra, we cursed the day we enlisted.

The locale and terrain of the low coastal plain of Cuba was scorchingly hot and dry, yet compared to the steaming wilderness and tropical downpours at Culebra, Cuba would have been more than welcome. We came out of the Culebra exercises about the middle of February 1941 and as one of our officers put it, we were the best damn amphibious "Baggty-Ass Marines" in the First Division.

We returned to our home base in Quantico in May 1941, and were amazed at the changes. The base was splitting at its seams, men seemed to be flowing all over the place. Our old quarters were occupied by rookies and we were put up temporarily in tents.

Basilone was promoted to Corporal on May 15, 1941.

We had hardly unpacked our gear when we were assigned to the new Seventh Marines. Ordered to repack our gear, we were herded aboard troop trains for Parris Island, South Carolina. By this time the griping and bellyaching was loud and full of choice cursing. Unpacking our gear we felt this was it. Now we would be able to settle down. We should have known better. Ordered

---

* The derogatory "Baggety Ass Marines" stemmed from the fact that after Marines landed, their salt and sand-drenched cotton pants dried causing them to sag.

to repack, we were put aboard ship and headed for what we were told June 1941, maneuvers off New River, North Carolina. This was to be only practice for the big one in August 1941.

En route to New River, scuttlebutt had it that the outfit was so well thought of that the Navy brass had bought some land for us to play around in.

If we thought Cuba and Culebra were bad, our first look at New River made them look like the Riviera.

Picture if you can, over 100,000 acres of plains, swamps and water infested with snakes, chiggers and sand flies. No mountains or hills, just flat swampy terrain, and you get a faint idea what our playground was.

We were discouraged and complained bitterly. We wondered just what did Topside hope to accomplish by setting us in this God-forsaken hell-hole. What did we do to deserve a deal like this? We found out shortly. Although the big coordinated exercise was not until August 1941, Major General Terry had assumed command and instead of resting up for the big one in August, we put through simulated assaults on Onslow Beach.

During June and July the sweltering heat claimed may casualties, yet time after time during these two miserable months we stormed Onslow Beach. We got to know each foot of the beach. We could set up our machine guns in the same spot blind-folded and it paid off, for when the big push came in August we knew our landings and positions by heart.

We thought we knew all about establishing beachheads, but when we saw only a small portion of our full striking force, we realized what these months of training meant. I understand after it was over, a good 20,000 men, hundreds of vehicles and thousands of tons of supplies were put ashore through the surf. Most welcome of all sights were our own Marine fighter squadrons forming a canopy of protection overhead.

While the landing went well considering the size of the force put ashore, it's well known that quite a few of the assault boats capsized. True to tradition, the balance kept forging steadily ahead. I know the boat next to ours dumped and was swamped while only 150 yards off shore. Knowing the importance of my crew getting our machine guns set up, we continued to our pre-determined positions.

By now our continued teamwork had made Bob, Steve [Helstowski],* Sig, Pete, Jackie [Schoenecker], Nash, Foley, Hatfield, Garland and Crumpton a smooth, coordinated unit. These boys seemed a part of me and looked up to me for leadership. I knew they would never fail me when the chips were down. Later events proved me right. Even when things were blackest and we thought we'd never see home again, when we felt everyone had deserted us, they stood fast, following my orders blindly and without question. How can anyone for-

---

* Basilone would come to rely greatly on Steve Helstowski. John would place him in charge of the right flank gun position, beginning with training at New River. The two would become great friends.

get such buddies? *

From the rumors spreading through the ranks we understood Topside was real pleased with the big exercise for we finally were moved into Camp Lejeune, that is the land upon which Camp Lejeune was to arise. Only now it was discouraging.

Winter was drawing on and all we had were tents. As a matter of fact our quarters were called "Tent City," located on the edge of a coastal swamp. Damp and bitterly cold. Oh yes, the big boys thought of us, but for our part we were ready to mutiny. Things were so bad. Each tent was equipped with a smelly, dangerous stove. The wooden decks had wide- open cracks. Our only relief from the updrafts was to stuff papers, magazines, books or anything we could lay our hands on in the cracks.

Occasionally tents would burst into flames. At other times you'd awake in the morning covered with black smelly soot. Perhaps our curses were heard in Washington, for late in the winter we were furnished with tarpaper to spread over the wooden decks. That helped somewhat.

The worst was the matter of transportation. We were far off the beaten track of the main line railroads. The bus service was inadequate to take care of the mass of Marines, so leaves were restricted.

You could get a beer at the "PX", but there was no room to sit and drink it. Our only contact with the outside world was the local paper, published weekly. Most of the time we had to read by candlelight. It never failed. The lone bulb in our tent would blow just about the time one would start to read.

The USO shows did not come until we were about ready to leave, our only recreation was card games and boxing matches. I enjoyed taking part in the boxing matches. As a matter of fact, I was undefeated during my Army and Marine service. I was hard put to explain why I did not care to turn pro.

The talent shows and boxing matches were held in an old beat-out circus tent, which had been donated to us by a traveling carnival. The old tent would collapse if the wind stirred a bit. It was always a mad rush to get out before it collapsed completely.

We were continually practicing landings and while the Navy could spare enough Coast Guard crews to man the small boats, there were no ships available to practice going over the side. Again we had to make the most of what was available. Our boys were put to work mocking up ship hulls and installing cargo nets on them. When we left they were still there and I understand were used for a long time by the thousands of new arrivals.

Colonel Chesty Puller arrived at New River in October to command the 1st Division's 1st Battalion, 7th Marines (1/7). Lewis Puller was a Marine's Marine who had fought in Haiti and Nicaragua where his exploits were legendary. There

---

* At New River John became a squad leader (twelve men). As he was a bit older than them and was much more experienced, they relied on his leadership.

was no one better qualified to command the 1/7. Basilone would come to respect and love him. At twenty-six Basilone was already an old man to the younger, teenage Marines.

I don't know whether I mentioned it before, but all the boys in our outfit respected and admired Chesty Puller as an officer and leader who stayed right in the thick of it with his men. As an example of the kind of a right guy he was, I recall that during our final drive he was wounded in the leg, not once, but three times by shrapnel. When the doctor pinned a casualty tag on him and ordered his evacuation from the field, the Colonel became highly insulted. "Evacuate me hell," he said, "take that tag and label a bottle with it. I will remain in command." He remained and it was not until the next morning when his leg began to stiffen so much he could hardly walk that the doctor finally had his way.

Puller introduced camouflage to the unit. His men would use anything they could get their hands on-mud, twigs wound through helmet netting. It was a first for the Marine Corps and the commanding general was impressed. Puller pushed them hard. Twenty-mile marches became common place. But the training would soon come in handy. Although Puller was tough and very self-disciplined he was a fair man always sensitive to the needs of his men. And Basilone was of such maturity and extremely disciplined himself that the relationship was tailor-made.

From Burke Davis' *Marine, The Life of Chesty Puller*:

One of his privates, Gerald White, a Yale man from East Port, Maine, also a diarist, began to take note of Puller:
'He is never obscene, remarkably, for the vigor with which he handles us. He is tough and demands the utmost, but there is always a kindly approach even when he is chewing you out that displays a touching sympathy with the miscreant.'

Basilone's "tent city" days were over. Puller kept his battalion on its own, separated from other units. From him his men would have bestowed upon them the years of experience in the wilds of Haiti and Nicaragua. They spent their days and nights in the woods, gaining the knowledge and experience that would carry them later in the jungle. They cleared land and built machine gun emplacements. They marched miles through the winter night's snow and pitched their pup tents there in the frozen ground. There was no escaping for the medical personnel either. They trudged along with the others and learned to survive in the woods with the rest. Basilone, always ready to learn something new in order to be a better Marine, worked a deal with a corpsman. He taught the medic the semaphore signaling system and he in turn taught John first aid.

There is no doubt that John Basilone later practiced what he learned from Chesty Puller. Again from Burke Davis:

Few details escaped Puller's eye. One day he watched a
Platoon under Lieutenant Willie Dumas practice an assault on
a hilltop position and became impatient with an elaborate
flanking maneuver which wasted time.

'Old man, there's mighty little room for fancy tactics below
Division level. The enemy are [sic] on the hill. You go get
'em. In the end you'll save men. There are times when you'll
have to flank, but don't forget that the shortest distance
between two points is a straight line.'

Even with the hardships of training at New River the Marines were able to
get liberty on Friday. Woman and fun were available at the Marine camp towns
of Morehead City and New Bern, but, if a few Marines pooled their money for a
cab, a trip to Washington, D.C. took about six hours and, by the score, they did
just that. It is a sure thing that Basilone did the same. Some Marines even
jumped on a train at D.C. and went home to destinations in the New York area.
This writer believes that John would have stayed in Washington to see the sights
since one had to be back at camp by Monday morning. This is not to say that
John did not frequent Morehead City or Bern. He did like his fun. He liked it
very much. Robert Leckie in his *"Helmet for My Pillow"* says:

In the towns of New Bern and Morehead City—where the
streets were thronged with green on Saturdays—there were
cafes at every turn: cheap, dingy, the air banked with clouds of
cigarette smoke, and the juke box wail so piercing that one half
expected it to stir up eddies in the lazy smoke. Always the
girls. They sat at marble-topped tables where the faded wide-
ringed imprints of soda glasses were linked to one another by
the newer, narower marks of beer bottles. This was the beer
hall superimposed on the soda parlor.

After Pearl Harbor, Puller drove his men even more relentlessly. He col-
laborated with Colonel Pedro Del Valle, commander of the 11th Marines.
Together they trained the 7th Marines in a unique way by having Del Valle's
artillery fire rounds over, but close to the 7th's position in the field. It would be
the first time a battalion of Marines would experience a live fire situation. The
exercise would come in handy later on Guadalcanal.

Puller's straight-on approach most definitely became ingrained in John
Basilone's mind. On a fateful day on Iwo Jima he would do just that. He would
go straight ahead.

Chesty Puller signed Basilone's promotion to Sergeant on January 23, 1942.

CHAPTER 14

On November 5th with negotiations at an impasse it was resolved by Imperial headquarters that Japan would go to war with the United States. Further negotiations would yield nothing, but the door was left open with November 30th as the final deadline for America to accede to Japan's ultimate offer which stipulated that America was to sell to Japan one million tons of aviation fuel in exchange for Japan's abandonment of southern Indo-China.

Japan's naval forces would sail very near November 25th to attack American bases in the Pacific. Concurrently, her army forces in Indo-China would then move against Burma, Thailand and the Dutch East Indies. With the United States on November 26th only re-stating its former position that Japan remove herself from China and Indo-China and with the explicit demand that she accept Chiang Kai-shek as the legitimate leader of China, Japan's commitment to war was sealed. Even with many Japanese Army and Navy officers against a Pacific War, it was too late.

Indeed it was realized by many in the government that Japan's China experiment was a true disaster sapping Japan of men and material. General Yamamoto, Japan's Combined Fleet Commander had said during war deliberations that he would in the first six months of war go quickly from island to island with success, but after that, winning a war with the United States would not be possible.

The United States, it must be remembered was not in a position of strength in the Pacific. The United States had since WWI maintained an isolationist position with little concern about conflicts overseas. The thinking leading right up to its entry into the war following Pearl Harbor was that should America maintain its neutrality, she should worry little about harm coming to her. And America's lack of readiness for war was the consequence.

The prospects of war in Europe and Asia would not be thought of as probable until 1940. Before that year funding for the United States military was minimal. With the expiration of the 1911 United States-Japanese Trade Treaty in 1940, and with increasing turbulence in the Pacific, the U.S. fleet presence in Pearl Harbor was maintained. But by 1941 the Japanese Navy had doubled its tonnage since 1922 with its force more powerful than the British and U. S. navies combined. It was reasoned that should they be able to bring a decisive blow to the U. S. naval fleet at Pearl Harbor, knocking out most of her naval firepower, Japan would then be able to seize the Dutch East Indies at her pleasure. Japan would then deal with the U. S. on her terms with regard to a peace in the Pacific.

So it was that the Japanese Navy attacked Pearl Harbor on December 7th. Wake Island would be next, then Guam and the Philippines, Malaya, Java, Burma, Thailand, French Indo-China, Borneo, the Marianas, Carolines,

Marshalls, and Formosa. Practically the whole of the South West Pacific including the Dutch East Indies was at their mercy. The ultimate threat to U.S. air and sea-lanes to Australia had by January, 1942 become a reality.

They needed now only to fortify their position, to strike further east toward New Guinea, the New Hebrides, Fiji, then on to Samoa, New Caledonia and, perhaps Hawaii itself. The South Pacific would be an Imperial lake. The strategic plan would entail first the securing of bases and attainment of materiel resources in the South West Pacific. The primary goal would be the establishment of a defense line defined by an arc through New Guinea, the Solomons, the Gilberts, the Marshalls, then, from Wake Island on up to the Aleutians.

So as the days of 1941 counted down to zero the United States and her allies were at a grim place. The allied armed forces, or what was left of them, in the western and south Pacific region were on the run from a formidable enemy who was now in control of that region. Utilizing the aircraft carrier, the Japanese attacked with stunning successes American, British and Dutch possessions defended by superior forces.

On January 23, 1942 the Japanese landed on Rabaul, just east of New Guinea, in the Bismarcks. This signaled the end of "Act One," their successful acquisition of oil, rubber and rice from the Indies necessary to sustain them for further aggression in the Pacific.

But now Japan had some choices to make. Her army advised against further expansion in the south seeking recognition of the fact that it had become overextended. With its headlong island conquering campaign so went the need for consolidation and defense in order to secure those islands. Fortunately for the Allies the Japanese did not choose wisely. Additionally, the Russians were a constant threat in Manchuria, and the China commitment was a constant drain on military and resources. The Navy, however, sought immediate expansion into the Solomons and New Caledonia. On January 29, 1942, the Navy won out and plans were laid for the occupation of selected areas within the Solomons and eastern New Guinea. These moves would consequently cut off Australia from its northeastern sea-lanes and threaten that continent directly. More concrete plans soon developed which specified the immediate invasion of Tulagi in the Solomons and later, Port Moresby in Papua (southeastern New Guinea).

In April 1942 Admiral Yamamoto presented his plan for the occupation of Midway.

As its name implies, the island lies about midway between the West Coast of the United States and the Japanese home islands. It would be there that Admiral Yamamoto would draw out the American fleet for a final showdown. There the Imperial Navy would once and for all eliminate the American naval threat to the Japanese advances made so far. With the Americans out of action for at least the short term, they would see the folly of their ways and negotiate on Japanese terms.

It was not only Admiral Yamamoto's popularity that gained the ultimate acceptance of his plan to take Midway, but it was also the famous Tokyo Raid implemented by General James Doolittle that pushed the imperial general staff into acceptance. From the carrier Hornet, Doolittle lead a small group of B-25 medium bombers that hit the homeland of Japan inflicting little damage, but yielding a great morale boost to Americans. Thus the Japanese forces coalesced into action against Midway with the decision made on May 5th.

The attempted seizure of Port Moresby resulted in the battle of the Coral Sea on May 8th which, though a standoff, denied a Japanese landing there and thus became a strategic victory for the Americans. The Battle of the Coral Sea did act as a brake on Japanese expansion beyond northern New Guinea thereby diminishing the threat against Australia.

June 3rd saw the commencement of the Battle of Midway. It was this battle which turned the tide in the Pacific naval war. Japan lost four precious carriers, the bulk of her naval aircraft along with their experienced pilots. Although the numbers of carriers that either country could put into action was made equal by the Midway battle, the blow to the Japanese Navy was devastating. Japan was, however, far from beaten. Japan remained in possession of her recent conquests and, although placed in a defense mode, she remained in control of that line of defense and would fight bitterly to keep it.

With base construction on Bougainville completed the Imperial Navy commenced exploratory ventures to Florida Island north of Guadalcanal. The Japanese crossed from Tulagi to Guadalcanal on May 28th. Guadalcanal—the perfect island for an airbase. The radius of operation from there gave chance for the interception of allied communications with Australia.

CHAPTER 15

Japan was the only important nation in the world in the twentieth century which combined modern industrial power and a first class military establishment with religious and social ideas inherited from the primitive ages of mankind, which exalted the military profession and regarded war and conquest as the highest good.

Samuel Eliot Morrison, *The Rising Sun in the Pacific*

Most Japanese soldiers had been battle tested in China. The Manchurian campaign had tested many intensely, so they were quite ready for combat in the Pacific. The American combat soldier had yet to be tested against the "invincible" Japanese warrior.

The Japanese soldier was well schooled in the ancient code of bushido, or "way of the warrior." The code endured from the days of Japanese feudalism that had spawned the "samurai" or warrior caste. In ancient days the warrior would gladly give his life for his clan lord. Now he would do the same for his Emperor. To surrender was to be disgraced and would bring dishonor to his family. If he should die in battle he would be revered.

With the code of the warrior went the belief in Japanese racial superiority. The American soldier was perceived to be just as inferior as the Chinese soldier had been. With the spirit of the warrior carrying him forward no foe could defeat him. And should the enemy surrender he would be shown no mercy, for his bushido code divined that surrender was cowardice. Should he fail in battle he would commit suicide. There would be no alternative. He would fight and win or he would fight and die. There would be no middle ground. This was especially true for the officer class. If required to do, so the Japanese soldier with his comrades would bravely charge the enemy in the infamous bonzai attack. But the code of the warrior inculcated ingenuity also. The Japanese soldier was known for his skillful night penetration of enemy defenses.

It was deeply ingrained into the Japanese male psyche that he had been chosen superior by the gods to other men by race itself. That indoctrination was carried then to his military service; his training, he was told, was superior also. There was no Japanese institution, religious, civil or military, that castigated suicide. Suicide would, to the contrary, be the soldier's ideal choice on the battlefield when facing death from the enemy. After dying he would be worshipped even by the Emperor as one of the spirit guardians of the empire. His death would bring true honor to his family.

John Basilone's beloved 1st Division* began operations in February 1942 at New River, North Carolina, and was commanded by Virginia born Major General Archer Vandegrift, a fifty-five year old seasoned veteran with thirty-four years of Marine Corps service. Archer Vandegrift, a gifted leader, was a man who knew and respected his men. His quiet demeanor masked his innate ability to grasp a tactically challenging situation and deal with it meticulously. Most of all he was a leader always displaying great optimism and resolve when faced with those challenges.

The 1st Division would be a blend of new recruits, those young men generally between the ages of nineteen or twenty who had enlisted following Pearl Harbor, and the

"Old Breed, " those who had been in the Corps some years and had seen action in Haiti and Nicaragua. Some had even seen the battlefields of France. The Old Breed also came from all points of the globe where they were known to be rough and tough, but also very capable. Lieutenant Colonel Samuel B. Griffith said about them as follows:

> ...Many wore expert badges with bars for proficiency in rifle, pistol, machine gun, hand grenade, auto-rifle, mortar and bayonet. They knew their weapons and they knew their tactics. They knew they were tough and they knew they were good. There were enough of them to leaven the Division and to impart to the thousands of younger men a share of both the unique spirit which animated them and the skills they possessed.

It was believed that the Japanese would soon invade the American base at Samoa. And although the Marine Raider Battalion had been training there since before May 1942, plans were made to have them hit the Japanese at Tulagi and others of their bases in the Solomons in order to slow them down a bit. So it was that John Basilone's Seventh Regiment, one of three 1st Division regimental units sailed from Norfolk on April 10, 1942. They arrived at Samoa on May 8th to defend against the impending Japanese invasion.

Manila John was in good company. He, along with most of the Corps' best noncommissioned officers (NCOs), went to Samoa. They had been hand picked from other units and sent with many of the most capable officers to provide the first defensive combat action of the war.

U.S. forces were not yet ready to go on the offensive in the Pacific. Luckily, the Japanese were not yet prepared to fight to the south and east of Tulagi. They would have to extend their supply lines and the range of their fighter aircraft. The extension of fighter range could most easily be obtained by gaining another airfield.

---

* See end of book.

Control of the Solomons was as of 1941 split. Its capital was Tulagi just to the north across Sealark Channel. The Australian Territory of New Guinea maintained control over Buka and the larger island of Bougainville to the northwest while the British Solomon Islands Protectorate held all others. Of interest to the Japanese was one of the few open areas existing on the island of Guadalcanal in the Solomons, the coastal Lunga Plain, located in the north-central area near the Lunga River.

From Guadalcanal the Japanese Mitsubishi Zero fighter's range would be extended. Then, further conquests to the south and east could be attempted. The airfield at Guadalcanal would be most convenient for supporting further expansion in the area by covering fleet operations out of the very nice deep-water harbor at Tulagi. Samoa would then be an easy target. Tokyo believed that surely it would be six months at least before the United States would be able to gear up its forces for operations in the Pacific.

Coast watcher Martin Clemens, to his horror, on July 1st verified information from Dovu, one of his scouts, who advised that the Japanese had indeed come in force to Guadalcanal. This force, though relatively small, consisted of advance units of the 11th and 13th Naval Construction Battalion. Work on an airfield at Guadalcanal began and increased in intensity with the aid of units arriving shortly thereafter. Coupled with the airbase at Rabaul, its Guadalcanal sister would do very nicely. So by the end of July a mix of about 3000 Japanese construction workers and naval personnel toiled diligently building an airstrip on Guadalcanal. On July 6th the Japanese Navy had arrived with their Kanae 13th Construction Unit consisting of 1,350 men under the command of Captain Tei Monzen. And Commander Okuma Tokunaga's 11th Construction Unit's additional 1,221 men had accompanied them. It should be mentioned that the Imperial Japanese Army had no idea that their own Navy had construction personnel on the island of Guadalcanal, or Tulagi for that matter. Such was the Navy's attitude of superiority that existed within its ranks.

With word coming from the coast watchers, Ernest King, Commander of the Atlantic Fleet, determined that something had to be done lest communications and shipping lanes to Australia be severed. Plans were set in motion to activate the 1st Marine Division. Indeed, as early as January 1942, King had decided that something had to be done to stem the Imperial advance. Aside from the heroic, but futile, defense of Wake Island the Allied losses since Pearl Harbor had been staggering.

On July 17th Lt. Colonel Merrill B. Twining and Major William McKean flew over Guadalcanal to evaluate the level of defensive posture posed by the Japanese. Their reconnaissance along with photos taken indicated that the northern beaches were just about clear of any Japanese defensive emplacements.

The U. S. Marine operation to take Guadalcanal would be a two-pronged amphibious assault organized as follows:

Force Yoke———————————Under BGen William Rupertus in overall command (Northern Force) would seize Florida Island, Tulagi, Gavutu and 1st Division, Marines Tanambogo across the Sealark and Lengo Channels twenty miles to the north of the Solomons.

Assigned Forces (Tulagi): 1st Raider Battalion
Commanded by the legendary Lieutenant Colonel Merrit "Red Mike" Edson.

2nd Battalion, 5th Marines
Commanded by Colonel Harold E. Rosecrans

Assigned Force (Gavutu and Tanambogo): 1st Parachute Battalion. Commanded by Major Robert Williams.

Assigned Force (Florida Island): 2nd Marines Reinforced. Commanded by Captain Edward Crane

Total Force: Approx. 3000 men

Force X-Ray———————————Under MGen. Alexander Archer Vandegrift in overall (Southern force) command would seize Guadalcanal Island, Solomons. 1st Division, Marines

Assigned Forces (Guadalcanal): Combat Group "A" consisting of 1st and 3rd Battalions, 5th Marines.
Commanded by Colonel Leroy P. Hunt

Combat Group "B" consisting of 1st Marines. Commanded by Colonel Clifton B. Cates

Support Group consisting of 11th Marines Artillery and remaining 1st Division units. Commanded by Colonel Pedro A. del Valle.

Total Force: Approx. 11,300 men

The loss of 7th Marines (Basilone) to Samoa was compensated for by assigning 2nd Division's Second Marine Regiment to the 1st Division. From San Diego the 1st Division proceeded to Wellington, New Zealand on May 1st. From there they combat loaded equipment for their impending embarkation to the Solomons. The 7th would remain at Samoa for a while as OPERATION WATCHTOWER, the invasion of Guadalcanal and its environs went forward. It would be the war's first amphibious assault. The brass would call it OPERA-

TION WATCHTOWER, but it would be known as OPERATION SHOESTRING to those who fought there.

CHAPTER 16

At the time Pearl Harbor was bombed on December 7, 1941, our total force was about 7,000 enlisted men and 500 officers. Small? Yes, but the rugged brutal training under primitive conditions had molded us into a hard-hitting division that could lick its weight in wildcats. That's exactly how we felt. If topside was striving to get us damned good and mad, they had succeeded beyond their wildest hopes. We were a rough outfit and proud of it. Now we were aching to get into action. Rumors were flying wildly and on the premise that the Seventh Division Marines would see action first, based on their length of service. Many of our best men asked for and were given transfer to the Seventh. In March 1942 we were detached and assigned to the defense of Samoa. A few days later the division got its orders for overseas duty.

We still thought we would be the first to see action and that Samoa was only a stopping off point to confuse the enemy. So it was with light hearts we sailed from Norfolk, Va., on April 10, 1942. From Prosner's *The Heroic Life of Sgt. John Basilone, USMC:*

> The ship rolled toward Samoa like a sick whale for almost a month. We started to feel like Columbus sailing toward the edge of the earth but he might have sailed faster. We had rusty merchant ships fitted out with racks of canvas hammocks below decks where cargo used to be. The riveted steel sides of the ship shivered and boomed from the pounding ocean and thumping engines. There was almost no ventilation and after a few days the smell was slightly worse than a feedlot.

After the long, uneventful trip our convoy reached Apia, Western Samoa on May 8, 1942, and set up camp. Compared to Tent City, our five-month stay in these beautiful islands was a luxury. Not that we didn't continue our training. We got it every day, only now it was real jungle warfare, camouflage, the works. There were some good times, however. The native women were only too eager to help the Americans and for months I don't think a single Marine had to do his laundry. Fresh eggs and butter were plentiful and for once the griping subsided.

By this time I had been promoted to Sergeant and my boys were the best damn machine gun outfit in the division.

Samoa was no picnic. Puller worked his Marines without respite again. Even aboard ship on the way he had them working hard. They broke out machine guns on deck and trained with them incessantly. On the island they did the same. There was no one to unload supplies from the transports so Marines worked at that detail also. But the weapons exercises continued through long days and almost sleepless nights.

Samoa, the land loved by Robert Louis Stevenson, was a beautiful place, a place of lush green mountains and sparkling ocean water of blue. Located a few hundred miles southeast of Guadalcanal this island chain presented an easy jumping-off spot for the 7th Marines. Friendly natives smiled and laughed at the strange soldiers who tramped down their streets by day and who danced with them in the evening aromatic splendor of the place.

One can picture Basilone there with his boyish smile and wisp of curly black hair drooping down his forehead smiling and teasing the native girls. His smile would be infectious and brother Marines would follow his lead as they sang and carried on to the sound of the native guitars. It was as if the war did not exist. The women were eager and the beer flowed beyond the rationed number of two cans per man. They became lost in the magic of it.

But Pullers endless marches in the boiling sun continued. He drove them hard, but he was caring at the same time. He knew what they would face, and it would be soon. It was more than a mechanical drill-sergeant thing with him. He knew instinctively what he must do with them. Something was driving Lieutenant Colonel Puller as well. Somehow the Chesty Pullers are sent. They come onto the scene as if from divine providence.

All sorts of scuttlebutt was drifting into the boondocks and the men were restless. We all had thought that we would see service first. One morning about the middle of August, 1942, word trickled back that our buddies from Quantico and Tent City had already locked grips with the legendary superhuman Japs.

In an effort to get the facts I dropped over to see Captain Rogers, an alright guy. Captain Rogers was sitting at his desk deeply engrossed in some maps. Looking up he said, "Yes, Sergeant?"

I asked the Captain if it was true that at last we had started our offensive. If there was anything I could tell the men as they were getting restless. Looking back, I think Captain Rogers was as disappointed as we were but he only said, "Sergeant, the 1st and 3rd Battalions of the 5th Marines landed on Guadalcanal. The First Raiders hit Tulagi. Florida Island was invaded by the 1st Battalion of the Second Marines and the First Parachute Battalion swarmed over Gavutu. Does that answer you question?"

Snapping out of my disappointment I answered, "Yes sir."

"Good, " he said, "now sit down. In these first engagements, reports are trickling back as to what we might expect. One thing we must overcome is the Japs ability to infiltrate through our lines at night. Now for the next few days we are going to run the men ragged. I know they bitch and gripe, but I still want to hear them gripe after our first action.

With that I was dismissed. The next few days were hell. All day long we practiced storming caves; then were routed out in the middle of the night to repel imaginary Japs behind our lines. While the men complained bitterly the prac-

tice paid off handsomely in the months to come. Instead of the confusion our buddies ran into, we profited by their misfortunes. I have no doubt that many lives were saved with the series of signals and codes we adopted. We became so proficient that not a man of our outfit was shot at by one of his buddies, as had been the case during the initial landings on the Canal. Every day different rumors drifted back to Samoa. We wondered whether we were ever going to see action. Just about the time we thought we'd sit out the war on our fannies doing garrison duty, orders were received for our outfit to move up to the Canal. I think this was about the latter part of August 1942. There was no doubt this time. We packed our gear and were transported out to our ship. The harbor was a beehive of activity. Small boats, LST's, Higgins boats and anything that could float was used to get the men loaded.

There seemed to be a tenseness generated by our officers and upon inquiring I found out that the boys on the Canal needed help quickly. The Japs were putting reinforcements in nightly and the talk was maybe our boys would be driven off the island into the sea.

We could not understand where our Navy was. Why couldn't they stop the Jap transports? We didn't know our Navy had taken quite a beating and lost some ships, even though they won the sea battle. Our losses were costly and the Japs were still pouring in. I was proud of our men. We knew a lot the boys fighting desperately on the Canal. All bitching and griping ceased. Our only desire was to get to the island quickly and help our buddies. The slowness of getting the huge convoy assembled was maddening and it seemed ages before we got underway.

Actually it developed we made record time.

Sig, Bob, Clyde and I were on the forward deck of our ship and looked in awe at the tremendous panorama spread before us. On the horizon as far as we could see were ships, freighters, transports, heavy cruisers, sleek destroyers, bulky aircraft carriers, awaiting us to join with the main body of our task force. It was an inspiring sight. I know Zig kept saying, "Jeez, we could go right into Tokyo Bay."

Bob and Clyde kept repeating, "What the hell is taking them so long to get started?" I laughed and said, "You jerks, look over the side." They crowded the rail and looking down saw the wake of the ship. We were well under way. They had been too engrossed in their thoughts; they didn't even feel the ship moving.

I yelled, "OK, you guys, get the rest of the crew here on the double." What a bunch. In no time the boys were crowding around. I looked them over, the finest, and shouted, "Set em up." In seconds flat each gun was assembled and set up. I don't think any crew could match our time. At least we never lost a bet. The first few days out were quiet and we spent each moment we could cleaning our weapons and setting up. I had to, any number of times, let the boys blindfold me while I took a gun apart and reassembled it. It seemed like a game at the time, but eventually paid off in a big way.

The men had settled down, grim, serious and but with the thought, to get at the enemy. The mortar squads were cleaning and setting up their mortars.

One could almost sense the caressing manner in which they handled their equipment, knowing their lives and their buddies depended on their being in perfect firing order.

Other Marines were honing and sharpening their bayonets. Others whetting down huge bolo knives so sharp they could take a man's head off with one sweep.

Meanwhile the talk drifted away from the coming action and centered on different gals they had met in the states. You could tell each Marine was trying to out do the other with his exploits. All in all it served to divert our minds from the thoughts that were spinning in our heads. I know Sig and the boys wondered how they would stand up under fire. Their main worry was no to be an "Eight Ball." I told them to forget it and follow me, no matter what.

God bless them, never once in the coming engagements did they do anything to lower my respect for their courage and guts.

One morning during our breakfast of beans, the plaintive beep, beep, beep, of general quarters sounded. The ship came alive as air defense stations were manned. It turned out to be a false alarm. However, it started the boys guessing as to the number of casualties we could expect. It also brought home the realization that we were getting close to dangerous waters.

Meanwhile the heavy cruisers in our convoy opened up firing practice. We crowded the rail and watched the yellow flashes of gunfire, heard the dull pom-pom of their guns and the whomp-whomp of the anti-aircraft guns. It gave us a feeling of security to know the Navy would be right by our side.

CHAPTER 17

If I were king, the worst punishment I could inflict
on my enemies would be to banish them to the
Solomons.

Jack London

Guadalcanal, situated approximately 6000 miles from San Francisco, is an island about twenty-five miles wide and about ninety miles long on an axis running approximately northwest to southeast. The highest of its center-spine chain of mountains reaches 7000 feet. The rain forest abounds with ridges interspersed with twisting creeks, rivers and swamp while the shoreline defends itself with treacherous reefs. In short, it is an extremely heat and humidity-locked jungle with annual rainfall estimated to be over 150 inches per year. It would be here that the Pacific War would have to turn. It would be here that the United States Marines, in America's first offensive of the war, would have to engage the enemy in decisive combat. Eric Bergerud in his *Touched with Fire* said it thusly:

> ...it is enough to note that both New Guinea and the Solomons
> are home to some of the most rugged mountain ranges and
> ridgelines on the globe. Precipitous ridges fan out, dissecting
> the landscape further.Near the coast are densely forested
> swamps and acres of tall, razor-sharp Kunai grass.

Martin Clemens was one of a few Coast Watchers who, from their remote jungle hideaways, watched the Japanese. Always moving their bulky radio transmitters to keep a step ahead of the pursing Japanese patrols, they risked their lives to keep the Americans up to date on Japanese movements in the air and on the sea in the Solomons. From his book, *Green Hell, The Battle for Guadalcanal*, William J. Owens quotes Martin Clemens:

> ...On the inside she was a poisonous morass. Crocodiles hid
> in her creeks or patrolled her turgid backwaters. Her jungles
> were alive with slithering, crawling, scuttling things; with
> giant lizards that barked like dogs, with huge red furry spiders,
> with centipedes and leeches and scorpions, with rats and bats
> and fiddler crabs and one big species of landcrab which moved
> through the bush with all the stealth of a steamroller.

Owens goes on, from historian Dan van der Vat's *The Pacific Campaign:*

> ...Even before one drop of blood had been spilled on its
> fecund soil or a single corpse buried in it, Guadalcanal stank...
> a queasy quagmire of superabundant vegetation, swift to rot,
> on a bed of primeval slime humming with malarial mosquitoes
> and nameless bacteria. Rich in mud and coconuts, the
> Solomons were wet from May to October, wetter from
> November to April and diabolically humid all the time.

Robert Leckie, a Marine machine gunner and scout, from his *Helmet for My Pillow*, memoirs about nighttime on Guadalcanal:

> ...It was darkness without time. It was an impenetrable dark-
> ness. To the right and left of men rose up those terrible form-
> less things of my imagination, which I could not see, but I
> dared not close my eyes lest the darkness crawl beneath my
> eyelids and suffocate me....My ears became my being and I
> could hear the specks of life that crawled beneath my cloth-
> ing....I could hear the darkness gathering against me and the
> silences that lay beneath the moving things. I could hear the
> enemy everywhere about me, whispering to each other and
> calling my name. I lay open mouthed and half-mad beneath
> that giant tree. I had not looked into the foliage before the
> darkness and now I fancied it infested with Japanese.

From Eric Hammel's *Guadalcanal Starvation Island*:

> There were 25,000 of them that first week in August 1942.
> They came from nearly as many neighborhoods and towns,
> and from every one of the forty-eight states. They had been
> trained to do a hundred different jobs, and could do them with
> 25,000 degrees of proficiency. They were dozens of nationali-
> ties and religions. They had parents who, among them, spoke
> over a hundred different languages and dialects. Their families
> had been American families for nearly four hundred years, or
> a few months, or were yet to become Americans. They had
> been raised in New Haven, Brooklyn, Boston, Bangor,
> Baltimore, Atlanta, Gary, Perth Amboy, Mine Ridge. Their
> names were Casamento, Kosanovich, Moran, Jachym,
> Hernandez, Weiss, Jones, Smith...
>
> A few had been to Shanghai, Culbera, Manila, London, Santo
> Domingo, Port Au prince, Managua. Others had spent their

lives within fifty miles of home, except for brief visits to such places as Parris Island, Quantico, New River, San Diego, San Francisco, Norfolk, and, more recently, Auckland and Wellington.

They had received the best training their technocracy could then offer. They were not, however, armed with the best weapons and equipment their nation could then produce.
They had little in common, but they were, most of them, U.S. Marines. They were proud; proud to be Americans, and proud to be Marines. They were too proud to admit fear. They were young men growing up or grown men growing old. Some had been Marines for as many as forty-five years, others for just three months. They were 1st Marine Division and they were on their way to battle.

The Marines thought that the heavy bombardment of Guadalcanal would devastate the island. Surely, they believed, nothing could live through that. Thus were their thoughts as they gazed from the ships. Then it was to the Higgins boats below and off to the shores of Guadalcanal. Again from Robert Leckie, on the transport *George F. Elliott*, in his *Helmet for My Pillow*:

The bombardment was lifting; I looked to both sides of me, clinging, antlike, to the net. Sealark Channel was choked with our ships. To the left, or west of me, hulking Savo Island. In front of me, to the north, but obscured by the side of the Elliott, stretched Florida Island and tiny Tulagi. The Marine Raiders and Paramarines were already at their bloody work on Tulagi. I could hear the sound of gunfire. Behind me, to the south, was Guadalcanal.

The U.S. Marines would call it the "Canal." On Friday, August 7, 1942 they landed, minus Chesty Puller's 7th Marines, on Red Beach at 9:10 a.m. They encountered no opposition. Their objective was the capture of the airfield at "Lunga Point" several miles west of the landing zone.

The 5th Marines left Red Beach and headed west for Alligator Creek. Behind the 5th Marines came the 1st Marines. Overtaking the 5th, 1st Marines headed southwest for Grassy Knoll, or where they thought Grassy Knoll should be. They slogged through the coconut groves into the steaming jungle hacking their way through the kunai grass wielding their machetes. As evening set in the 5th had reached their objective. 1st Marines would take longer. The Marines had no reliable maps so the going was slow.

The temperature on Guadalcanal was normally 100 degrees or more and the humidity was stifling. Late in the afternoon they were halted. Vandegrift believed they had gone far enough. Other than sporadic sniper fire there had been no opposition, so he had his men regroup. It was found later that the Grassy Knoll was not the mere 1000 yards from the beach as was earlier estimated, but rather, it lay eight miles inland. So, by midnight, Vandegrift changed the objective. The 1st would trudge toward the Lunga River south of the airfield and there, on the Lunga Plain, they would form a defensive perimeter around the newly completed airstrip. The 5th would continue on its westerly track as quickly as possible toward Lunga Point to the Japanese camp at Kokum.

Patrols sent to the airfield found that the Japanese had made a hasty retreat following the U.S. Navy's bombardment of the island. The airfield was taken during the morning hours of the second day on Guadalcanal with hardly any opposition. Falling into Marine hands would be equipment, food and supplies which would prove invaluable during the coming days. The airfield was key. It would allow the Marines the air defense required to hold the island against Japanese counterattack. Japanese counterattacks would come. But now the Marines took to completing the 2600-foot landing strip that the Japanese themselves had almost finished. Completing the airfield would present no problem. Holding on to it would be more difficult, for even now the Japanese were re-evaluating their first thoughts about the American effort on Guadalcanal. Even now they assumed that the Marine force there would be under strength and recapturing the island would present no problem. They were the victors of the South Pacific.

They would come in random fashion through the blindness of their arrogance, but they would come. Then they would come in force determined to regain the Solomon's and to push the Americans into the sea.

The Japanese construction workers, mostly Korean, would present no great threat to the Marines for they had no weapons and not much food. Many surrendered quickly. There would be nowhere to go. To flee into the steamy jungle would mean certain starvation.

Headlines at home gave the Americans the first word about Guadalcanal, an island they had never heard of: "Fierce Battle Rages in Solomons"...."Marines on Shore".... "Americans Hold Ground on Guadalcanal." Radio Tokyo reported it differently, "Summer Insects which have dropped into the fire."

While 1st Division Marines landed on Guadalcanal unopposed, the landing on Tulagi—Gavutu-Tanambogo was another story. They landed on Tulagi at 8:00 a.m. on August 7th and found bitter resistance there. The 1st Raiders and 5th Marines, 2nd Battalion would experience there the tenaciousness of the Japanese soldier. On Tulagi the Marines first encountered the camouflaged and fortified tunnels and caves that the Japanese would utilize all too effectively as defensive emplacements throughout the Pacific campaign. Of the 350 Japanese fighting from those caves and tunnels on Tulagi, only a few survived. The Raiders lost thirty-six men. The Japanese on Tulagi did not find out about the American landing for quite some time. If they had, it is probable that further Marine casualties would have resulted. Marines to make the first amphibious landing in the Solomons-the first of World War II—were those of Captain Ed

Crane's B Company, 2nd Marines. They landed on Florida Island at 7:40 a.m. and found no opposition there.

Gavutu-Tanambogo, off the southeastern coast of Tulagi and only miles from Florida Island's Halvo Peninsula to the east, was to be taken by the 1st Parachute Battalion. At about 10:00a.m. they were over the side of the transport Heywood and into their landing craft. Developed by the Royal Air Force and expanded by the Japanese, the islets offered great support facilities. The Japanese would not give it up easily. Upon landing on Gavutu the "Chutes" took fire immediately, but were all ashore in just twenty minutes. Tough fighting took place as the Chutes took many of the caves from which the Japanese fought fiercely. The islet was declared secured on August 8. Tanambogo, connected to Gavutu by a causeway, was similarly defended by the Japanese. After intense combat there, it too was secured on August 9. The Chutes lost twenty-seven dead and had forty-seven wounded.

The Japanese Navy would send their relief forces down the Slot, the narrow sea lane between Santa Isabel Island and New Georgia. Savo Island was its terminus just off the northwestern tip of Guadalcanal. Vice Admiral Gunichi Mikawa commanding the Japanese 8th fleet was eager to engage the American Navy in order to re-take Guadalcanal from the U.S. forces there. He was among the few who believed that the American defenders were larger in number than most guessed. Japanese 17th Army commander, Lieutenant General Harukichi Hyakutake, was not at all interested in gaining possession of Guadalcanal as he had not been involved in that area at the outset. This was a Navy problem. The inter-service rivalry was extensive. Hyakutake was more concerned with his governments overriding strategic goal of capturing New Guinea with Port Moresby his most immediate target. Imperial headquarters viewed the American incursion into the Solomons as insignificant. They would be removed with little effort. Surely the American force could not match Japanese strength of will and superior fighting ability.

Mikawa sent the transport Meiyo Maru with about 450 sailors and meager provisions down the Slot. U.S. Submarine S-38 sent her to the bottom with the loss of about 350 men. Jack Coggins describes the attitude of Imperial Headquarters the best perhaps in his *The Campaign for Guadalcanal*:

> ...Seventeenth Army was not particularly interested. Both
> they and the Navy consistently underestimated the strength
> and fighting ability of the American invasion forces.
> Mikawa's dispatch of the ill-fated handful embarked on Meiyo
> Maru was only the beginning of a haphazard method of rein-
> forcing the islands by dribs and drabs, putting ashore units
> never strong enough or well enough supplied to do the job
> assigned. This had been put down by a Japanese naval writer
> to 'victory disease'—a combination (born of a series of almost
> uninterrupted victories) of blind arrogance, supreme confi-

dence, and utter contempt for the enemy. This may be a splendid thing in the individual fighting man but at the tactical and strategic level it can prove a serious handicap. In Japan's case it was fatal.

Mikawa then devised a plan to attack the American fleet at Guadalcanal at night. Night maneuver and attack was the Japanese Navy's forte. And Vice Admiral Fletcher's sudden decision to depart from the area with the American carriers would leave the island with no air cover.

Savo Island would be the staging ground for the first naval engagement in the area. With the Japanese Long Lance Torpedo, the very best compared to any navy, its very fine telescope and binocular optics and their excellent spotters and superior night fighting tactics their victory was assured. The Naval Battle of Savo Island was brief. In just over half an hour on August 9th, the American cruisers *Astoria*, *Quincy* and *Vincennes* along with the Australian heavy cruiser *Canberra* were sent to the bottom. Mikawa would certainly have gone after the American landing forces had he known that Fletcher and his carriers had departed the area on the 8th. But precious supplies and equipment went with transports that also departed that day.

On Guadalcanal, patrols searched for the Japanese on the 8th and 9th in order to locate the enemy's fortified areas. A Japanese prisoner advised that a number of his comrades would probably surrender. But the team lead by Lieutenant Colonel Goettge that went in pursuit of the potential captives was ambushed. Only a few Marines survived the ordeal as Japanese hacked to death some of the wounded. Thus was the ordeal of the ill-fated Goettge patrol. More Marine deaths would follow. To the Marines on Guadalcanal the Japanese soldier's ability to fight at night was very much respected, especially when they came in small units.

Work on the airfield progressed with Seabees laboring in the construction of roads, revetments and storage facilities. By August 17th the airfield was ready to commence air operations and by the 20th the "Cactus Air Force," as it would be known, was in place and ready for the air war in the Solomons.

CHAPTER 18

ICHIKI FORCE—STRIKE ONE

Orders from Hyakutake's 17th Army Headquarters went out on August 17th and the first Japanese effort to re-take Guadalcanal began on August 16th as the Guadalcanal Reinforcement Force, commanded by Rear Admiral Raiso Tanaka, departed its anchorage at Rabaul. A detachment of 900 highly trained and battle tested men of Colonel Kiyono Ichiki's famed 28th Infantry Regiment, landed at Taivu Point 20 miles east of the Marine perimeter on the evening of August 19th. The Ichiki Force would do a reconnaissance of the area, but would await the remainder of their regiment before attacking the Marines. This unit had been scheduled to make the amphibious assault on Midway had the Japanese plans for that operation been successful.

Ichiki, thinking that the Americans numbered only about 2000 and believing in the invincibility of the Japanese soldier, decided to go ahead with his attack without the aid of his supplementary force. It was a mistake. The Marines wiped out a communications unit and gained the knowledge from captured documents that they were were fighting a respectable Japanese Army unit rather than remnants of the Navy personnel already encountered. The 5th Marines fought the Japanese in what would be the Matanikau River action. It was a battle in the treacherous jungle's deep ravines and swamp-bound undergrowth, and it would feature the first full-blown "Banzai" charge of the war.

The Japanese were attacked from west of the Matanikau and from the east across a sandbar at the mouth of the river. The Marines faced attack from west of the Matanikau, but the end for the Japanese was inevitable. And by now, unknown to the Marine forces, the Japanese had set up an observation post on Grassy Knoll. Marine airfield artillery emplacements clearly designated on maps in possession of dead Japanese Army officers, gave evidence that the Marines faced serious opposition. Ichiki struck again at 2:40 a.m. on August 21st. It was at the east bank of the Ilu River. Lieutenant Ed Pollock's 2nd Battalion, 1st Marines decimated a Japanese Bonzai charge with rifle and machine gun fire. Another desperate attack followed with the same violent end for the Japanese. 1st Battalion, 1st Marines under the command of Lieutenant Lenard Cresswell enveloped the enemy after crossing the Ilu. After a push toward the sea his men along with Pollock's caught the Japanese fighters in crossfire. Artillery, tanks and strafing by Marine aircraft finished off Ichiki's 1st Battalion in what would be known as the battle of the "Tenaru."

Japanese Imperial Headquarters had underestimated the American soldier's ability and fighting spirit. It had cost them 800 dead. Marine casualties were minimal. Ichiki committed hara-kiri. But the lesson for the Marines was that the Japanese soldier's loyalty to his emperor would be unconditional. He would fight to the death with surrender unacceptable to him. It was the Samurai's code. It was Bushido.

As Hayakutake sent Ichiki so would he send another. It would be Major General Kiyotaki Kawaguchi and his 35th Infantry Brigade. Hayakutake had dispatched them as Colonel Ichiki commenced his thrust toward the U.S. Marine defenses and his doom. Kawaguchi and his advance force of 1500 men disembarked from destroyers on August 31st. As had Ichiki, Kawaguchi's force landed at Taivu Point at the north east corner of the island. The relatively small attack force was another example of Imperial Headquarters' rank arrogance and short-sighted view of American intentions and strength on the island.

Vice Admiral Mikawa was the lone voice warning of the hazards of under-estimating the American force on Guadalcanal and of going in without a well thought out operational plan. What did result from Mikawa's admonishment was that Tokyo did pull back on their New Guinea first plan. They now realized that the Solomons would have to become the focus of operations with the re-taking of Guadalcanal the priority. And Admiral Tanaka, victor of the Savo Island sea battle, still owned the Slot at night. The Americans, however, were gradually taking over ownership of the air.

At this point, although American operations were becoming somewhat organized, support for the Marines was still very far from adequate. Admiral McCain, chief of air operations put it bluntly: "If the reinforcement requested is not made available Guadalcanal can not be supplied and hence can not be held."

But the U.S. operation in the Solomons had been a doubtful one right from the start. Perhaps only the Marines themselves believed they could hold on. Major General Millard F. Harmon, Commander of the U.S. Army and air units in the South Pacific said:

> The thing that impresses me more than anything else in con-
> nection with the Solomon action is that we are not prepared to
> follow up....Can the Marines hold it? There is considerable
> room for doubt.

And Marine air units on Guadalcanal had their troubles, too. Things were not progressing smoothly. Each day brought more shortages of equipment and supplies. The airmen lacked everything from ammunition to starter cartridges to bombs and aircraft were being totaled at an alarming rate. It became a nightmare as pilots went down with malaria. But they struggled on. Ground crew worked miracles. But time was running out.

Finally, on September 10th the airmen had some relief as 24 Navy Wildcat fighters were freed up by Nimitz.

KAWAGUCHI FORCE—STRIKE TWO , BLOODY RIDGE

Now Kawaguchi's turn came to have a crack at the Marine force, but he proceeded as ineptly as did Ichiki. Hyakutaki had ordered him to evaluate the Marine strength and terrain and move to the attack only if the conditions favored him. He would have none of it. The Marine defenders were small in number, he thought, and through the superior will of his force, he would overwhelm the enemy yielding victory easily. But his intelligence was erroneous. The Marines planned to stay, and they were there in large numbers.

He ordered a small force of engineers to hack their way through the jungle to a position south of the airfield. His battle plan was complex but impractical without knowledge of the terrain. To further his problems his supplementary force of about 1000 men was virtually annihilated by Marine fighter aircraft on September 5th. About 300 men survived.

The situation was this: Vandegrift had to hold an area about 1800 yards deep stretching from Kokum on the west to the Tenaru River on the east. Facing Vandegrift's Marines at this point was Kawaguchi's initial force along with Colonel Akinosuka Oka's 124th Infantry and its 2nd Battalion. Both of Oka's units had landed on the morning of September 6th at Kokumbona. It was fully expected that there would be little difficulty in taking the airfield back from the Marines. A short fight would ensue and Vandegrift's surrender would follow shortly thereafter. To Kawaguchi's dismay, however, "Red Mike" Edson's Raiders landed at Tasimboko on the 7th and were positioned at Kawaguchi's rear. So Kawaguchi could do nothing except plod ahead through the jungle with his accumulated force of about 3000 men. The trek through the swampy malaria infested jungle would more than wear them down.

One Raider company trapped the Japanese near Tasimboko and killed 27. Intelligence now reported that the Japanese force of 3000 was heading toward the Marine position from Tetere. Edson now knew that a major encounter with the enemy was on its way. The scene of action would be Kawaguchi's target area, a ridge running roughly parallel to the Lunga River south of the airfield. So Edson decided to move his men to a location deeper into the airfield area away from the Japanese shore area bombardment. On September 10th the decision was made to establish a defensive posture at a ridge south of the airfield. Marines were in a defensive posture in other areas, also, so Edson could use only the men he had.

The situation in the Pacific was even worse for the Marines. The reported superior Japanese naval strength at Rabaul and Truk was of grave concern, and the Japanese were even now loading aboard troop transports for probable debarkation to the Solomons. Worse, the U.S. Navy was strung out in the area. South Pacific Command stated flatly that there would be no support for the Marines on Guadalcanal. Vandegrift pushed hard on Turner, who came to believe, also, that Chesty Puller's Samoa based 7th Marines would have to get to Guadalcanal as soon as possible.

On September 10th the Raiders along with the 1st Parachute Battalion were in position south of the airfield where Edson believed Kawaguchi would strike. He placed his men on the high ground, a ridge that broke down gradually to the airfield. Here 700 Marines dug in and waited for the impending attack from out of the jungle. They would come. And they would come from the rainy blackness of night. Night fighting was their forte.

It started on the 12th with the shelling of the ridge by a few destroyers and a cruiser. Then came the Japanese probing the area, testing the Marines. But the Japanese attacks were disorganized and by dawn of the 13th they had been beaten away. Although Edson believed that the attacks were intentionally timid in order to evaluate the Marine strength, the truth was that the Japanese units were in disarray after their trek through the jungle. Kawaguchi had gambled that he could take the Marines with a swift and hard-hitting attack.

But by the morning of September 13th it became quiet. His force had dispersed into the jungle. Surely, Imperial Headquarters thought, Kawaguchi had retaken the airfield and in the process the Marines had surrendered. If they could not be sure of Kawaguchi's situation they did know that the airfield was still manned by U.S. Marines.

So Japanese destroyers pounded Henderson Field again for a solid hour. This time there were seven of them. The Japanese, almost 2000 of them, came again at the ridge in bonzai charges only to be thrown back again. And again, at eleven o'clock, they pulled back. The Marines waited. They came again just before midnight. Marine artillery cut them down with shells falling close to their own lines. Bloody hand-to-hand combat ensued with extensive casualties to both sides. But the Marines held at the ridge line and the two major Japanese attacks were thwarted.

The Japanese were not through. Supported by mortar fire they came again at 2:00 a.m.—and fell back again after thirty minutes. But by now their line was less than 1000 yards from the airfield. Edson moved his men back. Marine artillery was continuous and murderous, as was Henderson's fighter aircraft later in the morning. The jungle was strafed incessantly. Five hundred dead Japanese were left as their commander ordered a withdrawal.

Other repeated attacks against Marines were also taking place some 2000 yards east of the ridge against Lieutenant William McKelvy's battalion. From positions along the Ilu River the Japanese struck incessantly but, as at the ridge, they, too, were thrown back with many dead left behind.

But the Japanese attacks had caused great loss of life to both sides as what would come to be called the battle of "Edson's Ridge" came to an end. Total Japanese casualties were twelve hundred thirteen officers and men combined. Seven hundred eight were dead with 600 killed at the ridge alone. Raider and Parachute losses were forty-nine dead and about 200 wounded. The sure thing re-capture of the airfield had failed.

Kawaguchi and the remnants of his force withdrew through the jungle carrying their wounded to the Matanikau River. They would arrive at Point Cruz haggard and hungry. It was supposed to be a cakewalk. American rice and rations were to have been captured along with the airfield. Now they had next to nothing to eat, they were suffering from dysentery and after the slog through the stifling jungle many had malaria. Now, at Colonel Oka's rear guard position, they had to claw their way further west where they could find medical aid and food.

Imperial Command would soon be in shock. To them it was a certainty that the attack at Port Moresby, New Guinea, would have to be put on the back burner. A stronger and well-coordinated plan had to be developed and implemented if the airfield was to be re-taken. By September 12th, the 3rd Battalion of the 38th Division was moving along the coast to reinforce Colonel Oka. More would follow.

Adding to the problems facing the Americans in the South Pacific, on September 14th the Carrier Wasp was sunk by the Japanese submarine I-19. Minutes later the Battleship North Carolina was torpedoed, but she stayed afloat to see action again. Only the carrier Hornet remained ready for action in the South Pacific. The *Wasp* had been escorting the convoy carrying Basilone and the rest of the 7th Regiment.

CHAPTER 19

By now Seventh Marines had left Samoa and was on the way via Navy convoy bound for Guadalcanal. Little did they know at the time that the Japnanese had known of the convoy's existence. Why had the Japanese Navy not made a concentrated effort to shut down further American landings on Guadalcanal? They had the submarine capability and they had definite control of South Pacific waters. The only answer is that Japanese naval command's chief directive was specific. From Samuel B. Griffith II's *TheBattle for Guadalcanal*:

> …Decisive targets for their undersea boats and their reliable swift-running torpedoes were not, under the existing circumstances, carriers, battleships, or destroyers, but transports and supply vessels. However, submarine doctrine, which prescribed combat ships as primary targets, had apparently congealed. To naval officers in Tokyo, and indeed to Yamamoto, destruction of the American fleet had always been, and was to remain, a matter of exclusive priority.

On September 14th Basilone and his men experienced their first encounter with the Japanese while at sea on their way to Guadalcanal, same day the *Wasp* was sunk. Again from Prosner's *The Life of Sgt. John Basilone, USMC*:

> We'd started to see Jap spotter planes off in the distance and heard our battleship escorts testing their guns. The carrier *Wasp* was in our escort screen. Sorties were coming and going from her deck flying air cover for the column as we approached the Solomons. general quarters rang at all times of the day and night after the first week. We had the first shots fired at us on the 14th. Jap dive bombers and fighters swooped in and shot the hell out of us, putting rounds through he deck and superstructure and lining up for dive bombing runs until the carrier Wildcats shot a few of them up and chased the rest off. Every night the planes attacked and every day we were on the lookout for submarines.

Whatever the tragedy of their missed opportunity the Japanese had allowed the Marine Corps' "A" Team to slip through. On the 18th of September, 1942 John Basilone along with brother Marines of Chesty Puller's Seventh had their steak and egg breakfast and went over the side as the roll was called, down the nets into the Higgins Boats and headed in for their landing on Guadalcanal. The 7th was eager to fight. It had been a long voyage and they were tired of being shot at with no way to return fire and, most of all, they were more than ready to prove that the Japanese soldier was not invincible. They knew their brother Marines were in real trouble on Guadalcanal and they were hell-bent to help them.

Suddenly on Friday morning September 18, 1942, the loud speakers blared: "All Marines go to your debarkation stations!" We knew then the Canal lay low on the horizon. The entire ship hummed with activity. We climbed up narrow ladders to positions on the deck above the cargo nets draped over the side and heard the squeaking of the davits as they were swung out and landing craft lowered. The whole length of the ship was swarming with Marines scrambling down the nets into the boats. One by one the boats scooted off to the rendezvous areas where they waited circling. Breaking out of the tight circle wave after wave sped for the beach.

Our landing was unopposed and we poured in. Thousands and thousands of us, supplies, equipment, vehicles until the beach was a beehive of activity. We moved off the beach quickly as we had no way of knowing when any Jap bombers would fly over and I had no hankering to be on that crowded and seemingly hopeless jammed up beach.

Actually everything was proceeding according to plan and underneath the apparent confusion, equipment and supplies were being funneled quickly and efficiently to the pre-established positions beyond the beach area.

We were greeted wildly by our former buddies. Compared to their tattered appearance, we neat, clean and tough, while they looked like they had been through hell. Their baptism of fire had aged them beyond belief.

The 7th not only found Marines in real trouble; they found Marines in desperate physical shape. They were weak and worn from diarrhea, malaria and dengue fever and were thin from lack of food; some were near starvation. They had sustained themselves mostly on coconut milk and rice left by the Japanese. Many had that far-away look from a mix of nutritional deprivation and combat fatigue.

Our first night on the canal was made jumpy by a lone Jap bomber* who sailed over unmolested, dropped a flare and slowly without fear of retaliation released his bombs. Fortunately our first order of the day had been to dig foxholes and while we thought it foolish to spend our energy so, there was no delay that night in finding safety in our despised foxholes.

Some days after his landing on Guadalcanal a note written on brown wrapping paper arrived at the Basilone home in Raritan, New Jersey. On it was one sentence: "I have arrived safely." John's family mailed him paper and pencils.

---

* Probably "Wash Machine Charlie" who visited almost every night.

Basilone's men along with other units of the 7th Marines were first assigned to the reinforcement of Bloody Ridge (Edson's Ridge) by placing defensive networks of barbed wire and bamboo, as it was still believed that the enemy would attack over the ridge again with a greater force. Bloody Ridge was just south of the airfield, the best proximity for the Japanese attack. But Colonel William J. "Wild Bill" Whaling formed up special scout units* for probing the jungle west of the airfield to monitor any Japanese movement.

Intelligence gained from the scout patrols laid the groundwork for the next Marine offensive. Now, Basilone and his 7th Marine brothers in a force of over 4000 men went into battle almost immediately, heading west for Mt. Austin and the Matanikau River.

A few days later we received our first battle orders on the Canal. We were to move inland, cross the Matanikau River and continue on to the hills of Kokumbona. Light gear was the order of the day as the going through the jungle was known to be slow.

The Raiders who were to proceed along the coast, left three days after us with orders to meet up with our detachment beyond the Matanikau River.

Our training on Samoa came to the fore as cutting and hacking through the jungle was rough, back-breaking and slow. Our first night cramped in the jungle was eerie. The guards we had posted out got shadow-happy and the lead was flying. Sleep was almost impossible. Daybreak was a welcome sight and just as the sun's rays filtered down through the dense undergrowth we were on the move.

This was the morning of the 24th, and after about five hours of the roughest trail-breaking imaginable we halted for a breather. Our advance scouts sent word back that a heavy patrol of Japs was on the trail ahead. We had not expected to encounter the enemy this side of the Matanikau River.

Captain Rogers felt we should try and entrap this patrol by encircling them with a ring of machine gun fire. At the same time being fully aware of the enemy's reputation for trickery, he decided he would call on the Second Marines for help. Calling me to his side the Captain said, "Sergeant, take three machine gun crews up trail and clean up that nest of Japs. Be sure that none get away to warn the main body of our location." With that I turned to my boys telling them to follow me and we headed uptrail.

We had proceeded along the trail about a mile and a half, not seeing a single sign of the enemy. I motioned to the boys behind me to stop. The silence was oppressive. Standing in the shadows of the dense undergrowth, I listened. It seemed I could almost smell the Japs. Giving the boys a sign to stay put I dropped to the ground and crawled ahead, parting the dense foliage as I inched my way ahead. About 50 yards down the trail I spotted them.

---

* Phil Hernandez, one of Basilone's best buddies, was a member one of these elite units.

They were in a depressed clearing and evidently had stopped for chow, as they were all on their haunches eating. I could not count them, but it seemed to be a large patrol. Slowly turning I worked my way back to the boys, giving them the signal to follow me. Setting two gun crews 30 yards to the left and the other crew a similar distance to the right, I instructed them to hold their fire until I started blasting from the middle of the trail. I reasoned that with the crossfire we had set up we could get every one of the bitches. I figured when my chopper started blasting them in the center they would instinctively run for cover up the slopes and in that position my boys could chop them to pieces.

The boys gathered around me and I outlined my plan, making sure they understood I would need at least three minutes to blast the center of the clearing before they opened fire. They nodded they understood and silently set up.

I again focused my eyes on the unsuspecting enemy. Their officer was sitting off to one side with a map spread on the ground, studying it intently. Instinctively I edged closer until I reached a slight rise in the ground. The tenseness and weariness in me made breathing difficult. The sweat poured through my eyebrows and stung my eyes. The cords in my neck were knotted and bulging. I had but one objective-wipe out the Japs.

I took a second out to mop my brow and clear my eyes. Then sighting my gun in the center of the group I opened fire, slowly swinging my gun in a semi-arc. It seemed ages before the officer came within my sights, then he too joined the chorus line of the dancing Japs. Funny, I thought, they seemed to be dancing up and down. I forgot to realize the impact of the heavy caliber bullets was jerking them into all sorts of crazy contortions.

Out of the corner of my eye I could see Japs trying to get out of my withering fire, scrambling on hands and knees for the slopes, yet somehow not being able to make it. I screamed, "Open up, boys, open up, what the hell are you waiting for?" Suddenly, it hit me, they had been firing all the time, only I was too tense. No wonder these lousy bastards couldn't make the slopes. I should have known better; after all I needn't worry about Bob, Hatfield, Foley and the rest. They were right guys.

Seeing no further movement I signaled to the boys to cease fire and waited for some signs of life from the mangled and twisted bodies. Remembering our instructions, I held the boys back and slowly crept down the incline to the clearing. Cradling my gun in my arm I slowly and deliberately poured a short burst into each Jap for insurance. Bob Powell, who I think knew me better than the rest, yelled out, "Jesus, Sarge, what are you doing? Why waste ammo on the dead ones?" As I turned to Bob to pipe down, I heard a short burst from Zig's gun. Swinging about sharply I saw a supposedly dead Jap fall back, his rifle slipping from his hands to the ground. I heard nothing further from Bob!

Motioning to the boys to come out we walked around the clearing making sure every Jap was a good Jap and believe me folks, the only good Jap was a dead one. I patted Zig on his shoulders and said, "Glad you were aboard." Zig just shrugged his shoulders.

Bob came over and said, "Damit it, Sarge, I'm always shooting off my mouth.

"Forget it from now on, never walk by a dead Jap unless you're sure he's dead, and there's only one way," I answered. "Do we understand each other? OK, now let's get back and report."

As we turned to go, two of the boys got sick. After all, it was our first real engagement with the enemy and the reaction had set in. We moved back into the dense undergrowth and slumped to the ground exhausted. Lighting cigarettes, we lay back smoking and in a few short minutes we headed back refreshed, in light spirits over our first sortie, and leaving the smell of death behind-A smell that was to stay with us during our stretch on the Canal.

Reporting back to Captain Rogers, I told him, "All clear ahead." He questioned me as to whether we had taken any prisoners. I answered, "No, and none escaped." He just nodded his head and I saluted my leave.

The next two days were a repetition of the first day, slow tedious progress, hacking through the densest undergrowth, wet and slimy. All the newness was worn off by now. We were dirty, tired and mean. Suddenly we reached the east bank of the Matanikau River. Wheeling with the Fifth Marines we headed for the sea and our rendezvous with the Raiders. One hitch developed in our plans in that Topside had not figured how difficult it was to keep control of the units in the jungle country. So it was we were pinned down by Jap mortar shells and every time we tried to cross the river we were turned back by the Japs. Our casualties began to mount alarmingly. The Raiders upon arriving, found we still had not effected the crossing. Milling about aimlessly, it was decided that the Raiders continue on and try a crossing elsewhere. Unfortunately, no one thought about the Japs' tactics of infiltrating during the night.

True to form they had crossed to the east bank during the night and waited for the Raiders. Error followed error. The Raiders, attacking in a frontal assault, were beaten back, losing their battalion commander, Lieutenant Colonel S. B. Griffith, in the first push. The Second Battalion, Fifth Marines, joined in the attack. They too were repulsed with heavy losses.

Meanwhile, we found out later, Topside, unaware of what was taking place and assuming that the Raiders and the Second Battalion, Fifth Marines, had crossed the river and were fighting on the other side, approved a plan of putting two companies of Seventh Marines (held in reserve) in boats for a shore landing that would put them around and behind the Japs.

The two companies took off from the beach at Kokum just as an enemy air raid developed. The destroyer Ballard, instead of supporting the companies, had to take evasive action itself. The expected naval barrage from the Ballard never developed. The landings were made on schedule. Meeting no opposition, the two companies worked their way inland towards the higher ridges, which unknown to them were zeroed in by Jap mortar fire. Just as the leading forces reached the fringes of the ridge, the first enemy fire began to fall.

The first mortar shells killed Major Rogers, the battalion executive officer who was in command of the operation, and seriously wounded Captain Cox of Company B. Part of the battalion had been cut off. Word was sent back to us that while part of the battalion had succeeded in reaching the top of the ridge, the Japs with no one to harass them had worked their way around the defense positions set up by the battalion.

The situation was serious. Fortunately, a Marine pilot flying over the besieged Marines read their signal for help and contacted the Fifth Marines.

Meanwhile, Puller, who had remained behind, became worried and realizing that the enemy with heavy concentration of forces, had worked themselves between the ridge and the shoreline, took the only course open, which would be an evacuation by boats and landing craft. First, however, means must be found to clear a corridor to the beach. The Ballard came to the rescue. Laying down a curtain of fire, her guns cut a swath to the beach and withdrawal started. However, the Ballard's gunfire was too close in to us and caused heavy casualties.

It was during this withdrawal that one of my pals, Platoon Sergeant Tony Malinowski of Company A, was killed while he was covering the retreat of his company by rear guard action.

When we all got back to Kokum there was nothing but praise and admiration for the Coast Guard and Navy boys who had manned the landing craft during the forced withdrawal. The Japs had managed to concentrate their heavy fire on the beach and the first wave of landing craft were hit and placed in confusion. The second wave, while defenseless, kept coming in. Towards the end the same Marine pilot who had observed the situation on the ridge came in low strafing the Jap positions. The Japs had to take cover and our landing craft were able to pull away during the respite.

All in all we had the feeling that our first real engagement with the enemy left much to be desired in our tactics.

A week later Captain Rogers had us in and we went over the new battle orders. Topside insisted we had to occupy and hold a position on the east bank of the Matanikau River. Taking a costly lesson from our recent failure, the plans as explained by Captain Rogers called for six battalions deployed as follows:

The Fifth Marines, 2nd and 3rd Battalions, were to advance to the Matanikau River and await orders to cross. The 3rd Battalion, Second Marines, plus Whaling's Snipers, were to turn inland, cross the Matanikau at Nippon Bridge and turn back to attack toward the sea. Our outfit was also to cross the river and attack toward the sea.

This time we had the advantage of air and artillery support.

The entire maneuver went as planned. The Fifth Marines ran into a small party of the enemy, wiped them out and continued on to their objective, the river. Our outfit with Whaling's Snipers overran a few Japs and they were dispatched to their ancestors in quick fashion. We, too, reached our objective.

Again we got the sad news that Jap trickery had once more caused heavy losses to the company of Raiders sent out to help the 3rd Battalion, Fifth Marines.

As we got the story, the 3rd Battalion had bottled up a part of the Japs on our side of the river. The first night the Japs played possum and did nothing. The Raiders meantime had surrounded them. The next night, however, the Japs made their move and overwhelmed a small group of Raiders who had held the point, *killing most of the Raiders but not until the Raiders in hand-to-hand fighting had inflicted heavy losses on the enemy. Those of the enemy that broke through were trapped on the inside of a wire barricade we had strung along the sand pit. Our machine gunners made short work of the damned slantheads.*

Meanwhile division headquarters sent word back that one of our coast-watchers at Rabaul got a message through that the Japs had concentrated and loaded a huge task force of transports at Rabaul and were about ready to send in heavy reinforcements to Guadalcanal. Battle plans were changed to meet the coming invasion.

We were told to continue on with our flanking maneuver, but instead of forging on to the west we were to return to the perimeter. As it turned out, no sooner had we completed our flanking movement overlooking the coast than we were hit by what turned out to be the Japanese Fourth Infantry Regiment.

For once the terrain favored us. We were on a ridge and the Japs, as was their custom, charged at us frontally. Our machine gunners played havoc among their ranks, breaking up their charge with devastating results. Bodies were strewn to within a hundred yards of the crest of the ridge. They were fanatics and screamed and yelled as they met death. A few got within 30 feet of our guns and the sound of bullets smacking into their flesh was sickening. A few who evidently received a cross section of our fire seemed to disintegrate before our eyes.

Retreating down the hill the Japs centered in the bottom of the narrow ravine. Our mortar batteries bulls-eyed causing heavy casualties. The Japs had two courses open. They could climb the opposite ridge thereby exposing themselves to heavy fire, or they could again make an assault frontally up the ridge. They chose the latter, were beaten back with heavy losses, retreated once more to the narrow ravine where they were battered and smashed by our mortars.

The heavy battering and awesome loss of their comrades caused the Japs to break. Casting caution to the winds the remainder made a mad scramble up the opposite ridge placing themselves directly under our machine guns. We swept the slope of the ridge killing every last stinker. I was proud of the boys. They held themselves together, taking turns at the zig-zagging forms on the slopes. Their fire was accurate and deliberate to the extent that not a single Jap made the crest of the ridge.

We understood later that the enemy suffered losses well in excess of 1000 men and while we felt better about avenging our previous defeat, we did not escape unscathed. Our losses were 50 killed and about 125 wounded.

The Marine dead totaled 65 after three days of combat. The cost to the Japanese was heavier at almost 700 dead with about 70 more at the Matanikau head waters. Most notably, Basilone's C Company inflicted more losses on the Japanese in 150 minutes than had been caused by the entire two battalions fighting at Alligator Creek or at Bloody Ridge. Bloody Ridge had continued for two nights before action ceased.

CHAPTER 20

On that fourth day after the Battle of Bloody Ridge, the same day that Basilone and the 7th Marines landed on Guadalcanal, the Japanese High Command order was proclaimed; the Ichiki and Kawaguchi failures had caused great loss of face; the decisive battle for Guadalcanal must must take place. How could it fail? It would be back to the hard days of war against the Russians in Manchuria where Japanese night combat actions against an enemy of greater force had been successful, where the war had been won.

General Vandegrift now had 1st Division near full strength. At his disposal were infantry strength of nine battalions, artillery at four battalions, light tanks at two companies and the great Raiders in somewhat smaller strength than at the beginning of combat. But dysentery, various fungal infections, malnutrition and malaria, in somewhat small numbers, now plagued the Marines on Guadalcanal. The Marines did what they had to. They dug in. Vandegrift knew that further attacks were imminent. It was only a matter of time. They did their best to establish some kind of depth to their defensive posture. From this posture Vandegrift would attempt to strike with short punches at the Japanese. John Basilone and his machine gunners, in the first of these thrusts, had encountered some of Oka's men who were positioned ahead of his main units. They had then come in contact with stronger units in strength along the Matanikau. For by this time Japanese strength had reached more than 4000. And more would arrive soon.

By now "Red" Mike Edson was in command of the Fifth Marines. From well-concealed positions the Japanese had struck hard at the Raiders with mortars and automatic fire. It was at this point in the fighting that the troubles began. Major Otho Rogers was commanding Puller's (Basilone) 1st Battalion Seventh Marines as Puller had remained with Edson. But Rogers and the 1st Battalion were hit hard by the Japanese at their landing after being trapped in a closing vise almost preventing escape from the beach. Unknown to Basilone it was Puller, after rushing aboard the *Ballard*, who directed the escape from the trap at Point Cruz. This battle would be known as the "Second Matanikau."

Don't let anyone tell you about the glory of war. It's horrible. You see and feel your own buddies dying before your very eyes. You feel so helpless and lost. One minute you're splitting a smoke with a pal. The next second he's gone dead. At that you feel: OK, if I'm gonna get it, let it be fast. Don't let me suffer like Harry, Mike, Jim, you name them. Lying on the ground, bleeding, with their faces blown apart, stomachs split open, entrails spilling out and the smell of death upon them. All the while you're helpless. You've got to stay at your guns. The enemy doesn't stop to let you help or save your wounded.

You sob and trigger your gun until the heat blisters your hands. Meantime, the medics are performing heroic acts trying to save as many as they can. You see all of this out of the corner of your eyes but you continue on. You must hold your flank, regardless.

Suddenly there is quiet, so quiet you think your eardrums are going to burst. You look around you. The carnage is unbelievable. Your first thought is how did I come through this unhurt? All around you is death and suffering and you without a scratch. A few engagements like this and you accept the fatalistic outlook. The bullet didn't have my name on it. I got so I steeled myself and made myself believe that I could not get it. There was so much to be done and at this time so pitifully few of us to carry on. With that attitude I took chances that a more seasoned veteran would call foolhardy.

We had our objective. The enemy had inflicted some casualties and losses among us, small however, compared to his staggering losses. The advanced position along the Matanikau was ours and later developed into one of the turning points of the entire Canal campaign.

We had now proved ourselves. We were no longer the clean, cocky boys who only a short time ago had hit the beach. We acted older, our faces showed the terrific strain of the ordeal we had just gone through. We had seen and tasted death, seen our buddies blown apart. The taste was bitter. Now we had only one purpose in mind. To drive every Jap off the Canal. Our slogan was to the very end, "The only good Jap is a dead one."

We were pulled back to a rest area, where we licked our wounds and filled in our company to replace our losses. Our replacement were young, eager and every one a Marine. Looking at them one could almost feel sorry at the ordeal they were soon to undergo. Those who survived would be old overnight and join the ranks of us soldiers and so it would continue until this whole sorry, senseless slaughter was over.

A few days of rest and good food together with the opportunity to catch up on our mail put new life into us. Once more we were able to talk about what lay ahead of us. Scuttlebutt had it that the famed and dreaded Japanese Sendai Division had landed on the Canal. We doubted it as none of our battalions had run into them. However, it gave us something to jaw about as the Sendai Division was the cream of the Japanese fighting forces.

Up to this point the Japs had sent their famed Kawaguchi Regiment against us in September. This regiment had been sent in to reinforce the Ichiki detachments, which had landed in August. Outside of a few stragglers, who had fled to the hills and holed up in caves, both crack forces had been annihilated by us. Later developments revealed that Lieutenant-General Hyakutake of the Jap forces had complained bitterly to Tokyo that the Imperial Navy had not given him the support he needed, and would have to have, if he was to recapture the Canal as the American Commanders had put only their most stubborn forces ashore, the "Malines." I guess all the bitching was not confined to our side.

Hyakutaki assured Tokyo he could drive the "Malines" into the waters. He would send in his superior Sendai Division that he had been holding in reserve.

However, to insure its success the Imperial Navy must get them to Guadalcanal. Heavy artillery must be landed to support them and shell the airfield which must be knocked out.

Lieutenant-General Hyakutake was able to convince the Imperial Navy of the importance of knocking out Henderson Field and every plane based there.

In addition to assigning battleships and destroyers, plus submarines, to the Imperial Navy Southeast Fleet, the Japs also loaded land-based guns on a tender and with two destroyers to escort them, were to head for Guadalcanal on October 11. Following would be a full cruiser division with transports. The cruisers were to subject the Canal to a heavy and long shelling, with the purpose of knocking out Henderson Field and grounding the planes.

The transports would then be free to land their troops and if the timetable held up, the remainder of the famed Sendai Division would leave for the Canal the following day escorted by two battleships. At this time the Imperial Navy felt confident it would receive no opposition from the American Navy. For the past two months Jap ships had moved up and down the Solomons to the East China Sea without seeing any signs of our Navy.

It was about this time that our Topside underwent some changes. Vice Admiral William F. "Bull" Halsey took over command, bringing with him to augment our task force a few cruisers. Immediately Vice Admiral Halsey dispatched four of the cruisers from Espiritu Santo on the night of October 7 to "hit and destroy any enemy craft within sight of their guns."

On the night of October 11, in the vicinity of the Russell Islands, our ships sighted some Jap ships and closed in.

We were fortunate in surprising the Japs, and plastered them but good. We lost one destroyer. Ironically enough, we never knew just who sank the destroyer Duncan as it was fired upon by both sides.

The Japs in this engagement lost a cruiser and a destroyer and suffered heavy damage to two other cruisers. The enemy meanwhile under cover of the fast and furious naval battle had succeeded in getting their big guns ashore. They promptly blanketed Henderson Field with a thunderous barrage catching a few of our planes on the ground. The saturation shelling of the field rendered it unfit for use on the 13th.

According to the Japanese planned timetable the balance of the crack Sendai Division left Rabaul crammed into seven transports preceded by two battleships.

Upon reaching the Canal the two Jap battleships opened fire and for hours salvo after salvo thundered in on the defenders. All of our dive-bombers with the exception of four at Henderson Field were knocked out. The next morning the four, with a few fighter planes that could still get up in the air, searched for and sank one of the transports.

The other six transports put the Sendai Division ashore on the night of the 14th.

The following morning our dive-bombers knowing that the Japs could not have had time to put their supplies and heavy ammunition ashore, hunted out and sank three more transports. One more was sunk by one of our few PT boats *based on Guadalcanal.*

The famed Sendai Division already on the Canal was thus deprived of most of its much-needed supplies.

CHAPTER 21

The heavy shelling by the Jap battleships was an ordeal of torture. There was nothing you could do. Our planes were knocked out. Sprinting for the nearest shelter, whether it be foxhole or dugout, you crouched and prayed. The whole island was a spitting, flaming inferno. The very earth spewed forth sending its debris high into the air. Intermingled with the earth and debris were parts of human bodies, our boys, when a salvo would hit a dugout squarely. Through it all you raged, cursed and cried tears of frustration. There was nothing you could do. The Japs were slugging, this time for keeps.

We had been in the past subjected to all sorts of bombardments by every variety of enemy craft, but it had been on a hit-and-run basis. This time there was no let up. The din and concussions were unbelievable. Good brave men gave way and sobbed. Our planes were caught with their flaps down. The sky was full of twin-engine Jap bombers and they saturated Henderson Field. Later in the afternoon another flight of Jap bombers, escorted by sleek Zeros, scored direct hits on our aviation supply depot, sending flames gushing high into the air.

The carnage was such as to break down even the bravest of men and we were no exception. If only we could strike back. There was nothing we could do but hug the ground and pray.

In the late afternoon, the pall of death rising with the smoke and flames, we saw our first reinforcements shooting in from the beach. The landing craft looked like water bugs in the distance. I know one should always appreciate help, but I couldn't help saying out loud, "What the hell are they sending them in for? We need our fighter planes and where the hell is our Navy, why can't they stop the damn battleships. They're murdering us."

I watched the beach and marveled at the way our Coast Guardsmen brought in their craft and in seconds flat sped back to for another load. By now the beach, as it is in the initial stages of any landing, was becoming a milling mass of men and supplies.

It was at that very moment the Jap airmen flew over bombing and strafing the beachhead, the green troops getting their first taste of humiliation and death. The group still in the process of landing and receiving their baptism of fire were elements of the 164th Infantry Regiment, made up for the most part of National Guardsmen from North Dakota.

They were men from all walks of life, bank clerks, laborers, ordinary fellows who no doubt polished up and practiced drill once a week at home. Outside of two weeks of field training each summer they probably never fired a rifle or machine gun. Well you should see them on the beach under fire. It made you proud to be an American. They died like men and still they came, working their *way off the beach. One group even got their anti-aircraft gun set up and started popping at the low-level-flying strafers. At least they were hitting back.*

That evening the Jap field artillery guns that had been landed under cover of the naval engagement a couple of days ago, opened up and plastered Henderson field. Swinging about in a huge arc, they dropped shells on the base at Kokum. Completing a saturation shelling around our perimeter they finally swung out to sea seeking out the transports that had disgorged our Army boys that afternoon.

All night long it was in and out of foxholes. There was no sleep to be had. At two in the morning one lonely Jap flew over dropping flares over Henderson Field and lighting up the sky. Then for the next two hours it seemed the Japs were throwing everything at us.

Except for the heavy rumbling of the naval guns and the quivering of the earth as we clung tight to her bosom it reminded me of the fireworks display they used to put on at home for our annual fourth of July celebrations. Then it had been fun; now it was life and death. The enemy cruisers were hurling salvo after salvo and you could see the brilliant yellow green flashes of light and the red pencil line of the shells arching threw the sky. Flashes on the shore when they struck and seconds later the b-room-boom of the cannonading.

The worst I think, although at the time nothing was good, were the huge 14-inch shells that the Jap battleships were lobbing in. The earth shook and trembled when they hit and through it all you could hear the screams of the mangled and dying.

Intermingled and pulverizing whatever was left standing was the saturation plane bombing and blasting by the land-based artillery. All throughout the night this continued. At sunrise the heavy Jap field artillery started again. After about and hour they, too, let up.

Tired, glassy-starry-eyed boys climbed wearily out of their foxholes and with unbelieving eyes took in the holocaust. It didn't seem possible that anyone could have survived.

I found out later our Navy, which I had been calling upon to God to help us, consisted of four PT boats and, God bless them, one had the audacity to torpedo a large Jap cruiser before the sleek, swift Jap destroyers closed in on him.

We knew from this terrific bombardment and shelling that the Japs would not be too long in striking. What we didn't know was from which point would come the heaviest attack.

CHAPTER 22

Allied intelligence knew that something was going to happen and would happen soon. It was was nothing specific, but it was in the air. A decisive attack was imminent, probably from across the Matanikau.

The Japanese had indeed landed the bulk of the Sendai Division. General Masao Maruyama had them in place by October 8th. What was left of the Kawaguchi and Ichiki regiments rested and tried to regain their strength at the rear. Their rations were practically non-existent and malaria had spread widely through their ranks.

But Japan's most powerful attempt to re-take Guadalcanal—and from that effort regain command of the Southwest Pacific—was in the making. They had been landing about 900 men each night since October 9th. With promised howitzers Maruyama and Hyakutake would bombard the airfield prior to a driving attack. Japanese units dug in along the Matanikau and sparred with Marine patrols sent in by Vandegrift.

A Japanese force of cruisers, destroyers and transports was spotted by the coast watchers. And on October 11 the Japanese force was observed coming down the Slot. The sea Battle of Cape Esperance ensued causing the loss of the destroyer Duncan as told by Basilone. It ended with no great triumph for either side. The Japanese, although shaken, landed another 4000 of their forces at Tassafaronga on October 12th.

Imperial Headquarters was in a quandary, not as to the overall aim of the plan, i.e., the re-capture of the airfield, but the question remained regarding the overall tactical plan. From which direction should the main attack emanate, and which units would take part from the jump-off points decided? One point was agreed upon right from the start: the forces must be focused and tightly knit and the American defense would have to be overrun with swiftness. So the Japanese 17th Army and the 2nd Division deliberated.

On October 11 Colonel Tamaoki, 2nd Division Chief of Staff and his Operations Officer, Colonel Makumoto, climbed to an observation post atop Mt. Austen. From there they observed that defenses south of Henderson field were light, so with Hyakutake's blessing, they planned an attack from that direction. The next day engineers began to cut a path through the jungle via what would become known as the Maruyama Road, a two-foot wide treacherous ridge-laden steaming trail that wound through the dense jungle between the Matanikau and Lunga Rivers.

Formal orders issued by the 17th Army on the 15th directed that a well-coordinated and simultaneous attack would be mounted from three positions south of the airfield. It would go forward at dusk on the 22nd. The main effort total force would consist of 7000 troops of the 2nd Infantry Sendai Division and would be lead by General Maruyama. Their attack would penetrate what they believed was a thin Marine line south of Henderson Field.

The main attack would consist of two wings. At the left would be Major General Nasu's 29th Infantry Regiment. On the 16th they would start the trek through the jungle to the jump-off point. Following directly behind would be the right wing consisting of the 16th and 230th Infantry Regiments, commanded by General Kawaguchi. Included in each five-battalion wing would be three infantry battalions carrying mortars, artillery, anti-tank guns and artillery pieces. The two wings would advance parallel to each other and roughly parallel to the east bank of the Lunga River.

Distracting the Marines would be a diversion by Major General Tadashi Sumiyoshi's 17th Army attacking along the coast with heavy artillery and five infantry battalions.

It was Sumiyoshi who said, "The operation to surround and recapture Guadalcanal will truly decide the fate of the war."

On the 23rd, the 1st Battalion of the 228th Infantry Regiment was to land at Koli Point and wait for orders to attack the Marine perimeter from the east. Lastly, Colonel Oka's 124th Infantry Regiment along with a 4th Infantry Regimental group was to cross the Lunga and engage Marines defending that area.

Concurrent with the above, battleships and heavy cruisers would shell the airfield from the sea while aircraft would do bombing runs. Of course the whole of the Japanese plan depended on timing, and a struggling trek through the Guadalcanal jungle along with a required pre-attack regrouping and set-up, would not help with the timing. Complicating matters for the Japanese was the load that each soldier was to carry through the jungle, as he was expected to hack through the vine-entangled bush, climb steep ridges and plod through swamp. Each soldier would carry the added weight of an artillery shell. Mortar men carried their weapons broken down along with ammunition, etc.

The Marine situation was tenuous at best. Vandegrift had thirteen battalions to cover a 12,000-yard run along the beach from the Ilu River to the Matanikau River, then a run from the Matanikoau south that stretched about 15,000 yards. From the Lunga River the perimeter ran west then turned north to the beach at the Matanikau. More of a concern was the condition of the Marine force. Six of the thirteen battalions were worn down from combat and were riddled with malaria. Hundreds were infected. The second week total was about 700 cases and the third week brought about 650 more. Luckily Puller's Seventh Marines were in relatively good shape.

Vandegrift's greatest fear was an attack from the sea against the Matanikau - Ilu line. He was aware of Sumiyoshi's howitzers and knew that he had nothing to effectively defend against them. He knew, too, that through all the fighting whether on land or in the air, the Japanese were landing in force, both in men and in arms.

It is interesting to pause here and examine the scene in the Solomons as visualized by the outside world. Tokyo said nothing much at all. In Washington the news was grim. Secretary of the Navy, Frank Knox, was non-committal when queried by the press. When Chesty Puller's radiomen set up a radio at his command post his men heard Knox say that the Marines' chances of survival on Guadalcanal was impossible. It looked to him that it would become another Bataan. President Roosevelt, all-consumed by the situation in Europe and North Africa, was silent. The New York Times reported that [Guadalcanal] was "likely to develop into one of the decisive struggles of the war in the Pacific." Vandegrift kept the pressure on for more support. Then, a good thing happened.

Halsey arrived. On October 18th from CincPac he was told to take command of the South Pacific "immediately." He advised Vandegrift that he would give all the support that he needed. Morale soared.

Maruyama's men trudged through the humid menacing jungle. They struggled forward and were exhausted after only two days. It was an agonizing ordeal. They slipped down ridges and dropped or abandoned equipment—field pieces, shells, and mines—to the undergrowth. Their rations were meager, a small scoop or two of rice each day. But Maruyama remained confident that with or without his firepower his forces would overwhelm the Marine defenders.

By the 19th forward Sendai units believed they were about four miles from their designated Lunga crossing point. They prepared for the up coming battle. Maruyama and his headquarters personnel arrived at the same point on the 20th. Though he thought he was closer, Maruyama was now only eight miles from the airfield, within a mile of the point of attack. And Sumiyoshi's 150mm howitzers had now been bombing the airfield since the 12th from positions west of the Matanikau. As Maruyama expected, this caused the Americans to focus their attention there. 17th Army morale was boosted as they listened to pessimistic American radio broadcasts about the critical situation on Guadalcanal. The Japanese were in relatively good shape now with 20,000 troops readying themselves for the decisive battle for Henderson Field. Defending against the impending attack was about an equal number of American Marines and Army soldiers combined.

Colonel Nakaguma's 4th Infantry Regiment created a great stir at the coast to convince the Marines that they were concentrating their forces there in preparation for a main offensive from that area. Sumiyoshi's bombardment continued.

Although the Marines had come across a map prepared by the Japanese showing thrusts from the east, west and south, no activity was detected in those areas, so the upper Matanikau remained the main defensive area. The Army's untested 164th Regiment was placed east of the Henderson field where activity was least expected. The Army's right flank was interwoven with the 7th Marine's right.

The 7th's position, south of the airfield, extended west to east with Edson's Ridge (Mt. Austen) just west of their position. The 7th's C Company was immediate to the Lunga. Following, west to east from Company B were Companies C, with Sergeant John Basilone commanding three machine gun positions in that company, and A in that order. 7th Marines now had to defend the 2500-yard sector south of the airfield with an under-strength 1st Battalion of 700 men. A force of regimental size would normally defend a sector of this length.

The problem for the defenders of Henderson Field was that they were bound and pressed tightly to the perimeter with the sea controlled by the Japanese Navy at night. With expected action at the Matanikau, Vandegrift assigned two battalions, most of the division's strength, to the mouth of the river. The consequence was a thinning of other defensive positions. The south portion of Edson's Bloody Ridge descended at the right of Company C and proceeded southwest for a good distance. A Company, situated on lower ground than the other two, had the worst of positions as it faced thick jungle above them. Over Puller's strong objection, one A Company platoon was assigned an outpost about 1500 yards out front off Puller's left flank thus weakening their position further. That early warning outpost commanded by Sergeant Ralph Briggs had been in place for over a week when Puller's protests got the men withdrawn some distance, but they still remained out in front. Intense combat was still not expected from the jungle south of the airfield.

CHAPTER 23

The boyish face now took form—the wisps of curly hair, the eyebrows. It radiated mischievousness, but also innocence. But now his eyes—eyes once filled with light and laughter. Orlando hesitated and breathed deeply and imagined looking out through those eyes. He gazed transfixed as John Basilone did at the rain-drenched blackness before him beyond the Lunga Plain. The laughter in those eyes replaced now by a tense apprehensive stare as he waited—wondered, sensing the epic battle to come.

SENDAI FORCESTRIKE THREELUNGA RIDGE

Somber warning from Imperial Headquarters in October had been ominous:

It must be said that the success or failure in recapturing Guadalcanal Island, and the vital naval battle related to it, is the fork in the road which leads to victory for them or for us.

On Sunday, October 19th, mass was said on the beach.

Our boys holding on to the advance position we had secured at the Matanikau River so dearly, heard on the night of October 20th some Japs milling around on the other side of the river. It was not until the 21st, however, that the Japs made their presence felt. Shortly before dark they began shelling our positions at the mouth of the river.

As soon as darkness set in the Japs tried to push across a tank force followed by infantry. Our boys were waiting and repulsed the attempt, the Japs leaving one of their tanks on a sandbar and retreating to the other side of the river. We had learned our lesson now. Figuring they would bunch together before attacking again we had our artillery zeroed in on the banks of the opposite side. Sure enough and true to form the enemy, confused at the rapid fire, bunched together so that our exploding artillery shells killed hundreds before they could scatter for cover.

We had set up our defensive positions for a full-scale frontal attack by the enemy, fully expecting an assault in full force.

However, the next day, the 22nd, except for some light bombardment, noth-

93

ing happened. The 23rd was quiet until the sun began to sink in the west. Just as the last rays were fading out, the Japs opened up with their heavy artillery and laid down one of their heaviest barrages.

We felt this was a prelude to an all out attack. But the Japs tried only to push a heavy force of huge tanks across the spit and ran into a veritable curtain of fire laid out by our anti-tank destroyers. One tank did succeed in getting through our wire, but was directly scored upon by an anti-tank unit that blew it back off the spit into the ocean.

Evidently the Japs had had it for the night. Nothing stirred.

With the coming of daybreak we were able to see the frightful wreckage our guns had created. The huge tanks stood high on the sand spit, twisted and torn. The coconut grove was nothing more than blasted stumps. The Jap dead interwoven in the debris were already in the first stages of decay. The stench rising in steam at the water's edge was sharp and pungent. The corpses swelling in the hot sun seemed about ready to burst.

No one knew exactly where the Japs would hit next. The most likely spot was the flank of advanced Matanikau River position. This flank being spread out and thin was immediately reinforced by pulling in two battalions of Seventh Marines stationed at the ridge south of Henderson Field. This left the ridge protected only by our battalion, the First, under Lieutenant Colonel Puller.

This maneuver seriously weakened our defenses on the south ridge, forcing us to spread the balance of the men out. Topside had figured the advance position along the Matanikau River would be the focal point of the big assault. For a while it seemed they had anticipated the enemy's next move. The fact that our scouts reported to division headquarters a heavy Japanese column had crossed a ridge bound for what appeared to be a full scale rear attack on our exposed flank along the Matanikau River practically gave confirmation to Topside's thinking. The anticipated attack did not materialize and by nightfall, reports filtered back that our position on the ridge south of Henderson Field was being scrutinized by Japanese officers.

I hoped the Japs would not try to reach Henderson Field through our section of the front in full regimental strength as I had only sixteen boys and four heavy machine guns. Rumors had it that the enemy had landed their crack troops in heavy force and were going to overwhelm us by sheer force of numbers.

Maruyama was not in position to strike on the 22nd as he had planned. It was indeed foolish to think that a three-pronged coordinated attack could be brought into action after a grueling jungle trek. He put off the attack until the 24th. But communications with other units had broken down. On the 23rd Sumiyoshi, suffering from malaria and not having gotten the word that the attack had been postponed, was out of action.

Colonel Oka's 124th Infantry and Nakagama's 4th's under Oka's command proceeded with the diversionary effort, but were stopped at the Matanikau after heavy combat. So by midnight on the 23rd the Marines had secured the Matanikau. Sumiyoshi's failed attack, however, did achieve its goal. American focus remained at the mouth of the Matanikau.

To complicate matters the rain that had been pouring down for some days now hindered Maruyama's movement, but also turned Henderson field into a sopping mass of slush. This made Marine air cover impossible.

On the 24th Maryuama had his command post set up south of Edson's Ridge and was ready to go. A 5:00 p.m. jump-off time was set. Unknown to Maruyama, Marines had observed a Japanese officer looking toward the Marine positions at Edson's Ridge through binoculars and a column of Japanese soldiers was seen moving through the jungle near the ridge. A Marine scout saw campfires along the Lunga River.

This alerted the Marines to the fact that the Japanese were preparing to attack Henderson Field from the south. All they could do now was brace themselves for the coming battle. The allocation of their defensive force was set; realignment was not possible.

Looking over their machine guns, Basilone and his men of C Company, facing south, had before them first a grassy plain, a decline, then the jungle just beyond. This was Lung Ridge. Earlier in the day Basilone had walked the area occupied by Lieutenant Colonel Herman Hanneken's battalion before they were pulled out and sent to the Matanikau River mouth area. After, the area facing 7th Marines was plowed to slow down the enemy attackers.

John saw to it that sandbags were placed around the gun emplacements. The Marines then hung tin cans filled with stones* from barbed wire strung in front of their positions. They placed grenades in the cans and pulled the pins half way out with hopes that they would fall out if jarred. As there were no staples, the wire was wrapped around trees.

The darkness of night closed in on that Saturday, October 24th as Puller made sure all field phones were turned on as he walked the line. He knew it was coming—the moonlight was dim and the rain would begin soon. The Marines went back and forth from the gun pits to the wire line to string more barbed wire thus creating a second and third line. Bob Powell went to a jeep at the rear for another bail of barbed wire that Puller had found. Now a fourth wire line was created. Puller double-checked the single communication wire between each emplacement and again ordered that the line be left open.

The terrain favored us somewhat and taking every advantage of it, I placed two of the guns close together on my left and two further over to my right. I knew there was plenty of barbed wire out front and if we could only hold the lousy sons of Nippon at the wire, I felt sure we could give a good account of ourselves.

At any rate as we settled down we could hear scattered far up and down the

---

* Benjamin Montgomery, a machine gunner on Guadalcanal, remembers that they also placed stones in the cans at times and found that the ever present crabs would somehow crawl into them causing the stones to rattle; the Marines would of course start shooting. Noisy crocodiles in the creeks caused the same comotion.

line an occasional burst of grenades and mortars. Hell, I thought, this is not too bad. They're going to have to blow up my whole damn outfit to kingdom come before they can get through the pass.

Basilone's gun positions of two heavy Brownings each were installed in shallow trenches at either side of the clearing 150 yards apart. As darkness crept in he went to do a final check on his right hand position that unfortunately was not visible from the left one. His men, Nash, Foley, Hatfield, Crumpton, Evans and LaPointe on the right seemed ready for the battle they knew was coming so he returned to the left position.

The rain came, and the gun pits filled with a grimy sludge of mud and urine. The chaplain came through and prayed with the men, for it was coming now. John knelt, field phone in hand, between the two machine gunners wanting to control the timing of the first bursts.

It was John's buddy, Sergeant Ralph Briggs who spotted the Japanese first. Briggs' platoon had been pulled from Company A and placed 3000 yards directly in front of Basilone's position a short distance into the jungle. Puller became incensed at the decision to place Briggs out there and angrily called General Sims to rescind the order saying that there was no need to have them out there to be sacrificed. But there was some indecision by Sims. Minutes went by.

Briggs stayed in position at his outpost in the jungle, but it didn't take long for him to phone Puller at the battalion CP. As instructed, Basilone listened in. Briggs reported that the Japanese were coming in from the south. "Colonel, there's about three thousand Japs between you and me," he reported in a whisper." At first they did not spot Briggs as they literally brushed passed his platoon. It is known that the first contact beyond the perimeter guarded by Puller's 1st Battalion, was made by Shoji's 1st Battalion 230th Infantry. Shoji engaged Briggs during his retreat and a few men were lost.

Major General Nasu ordered his men to attack east of Bloody Ridge in the area that would be known as Lunga Ridge. The rain poured as flares from Colonel Furimiya's 29th Infantry pierced the sky signaling the commencement of the attack. Captain Kihei Nakajima lead his 3rd Battalion, 29th Infantry forward with Captain Jiro Katsumata's 11th Company just ahead assisted by a scout team. Now at about 12:30 a.m. on October 25th, about twenty yards from the perimeter, Katsumata's engineers began to cut through the barbed wire. Katsumata's men behind them crawled through the grass quietly. A few men overcome by exhaustion stood and staggered sideways while others screamed out in anticipation of the attack. It would be the 9th Company that would hit Basilone's line, out of the planned sequence of attack; they were supposed to come in behind the 11th company, but in the confusion they became mixed with the 11th charging Basilone's C Company. Japanese sappers cut the barbed wire facing A Company.

It was about 10 o'clock when the field phone rang sharply.
[Bob] Powell said, "Take it, Sarge, it's probably for you."

96

Garland chipped in, "Yes, Sarge, one of the outposts is getting lonely."

I picked up the phone and at once the wire crackled sharply. I heard Jonesy* on the other end calling, "Sarge, " he screamed, and through his excited yelling I could hear the sounds of heavy fire and deep explosions. "Sarge, the Japs are coming. Thousands of em. My God, Sarge, there's no end to em. They just keep coming. Sarge, we can't stop them. Sarge, I got...." Suddenly the wire went dead. "Jonesy, Jonesy, " I yelled, "Are you OK?" Answer me." Nothing but silence. I turned to the boys and said, "They got Jonsey."

Puller shouted to his men to hold their fire after one of the Marines along the defense line advised via phone that the Japanese were cutting through the barbed wire. It was ten o'clock. Through the drenching rain Marines and Japanese exchanged obscenities.

The rain slowed a bit as Basilone, tensely waiting at his left flank position, strained his eyes peering into the shadows of the jungle beyond the clearing. But the shadows were real. They came menacingly forward, slowly. They had snaked through the barbed wire now and were advancing. Basilone cautioned his men, "Steady, boys, hold your fire till I give you the word. Time seemed as if to stand still, "The Japs came—60 yards, 40 yards, 30 yards." The order came from Puller, "Fire!" The machine guns blazed. The battalion's mortars and artillery open up immediately. Colonel Del Valle's artillery had been sited to the area fronting the jungle close to the Marine line.

Katsumata's plan was to feint one platoon to his left into Company A while sending the rest of his company to the center toward the opening developed by the feint. This would put the bulk of his force into the guns manned by Company C. At about 1:00 a.m. Company A along with Marine artillery and mortars killed most of the feinting force as they became snagged on the barbed wire. Then the 9th Company, at about 1:15 a.m., charged Basilone's Company C position. They came screaming, "Totsugeki!" And they would continue to come in waves.

Tracers flashed and intersected across the clearing from each of Basilone's gun positions. Japanese tumbled as they were ripped apart, some dropped and went prone as they continued to advance. As they went low so did Basilone's guns as his men lowered their trajectory chewing up ground and Japanese soldiers at the same time; 500 rounds per minute from each gun ripped through the charging Japanese. John was thankful that he had not set the guns up himself as he believed that he probably would have set them too high causing them to fire "over their heads."**

---

* Just who Jonesy was or what his position in the field was, is not known. It is probable that he was one of Brigg's men at the jungle outpost.

** This does make sense when one knows that Basilone trained these men and would have come to have faith in their ability to set the guns up.

"The noise was terrific and I could see the Japs leaping as they were smacked by our bullets. Screaming, yelling, and dying all at the same time. Still they came only to fall back, twisting and going through all sorts of motions as we dispatched them to their honorable ancestors."

Then the action ceased as the Japanese retreated back into the jungle. Basilone and his men relaxed for a moment. "Keep your eyes on the clearing," he snapped. "That was nothing, just a probing party to give the location of our guns. In a minute you'll know what a head-on attack really is." It was only a matter of time before they would be screaming back at them. Instead, they sent their mortar* shells in, but they were short.

Basilone shouted, "Get your heads down!" Dust and stone fragments showered down on their helmets as they hugged the earth.

The rounds came in closer now, but Basilone could hear explosions far into the front as Marine artillery rounds flew over Company C toward the Japanese positions. He sensed that their fire also was short. His thoughts were interrupted as the Sendai came again, this time from the right and left throwing grenades as they charged. Basilone and his men met them at each position with machine gun fire. He thought in amazement that these Japanese are truly not afraid to die. A Company, too, with great massed firepower blew great holes in the charging ranks.

Puller, now knowing that the enemy was hitting the Marine line with a concentrated experienced force, augmented the line with three platoons of the Army's 3d Battalion, 164th Infantry which had been held as reserve.

From Prosner's *The Heroic Life of Sgt. John Basilone, USMC*:

> Calls for help were coming over the wire from every sector. The whole front was completely engaged—two 37-millimeter anti-tank guns firing canister shot, six 30-caliber machine guns, four 50-caliber guns, a full rifle platoon, six old Lewis machine guns, most of which jammed early on, eighteen Browning Automatic Rifles [BAR's] and a 60-milli-meter mortar.

Puller's Operations Officer, Capt. Charlie Beasley, noting the enemy's strength and blind determination to pierce the Marine line, murmured to Puller, "Colonel,

---

* Most feared by the Marines was the Japanese Model 89 50mm Heavy Grenade Discharger, known as the "Knee Mortar" since it was generally fired from the kneeling position. Known as the *Juteki* to the Japanese, it was a weapon of standard issue to all Japanese ground units and was encountered in all major battles in the Pacific War. It could fire a powerful 1-pound, twelve-ounce high explosive shell or the Model 91 fragmentation grenade. It was easy to transport, relatively light and straightforward in operation.

we're gonna lose Henderson Field tonight. I want to call General Vandegrift."

The Japanese, literally mowed down in front of Basilone and his men, were beginning to pile up. Still they came. But now another lull.

Basilone continued to focus on the jungle, his eyes straining as he looked for movement. Garland, pointing to the left, nudged Basilone's arm. "Sarge, I think there is something moving in the trees—over there." Basilone looked both left and right seeking out any movement. "They're coming in from the flanks," he yelled, "swing the guns around." As they re-positioned the guns he crawled to his right gun emplacement to tell them what was happening, then returned. As expected they came again; this time from the flanks, but they were met with the same concentrated fire as before and were cut down again. Another lull.

Basilone and his men had been firing constantly and the gun cooling jackets were sizzling. He thought, my God, how long would the barrels hold out. The ammo was getting low and they needed water for the cooling jackets.

Basilone believed that his men would not be able to find their way back to the ammunition dump as it was a treacherous minimum of one hundred yards through enemy pockets to get there. So he went.

Henderson Field is buffered by forest, and through that forest runs a tortuous pathway to the gun emplacements that has been cleared by buldozers and Marines using bolo knives. Should the Japanese overrun the machine gun line to that pathway, the airfield would be within their grasp.

Basilone must run that pathway.* He crawled to it, then jumped to his feet, went left and started the hundred-yard dash knowing that some Japanese have infiltrated into the forest and he will be exposed to sniper and automatic weapon fire.

It did not take long before he knew he was right. There is an eruption of gunfire from the woods. He kept going knowing that bullets were only narrowly missing him. Snipers shoot at him and grenades explode behind him, but he runs on amid the shrapnel. One explodes so close that he is knocked to the

---

* From *Guadalcanal Starvation Island*: "Manila John discarded his disintegrating boondockers and ran barefoot along dark, muddy, rainswept trails..." Nash Phillips, also with Basilone that night, says that Basilone was barefooted when he (Basilone) visited him in the hospital tent after the battle, later that night. From Prosner's *The Heroic Life of Sgt. John Basilone, USMC,* Basilone says, while waiting for the epic battle to begin: "Our hole had inches of water in it and the bottom was slick with mud. I could feel my boots slipping on it so I just took them off." Corporal Richard Greer, encountering Basilone that terrible night during one of Basilone's harrowing trips to the ammunition dump disagrees saying to this writer, "Well he wasn't [barefooted]." The only conlusion this writer can come up with is that during all the terrible confusion of combat, John may have taken his boots off not earlier, but later in the battle during a lull in the fighting. Also, it must be remembered that John made at least three trips to the ammo dump. Greer, then, may have seen him when he (John) had not yet removed them.

ground. Examining himself he cannot believe that he is not injured or killed.

Finally at the ammo dump a sentry questioned his pulling of the 50 caliber ammunition boxes from the stack without authorization. Basilone fired back, "What do you want, a requisition? A hundred yards up that path is a whole regiment of Nips and the only thing standing between them and the goddamned airfield is three machine guns. And those guns are just about empty."

At any rate the ammo dump was intact, no Japs had broken through. I broke open a box and pulled out cartridge belts, throwing them across both shoulders. Picking up a full box I started back. The belts hanging from my shoulders banged against my legs. I had to stop and adjust them. The box was awkward and I had to slow down.

Basilone, staggering from the weight now remembered the water and manages to swing by the CP where a Marine throws a string of canteens over his shoulder. He starts the gruelng trek back down the path toward his gun emplacement. He is again under sniper fire during the return trip as bullets whiz by and slam into the trees, so he drops to the ground and crawls. He is close, yet so far. The ammunition begins to weigh him down, but he struggles on and does the hundred yards back in fifteen minutes. Dropping exhausted into the left flank gun position he quickly unloads six ammunition belts as a sniper opens up on him.

Bullard, now down to 50 rounds at the left gun emplacement doesn't believe his eyes as Basilone drops the ammunition belts down. Powell and Garland, elated, hug him telling him that they are completely out of ammunition. "Just like in the movies," Powell exclaims, "They could have taken us any time they wanted."

Now the third wave is coming at them. Basilone's stomach tightens as he sees through the corner of his eye Japanese breaking through his right flank gun position.

Not having time to set up his gun John went prone with the trigger grip set high so his fire would skim the grass so as not to miss those attackers crawling at him. From their left the Japanese charged again, but now two machine guns were ready to stop them. They had mistakenly assumed that the emplacement was out of action. The Marines mowed them down. Those that remained, retreated to the jungle.

Climbing over the dead bodies of their fallen comrades a few of the Japs managed to get within five feet of my gun. Whipping up my pistol I let them have it. One practically fell on my gun as his face vanished into a deep crimson blob as he hugged the ground in death. Powell, Steve, Garland and the boys were all firing steadily and the ground was beginning to get choked with dark figures. Only they were not wriggling. Suddenly over to my right there was a loud explosion and I missed the chatter of the Brownings set up in that direction.

A Marine private crawled into Basilone's emplacement.

It was Private La Pointe. Spotting me, he inched over. "Sarge," he said, both right flank guns are knocked out and the crews are all dead or injured." Good God, I thought, not them boys, not the ones I trained and was so proud of.

Knowing that his right flank guns had to be put back in action to hold the line, Basilone raced down the trail to the right flank gun pit averting those Japanese who had broken through at that position. He felt terrible anguish knowing that his men had probably been killed there.

Crumpton and Evans, raging with anger, were firing .45's to hold off as many Japanese as they could. John, seeing the dead Marines, three of them still bleeding in the mud, could do nothing except pull them out of the pit to make room, and question himself as to how he might be able to get the right postion going again. But he knew how—instinctively. He yelled at Crumpton and Evans to hold as best as they could, then yelled to the other two, "Nash! Go back— you, too Foley!" Nash's hand was almost completely shot away and Foley's leg had been hit. He was now down to two men left at the right gun position.* He jumped from the pit and ran back to the left emplacement. Luckily there was now another lull in the battle.

Arriving back in seconds, Basilone jumped down into the emplacement and yelled to Cpl. Powell and Pfc.Garland to follow him as he grabbed the Browning they were firing at the right side of the pit.** Basilone knew in that brief moment that unless the right flank guns were put back into operation the Japanese would break through in force and his position, too, would be overrun from the flanks. He yelled for Powell and Garland to follow him as he grabbed the gun, leaving Bullard with the remaining Browning.

Basilone stood straight up with the gun ignoring the bullets now whizzing by. With the 40-pound machine gun cradled in his left arm Basilone headed for the silenced gun position with LaPointe, Garland and Powell following with the tripod and ammunition. They entered the trail and moved in silence.

Knowing that mortar rounds had now been dropping into both positions, Basilone could not go directly across the plain to it. It was just too dangerous; another round could come screaming down on them. He had to work around to

---

* Basilone, then, had more than six men at the right flank position: Evans, Crumpton, Foley, Nash and three dead (One of the dead is, in all probability, Hatfield.).

** In Phylis Cutter's compiled narrative, from Basilone's letters, she has Basilone saying that it was Bullard's gun that he took posession of. In a piece by Burris Jenkins, Jr., a copy of which Basilone sent to a friend in 1943, it was Garland's and Bob Powell's gun that he picked up, as detailed in most narratives of that evening. Basilone's recall in the Burris piece makes more sense; he would not have taken Bullard's gun from him while taking Powell and Garland to the right flank gun. Further, Bullard's name is never mentioned during his movement to the right flank position.

it through the jungle path. As they worked their way through the rain-soaked and muddy foliage toward the right gun position, Basilone sensed the presence of the Japanese. Thomas Gallagher of *Real Magazine*:

> But Basilone kept on walking, and his failure to look back to see if they were still with him was despotic. Without a word or gesture he forbade them to attend to their anxiety. He allowed them time only for the grinding labor of the moment, the ennui of foliage and heat. He might have been alone, so they followed him, enraged and faithful. He had trained his ears to hear through the sounds of life here, and he had the sudden grace and uninterupted reflexes of a deer. He'd caddied and played golf as a kid at the Raritan, New Jersey Country Club—whacked balls straight from the moment he'd picked up a club. He had a feeling for movement and terrain, and he always sensed rather than decided what to do in an emergency.

He signaled his men to halt. It was not the presence of living Japanese that John sensed. It was that of the dead.

The stench was almost unbearable. Crawling around the dead bodies we came to what appeared to be a clearing. The mutilation there was unbelievable. Evidently one of our artillery shells had cut a swath through the trees and exploded in the midst of an enemy patrol. The smell of fresh blood was strong, and dismembered portions of bodies were scattered like so many broken scarecrows. For the moment we threw caution to the wind, getting out of there fast.

They were almost there. But now Basilone halted, instantly raising his hand without turning. He lowered himself down signaling them to get down, also. Their eyes followed his outstretched arm as he pointed to a clearing hardly visible through the creeping, twisting vines. There, another Japanese patrol sat quietly in the muted staccato of shell and machine gun fire. It is probable that they were just not sure of the direction in which to go from where they found themselves. So there they paused, waiting—waiting for what? They had to know that they were into the American lines, and they must have been seeking out the right gun emplacement from behind to finish off the Marines still alive there. Then they would signal a break-through point to their commander.

Basilone's men waited in the stillness for his signal. How would Basilone handle this one? They stood exhausted and sweating—waiting. Basilone turned and came silently back to them. "Keep quiet and stay here," he ordered. He turned away from them again and went again toward the Japanese.

He had to get in close enough to clear the foliage for a clear field of fire. There was a tree close in to them. He cradled the machine gun as if it were a BAR (Browning Automatic Rifle) and creeped silently forward. Every step was calculated, made with an eye toward side stepping a twig or root sticking up through the putrefaction that might give him up. Getting into position seemed like it would take forever, but he persisted ever so slowly with intense concentration, sweating profusely, first glancing at the Japanese, then instantly back to his footfalls. He reached the tree that would be his firing position.

He was too focused to be afraid. His men looked on nervously and mentally walked every step with him. He slowly dropped down as he came closer to the tree that would be his firing position. He stood back up behind it. He could not wait another second. The weapon was too heavy to hold near vertical behind the tree forever. All five were in clear view. It was time.

Stepping out from behind the tree he brought the Browning down toward the enemy. Now, in their full view, and without hesitation, he fired one long burst from the hip. The gun's terrific blast and spray caught the Japanese by surprise. There was no chance to escape as it was over in seconds. The two Japanese who were standing twisted and crashed to the ground, the others being blown down from their sitting position. When it was over he noticed that the heat from the gun barrel had burned his arm.

Reaching the right gun emplacement Basilone and his men jumped down into it. Powell and Garland instantly set up the gun they were carrying, but Basilone ordered them to hold their fire to make the Japanese believe that the position was down for good. He then went to work on the damaged Brownings with Powell and Garland yelling at him to get down. Basilone yelled back, "I have to take a look at these guns." It did not take long to see that the first machine gun was too shot up to work for them. The second gun was jammed. Quickly scanning the second gun he tore into its disassembly.

"What are you doing?" Powell asked. "Taking the damned thing apart," he responded casually as if he were going to teach a lesson back at Pendleton.

"In the dark?" Garland blurted out.

"Yes, remember boot camp when they told you that a time like this might come?"

Down low in the blackness he ran his hands deftly over the jammed weapon feeling for every fitting. Ever so carefully, in intense concentration, he dismantled it. Japanese machine gun fire tore the ground around Basilone's head and shoulders as he crouched down. Again, one of the Marines yelled, "For Christ's sake, Sarge, get down!"

Basilone felt for the spacer. Japanese 25 and 60-caliber machine gun fire increased. He knew he had only seconds before another charge. He yelled to Powell that the head spacing was out of line. "Tough," Powell fires back, "that gun is finished." Basilone roared back, "Just cover me!" They forgot that it was Sergeant John Basilone who was rebuilding a machine gun. Darkness was no imposition.

Basilone also had to make a split-second decision. He had a choice—take whatever chance they had with rifles, side arms and one machine gun or increase their chances by making the second machine gun work. He confidently continued the tear down. Seconds went by. Finally, he worked at reassembly. The whole show depended on the next five or ten seconds. If they went down so, too, would Henderson Field. Retreat was out of the question. He finally managed to set the spacer, scraped mud from the receiver and slammed the gun into the tripod that Crumpton, with his leg now torn up from a grenade hit, had already set up.

Powell yelled, "Jesus! Here they come!"

Powell's machine gun along with carbine and rifle fire met the oncoming Japanese. It was effective, but not enough to break the charge. Their position would soon be overrun.

A Japanese soldier fell so close that his arm dropped at the muzzle of Powell's gun. A wounded Marine started to recite the 23rd Psalm.

Suddenly, to the amazement and relief of his men Basilone was firing the repaired machine gun with Evans feeding the belt in. More and more Japanese went down as the increased firepower took effect. Powell literally jumped for joy throwing his helmet in the air, then immediately began to fire again. The next wave of Japanese held back for a moment. With Japanese bodies now piling up so high in front of them that they cannot see the field of fire, Basilone yelled to Garland to go out and clear them away. Garland courageously ran out and cleared the field by pushing the bodies, piled in front of each machine gun, aside as Basilone provided covering fire.

Now we got two guns working. I thought, how the hell can we keep them from coming? They were working a pattern and by now we knew just when to open up. First they would drop their mortar fire on us, and then coming from all sides, having dynamite and grenades and yelling, 'Bonzai, bonzai,' they would throw themselves at our guns. We'd yell, 'bonzai, bonzai,' right back with a few choice words of our own as we dispatched them to the bosom of mother earth, by this time running red with the life blood of Hirohito's legions.

The Japanese charge had been routed, and the charge subsided.

Lost in the excitement of the moment Powel swept the jungle over and over again. Basilone held him from further firing patting him on the back saying, "Easy boy, easy! They're gone. Don't waste your ammo."

Seeing how badly Crumpton's leg was hit John asked if he was able to walk. Answering yes, Basilone told go him to go to the rear, but he resisted. Basilone insisted. "Crumpton, get the hell outta here, I'm boss, go on back and get fixed up. If anybody asks you, tell em, Evans, Powell, Garland and Basilone are hold- ing the right flank and we think we're slightly out numbered."*

It was now about three o'clock in the morning, the gun barrels were dan- gerously overheating and Powell and Garland were almost out of ammunition. A grenade had blown much of it away. Powell was down to a half belt and Garland was out completely.

For a while now Basilone had not heard fire from the left emplacement and

---

* On his way to the aid station, eighteen-year-old Billy Crumpton was killed by those Japanese who had broken through the perimeter.

feared the worst. He yelled, "Let's go, grab everything, we're getting out of here!" They followed him to the left gun position only to find that all were dead there. Bullard was lying there. John felt that mix of pride, anger and sadness as he allowed himself to gaze at him. They had indeed held as long as they could. They were gone and the guns were blown apart.

Basilone called the CP advising that the right position was out of action.

With the blessing of another pause in the battle Basilone had to make another decision. "OK, fellas, hold on, fight with your pistols till I get back. I'll bring you some ammo." Garland and Powell, in shock, tell him that he doesn't have a chance. They knew the enemy has infiltrated the line and were all around them. To Garland Basilone said, "There's not many behind us, and I'll take care of them with my .45. If I'm not back in ten minutes with ammo, put an ad in the paper for me." He turned to Powell, "Hold the fort till I get back." So Basilone went again, back through the gauntlet of fire and death, and returned unscathed.

It now began to rain again. Another lull. At this point Basilone knew that the Japanese had chosen his position as the focal point of their attack and he wondered if he and his men could hold out. He knew, too, that he and his men were cutting the best of the Japanese Army to pieces. He had lost all track of time and was seeing his life pass by. He thought, am I to die here in the "stinking jungle thousands of miles from home." He tried to comprehend the carnage. Those piled up in front of him. Who were they? They had homes and families. But he can't think about that. He had to survive and the only way to survive was to do his job, to think of them as not human. He must fill them with enough lead so they can't hurt him or his men. But it's all so crazy and they are fatigued and weary from battle.

Powell stirred him from his stupor "Sarge, Sarge, They keep coming, nothing stops them." Through the heavy soaking rain they were coming again. Basilone saw them. Their screams sear his brain. They come on again, "Relentless, screaming, 'Bonzai,' their faces contorted in savage inhuman grimaces." He had to change tactics.

They will not hold out unless he can further increase the amount of firepower during each charge. His only emplacement was down to three men and he had to have both guns firing. He had to have freedom of movement as he fired and he had to make them think there were more guns than he had. So he improvised. American soldiers improvised all the time, and they did it well. It is what Americans always do well in times of struggle and turmoil. It is what made them Americans. And it is what made American soldiers better than their enemy.

He told them that he would fire one gun at a time; he would roll from one to the other.

"Hold the fire on the other gun," he yelled to Powell, "just make sure it's ready when this one is empty." Having the gun barrels cool a bit at each loading would add to their chances for survival. Powell reloaded one, then the other, as Basilone skillfully fired at the charging enemy while Evans and Garland protected each flank with their carbines. Powell pees into one of the water jackets to cool the barrel.

I was firing in a blind rage. Nothing we did seemed to stop them from coming. Suddenly there was a lull in the charge. The stillness was almost deafening.

It went on like this for hours—a lull, then a charge. Japanese bodies began to mount in front of him. He was up; the guns were pulled from the pit and placed to one side so that he could gain height over the mounting bodies. He went prone and repeated the process—one gun, then the other. He moved one gun over two feet to clear the bodies again. It was automatic now— all of it was taking hold—the microsecond responses that come only from the training and instinct that was the totality of his Marine Corps being. They continued to charge at him screaming as they came. Another lull.

He ran again to the ammo dump and reported to the CP that gun barrels were burning up and his men had to urinate into the cooling jackets to keep them going since they had no water. One of the ammo dumps is six hundred yards through intense enemy fire. Corporal Richard Greer handed him the ammo belts.

Incessant enemy machine gun fire and grenades seek him out, but he went on not thinking or even fearing anymore. It is as if in a dream. He loaded up on ammo, filled his canteen with water, grabbed a spare gun barrel and started back. He knew it was a miracle that he was not dead yet. He focused only on the struggle back through the tall grass. There was no time to rest. He is possessed with only the mission. "Only one thing scared me. I was afraid if I stopped, I'd never get enough strength to start again."

Puller knew his line was close to disintegrating so he calls Colonel Pedro Del Valle, the artillery commander, as he had once or twice before and said, "Give us all you've got. We're holding on by our toenails." Del Valle, his good friend, pledged his support and his men fired in shell after shell adding to the carnage caused by Basilone and his men.

The Marines had allowed the ammo belts to lie on the ground to save seconds and they were now soaked with mud. But the Brownings miraculously continued to fire. Prescribed firing lanes and coordination gone at this point they just had to keep the guns going.

"Just when we'd think we could not go on a minute longer the Japs would retire to the woods and regroup."

They came at the emplacement again and again. All the time Japanese mortar rounds came in at them, somehow missing—some in front of them, some behind. Enemy machine gun fire ripped at the rim of the emplacement. Miraculously no one was hit. Garland and Evans throw grenades one after the other. Would they run out of them? Then what?

Garland yelled to Basilone that they soon would be pinned down. Basilone yelled back to him, "Like hell! Open that tripod as far as it will go."

I let them get close and then would mow them down. Their screams filled the night. Bodies were hanging on the wire, crazy-like...Their yellow brothers climbed over them and it was like picking off crows on a fence, only these crows won't stay still. But they are getting closer at each charge.

That day in Coney Island flashed through his mind, at the shooting gallery; the endless number of ducks moving from left to right. He would swing the gun back and forth in wide arcs picking off the ducks as they appeared.

Now Basilone could see that some of the enemy had broken through at the rear of his line. Powell called out, "Watch it, Sarge." John turned his head just in time to see a Japanese soldier coming at him with a knife. Grabbing his .45 that had been down at his side he shot the attacker in the face. "Spellbound, I watched him crumple to the ground, grabbing the hole in his forehead as he died in front of me."

This went on at intervals and subconsciously I listened for Powell's call, turned and sent another Nip to his ancestors.

I watched as in a trance, saw four Japs slip through the wire set up a heavy machine gun and just as they got ready to fire it, wiped them out with one short burst.

Powell and Evans shot Japanese as they crept up from behind so Basilone was secure knowing that his back was covered. Garland was loading for him and he was free to shoot with his .45 those of the enemy who crawled through to his gun muzzle.

The Japanese now blew the barbed wire with dynamite and threw more grenades at the Marine line. They come at the Marines in heavier waves. Shrapnel flew showering Basilone's position. Marine artillery dropped dangerously close to the Marine machine gun positions.*

Basilone was afraid to feel his head or neck fearing that he had been hit by enemy grenades, exploding close to his position. As he rolled from gun to gun he heard another warning, "Look out, Sarge—to your left!"**

Turning quickly, I just caught the spinning flash of a wicked machete circling

---

* John Setteducatti, 11th Regiment Marine artilleryman from Warren, New Jersey, and his men set the 105mm howitzer charges "2/3" so that the projectiles would fall almost vertically in order to take out Japanese who had broken through the wire, close in to Basilone's emplacements. Setteducati had walked the one-mile distance from his three-battery, four-gun each, position to Basilone's emplacements the day before. He emphasized the fact to this writer that they were trying to give the "guys as much ammo as possible." Marines R. A. Marsolini and Richard Smith were giving firing orders.

** Whether it was Powell or Evans who swung the machete is unknown. Basilone never knows who warned him and never asks. The image will come to haunt him.

over my head. Transfixed, I watched as the Jap's stomach split open as the machete sliced him through the middle. Horrified, I saw his entrails spill out and got sick as the hot blood and pink, red and white blue guts splattered the water jacket of my gun.

As Powell loaded the left gun he discovered that the right gun was damaged due to gunfire. Telling Powell to cover him John used parts of the knocked out gun found earlier to repair the damaged one. The repair was completed just in time for the all out enemy charge. Again, the ammo is almost gone. He has to get some—and fast. A lull. He must go. But he can't make the run and get back in time for the next attack. They are coming at them more frequently now. So he goes to A Company down to the right for ammo and water. He drops to the ground and gives the call sign, "Yankee Clipper." They respond, "Joe DiMaggio." In minutes he is back with water and ammo. But Garland has been hit bad; he is dead.

It was after 4:30 a.m. John Basilone knew it was coming. The most vicious effort by the Japanese to take Henderson field was about to commence.

I could sense this was the one to beat back. They must want the field badly to waste all that manpower that was rotting and swelling in the field ahead of us. They almost had perfect range now and their bullets were driving desperately close. I opened the tripod and flattened the Browning to the ground pressing myself to the earth's surface, but my helmet again got in my way. Ripping it off, I pressed the trigger in short bursts as the Japs charged.

The fanatic bonzai screams shriek from the massed enemy force as they dashed toward the Marines. "Malines, you die, bonzai, bonzai." And they are killed as they come. Basilone did the roll from gun to gun, again and again. Powell loaded—again and again. Japanese climbed over their dead comrades as they came at the Marines, and continued to pile up in front of Basilone's guns. The guns were so hot that they burned his hands. He wondered how they continued to fire being so hot, but he continued. Ammunition was getting low again.

With the right gun position down the Japanese had breeched the line and were through in force. Basilone's position was almost surrounded on the right and rear. But units from the Army's 164th Regiment had been sent forward and had been attempting to seal the gap with concenrated rifle fire.* It had been light for some time now and the corpses of Japanese piled high in front of Basilone's emplacement began to give off a stench as the sun beat down on them.

The pile of dead Japanese was beginning to mount up so he ordered the

---

* Although the main attack had not been expected from the south and, as the action increased and reality set in, Puller repeatedly called Colonel Sims, the 7th's commanding officer, for additional support. But only later at 2:00 AM did Sims send in men from the 3rd Battalion, 164th Infantry, a green Army unit under the command of Lieutenant Colonel Robert Hall.

tripods elevated to enable him to fire over the pile. The Marines watched entranced as the Japanese also piled their dead high building a wall. They were trying to work their way in closer to Basilone's emplacement. Basilone knew that the men were thinking about withdrawal. A feeling of abandonment had set in. One of Basilone's machine guns was now hit by mortar fire and is out of action.

The cooling jacket on his remaining gun is steaming now; there was no water. He fired knowing that it would quit on him any second. He will fire until it does.

But now American mortar fire was saturating the Japanese force that had filled the gap between Basilone's guns, and the Marine 11th is raining down artillery fire on the area behind the infilltrating Japanese force. They became trapped. The 164th fired into them relentlessly as the Marine mortar fire dropped on them. A Japanese machine gun squad got in close, out in front of Basilone's gun.

"Behind the soggy flesh, now resembling bags of meal they set up their machine guns."

Basilone reacted by shifting position. He was able to shoot from a different angle and wiped out a newly created Japanese machine gun position. Operating on automatic again he was way beyond fatigue.

From William J. Owens' *Green Hell, The Battle for Guadalcanal*:

> Manila John's guns were near the company center, placed with a decline to the front. Soon the hill was covered with bodies, and when the fury of the attack abated, he sent men down to push aside the corpses to once again clear his field of fire. Still the attack waves came, about once an hour, each more vicious than the one before and lasting about fifteen minutes.
> Basilone scampered barefooted so he could move more quickly through the mud in his trousers with a .45-caliber automatic pistol strapped on his hips, back to the battalion command post during lulls in the fighting to report the guns in trouble. He then returned to the front lugging spare parts, and most important of all, several 14-pound ammunition belts.
> Once near the Company A area, Basilone reported to Fuller that his water-cooled guns were beginning to burn out from the continuous firing and that his men were urinating into the gun jackets to keep them cool enough to fire. The killing or wounding of his gun crews left him short-handed, so he set up several guns, then rolled and ran from one to the other firing each in turn to confuse the enemy.

Our mouths were parched and our lips crusted with dry saliva and dirt. We had lost all resemblance to the human race. Our replacements were not coming.

But it was ending. The charges were fewer; the number of Japanese in each assault was dwindling; they were worn down. The Marine and Army units had held. Company C had held.

CHAPTER 24

orning dawns on October 25th and the horizon is red with sunrise. It would become known as "Dugout Sunday."

All day long firing continued along the line. Teaming up with the boys of the 164th Infantry we set up a crossfire cleaning out what few Japs had pierced our lines. All the time the 11th Marines poured a devastating curtain of fire beyond our sector, cutting off the possibility of the enemy being able to reinforce his position.

The Japs were fanatical in their efforts to push through to the field and it was weird to see them come waving their arms wildly shrieking and jabbering like monkeys, then the piercing screams of the dying as our bullets smacked into them rose above the clatter of our Brownies.

There never was an enemy like this. If nothing else you had to admire their utter disregard for death. It seemed they opened their arms and embraced it as they melted into globs of soggy flesh. I was taking no chances. After each assault I stood up and, cradling my Brownie in my arms, I would spray the crumpled up bodies in front of me. I had seen some of these dead come alive and snuff out the life of some of my buddies. No sir-ee, I wanted to make sure they were good Japs.

Meanwhile the Japs who were observed near the Matanikau came out of hiding and launched an attack against the 2nd Battalion of the 7th Marines. The attack was so fierce and relentless that the position of Company F on the left became untenable and the survivors began working their way back to our rear positions. The Japs then pushed to the top of the ridge, setting up their heavy machine guns.

Then a sight opened up before us that was hardly believable, but so typical of the Marine Corps.

Lieutenant-Colonel Odell Conoley, sizing up the situation and the advantageous position the enemy had obtained with his heavy machine guns set up on the ridge, decided to rush the position and clear the ridge.

All he had in the way of a fighting force was a grand total of 17 men, which included communicators, bandsmen, runners, messmen, etc.

Charging the position using grenades in overwhelming numbers, this small group surprised the Jap gunners and cleared the crest.

But it is whimpering down. Basilone knows that the strength has been whittled out of them. It is over. He slumps down in the pit. He cannot believe that now, for the first time, he is aware of cordite in the air. He is actually alive.

From the twisted bodies in front of him Basilone sees movement and he goes for his .45, but hesitates. Sergeant Mucha staggers to the emplacement. He has been lying unconscious among the Japanese dead subsequent to a mortar blast.

From *Leatherneck Magazine*:

> At that moment there is the sound of activity on the pathway leading back to Henderson Field. Marines—lots of Marines— pour out of the jungle and fan out across the clearing. A squad leader drops into the hole beside Basilone.
> "What the hell!" He says. "We heard there was a fight going on up here."
> "So what do we find, a bunch of gold-bricks sitting on their tails." Basilone feels a surge of anger and starts to snarl something at the flippant visitor. Then he observes that the corporal's eyes are surveying the mound of dead Japs before the emplacement with total understanding. He relaxes again, grins broadly.
> "You our relief, corporal?"
> "What else?"
> Basilone jerks a thumb toward the mountain of corpses.
> "You'll pardon us if we don't police up the area before we leave."

*I rested my head on the edge of the emplacement, weary, tired and thankful that the lord had seen fit to spare me. Then I heard my name being called. Looking up I saw Chesty Puller, my commanding officer, standing with his arm outstretched. He shook hands with me and said, " you came back for ammunition, good work.**

Puller walks slowly toward Basilone. He hestates and scans the plain beyond. He looks down at Basilone.

"Do you know what you boys did out there, sergeant?" Puller asks, "You wiped out an entire Japanese regiment. Almost 3000 men. It's the most dramatic military action since Custer's Last Stand. Only you're still around to tell about it." Puller's Marines, along with the U.S. Army, indeed had annhilated over 2900 seasoned Imperial Japanese troops.**

After sending his men to the rear Basilone remained with his guns until six o'clock in the afternoon when he, too, was told to return to the command post.

---

* *Starvation Island*: Puller noticed Basilone going and coming during the action with gun barrels, ammunition and spare parts, but he pulled John aside only once to ask how the fighting was going.
** Two hundred and fifty are found within Puller's lines. Thirty-eight enemy dead are piled high around Basilone's emplacement. 1st Battalion had lost nineteen men and counted thirty wounded. Total casualties as per Vandegrift were 86 killed, 119 wounded. Twelve were missing.

"After all, they were my guns and I didn't want to leave them." Later in the day he is ordered to a position about 1000 yards to the right where he encountered sporadic enemy resistance.

Finally, Battle-worn and hungry, Basilone trudged to the rear. On the way he met Sgt. Paul Plyler who reached out and gave him a spam sandwich. He continued on to the hospital tent to see those of his men who had been wounded at the gun emplacements.

While there he stopped to see Nash Phillips one of the men in his section who had his hand blown off during the fighting. It is Phillips who gives us the grandest picture of John Basilone immediately after the Lunga Ridge battle.

> He was barefooted and his eyes were as red as fire. His face was dirty black from gunfire and lack of sleep. His shirt sleeves were rolled up to his shoulders, revealing tattoos on each arm. One was a sword plunged into a human heart above the words: 'Death before Dishonor.'
> On his other arm, below the shoulder, was a figure of a full-blown Wild West girl and the caption: 'Manila-1936.' He had a .45 tucked into the waistband of his trousers. He'd just dropped by to see how I was making out—me and others of his section. I'll never forget him. He'll never be dead in my mind.

From *Marine! The Life of Chesty Puller* by Burke Davis:

> It was clear that, for the time being, 1/7, with the aid of Del Valle's artillery and the final support of the Army battalion had saved the perimeter against almost staggering odds. It had cost the Japanese dearly to leave their artillery on the rugged trails and to confine their attacks to a narrow front. Guadalcanal saw no fighting more furious, by land or air.

A few days after the October 24-25th battle, Puller requested Division headquarters to make an official count of enemy dead. A burial detail counted 1462. Bulldozers dug great pits and the Imperial dead were thus covered over.*

Colonel Furimiya with the 29th's regimental colors and a small band of his men had managed to penetrate the Marine lines and survived for about two days. They did not last long, however, and with the exception of a few most were killed or were among the missing. Furimiya, surrounded by Marines wrote in his diary:

---

* *Green Hell*: Puller first estimated that his under-strength battalion had been attacked by a regiment of about 2000 men. Captured documents later revealed that there had been nearly twice that number. The appalling attacks that had resulted in the deaths of so many Japanese soldiers had been made by three regiments—the 16th, 29th, 230th and the remnants of Kawaguchi's 35th Infantry Brigade.

"Those who followed me in the charge...are the eight persons...whose names are written on the back of this page...."

He regrets the fact that his army was not supported by artillery and emphasizes the need for firepower in combat and believes that his troops became dispirited without it. He goes on to say, "At daybreak (of the 29th) we gave up hope of escaping and began to make last preparations." * Knowing he had been defeated, he ordered a retreat. He who had stated that he would "exterminate the enemy with one blow" now retired with the loss of approximately thirty five hundred soldiers. And the arduous jungle trek would claim the lives of many more. Furimiya coninued: "I am going to return my borrowed life today with short interest." To General Maruyama he wrote, "I do not know what excuse to give. I apologize for what I have done." He and Captain Suzuki were then prepared.

Suzuki shot him once in the temple, then he killed himself.

Japanese headquarters at Rabaul believed surely that the airfield had been won and sent fighters in to land, only to be greeted by anti-aircraft fire. Many are shot down as they come in low over Henderson Field.

Dr. Edward Smith operated on wounded and dying American fighting men in what amounted to a crude tent. Conditions were terrible, but he worked feverishly to save those he could. The rain fell and mixed with Marine and Army blood in the ditches near the operating table. From the 25th on, conditions did not get much better although Puller succeeded in having more doctors sent in. As each day passed more men got malaria. But they fought on, with or without it.

The first thing I thought about was that I was hungry. I don't remember when I ate last. I worked my way over to the "CP" to get some chow. All they had was crackers and jam. I was so hungry I could have polished off half a cow. Smacking my lips over the thought of meat, I rushed back to my emplacement cramming some crackers in my pockets; there was no time to sit and take it easy.

We were still groggy and dazed and did not realize that a battle was progressing far to the east. Actually Lieutenant-Colonel [Herman] Hanneken and his 2nd Battalion, 7th Marines had engaged enemy forces, but was unable to get word back to headquarters until three days later with the dismaying news that the enemy was trying to land an entire division east of the Metapona River and had already succeeded in landing the advance party who were to establish a beachhead for the remainder of the division.

Upon receipt of this news we were immediately pulled out of the Henderson Field defense perimeter and under cover of darkness we moved out to Koli Point in boats. No sooner had we embarked than two Army battalions moved out up the Malimbiu River. Whaling's scouts, on a forced march, moved inland from the mouth of the Malimbiu River. The following morning two tank companies were ordered to cross the Ilu, and for heavy reinforced support, a battalion of 75-mil-

---

* By this he meant the most important one of tearing up the regimental colors and scattering them in the jungle.

114

limeter pack howitzers (33rd Battalion, 10th Marines) was withdrawn from the perimeter to support the 7th Marines. To insure success of this maneuver, Colonel Del Valle's Special Weapons Battery moved to cover the artillery's south flank.

The Ilu swollen and made treacherous by torrential rains was too deep and swift running for the trucks to cross. However Lieutenand Colonel Curry moved his guns and ammunition across by hand.

An Army battalion relieved the beleagered 3rd Battalion, 7th Marines, west of the Matanikau and they were rushed back to plug the gaps in the Henderson Field perimeter, which defenses by the withdrawal, had become dangerously thin and spread out. The 8th Marines under R. H. Jescake were expected to arrive on November 4th, to further seal and strengthen the gaps in the field defense perimeter. Fortunately they arrived on the morning of November 4th, landing east of Lunga Lagoon.

As was his custom, no sooner had the enemy spotted the landing he opened up with his still intact field artillery. This time however he was rocked back on his heels by the thundering reply of our 155-millimeter battery and a concentrated curtain of murderous fire from the guns of the escorting destroyers. Swinging about, our destroyers bombarded the Jap positions east of the Metapona churning up their beachhead into a fountain of chaos, setting fires to the stores and equipment that the invading Japs had stashed in the woods just off the beach.

We pressed eastward and, with the help of the 164th Infantry, closed in on the enemy east of the Metapona. We had the yellow-bellies in a noose. The 164th Infantry, which had crossed the river behind the Japs, now began to move northwards towards the beach, closing the neck of the opening so that the Japs had only one way to reach the beach.

They took refuge in a clump of woods with the beach to their backs. Between the heavy mortar fire and our machine guns' penetrating long bursts, the woods resounded with the screams of the Japs as they tried to evade the hell that was being poured into them. In a last attempt to evade our singing messengers of death, they fled south only to run into the 164th Infantry. These boys having received their baptism of fire on the defense perimeter of Henderson Field, met the Japs head on in hand-to-hand combat, cuttng them to pieces.

It was a fast and furious action while it lasted and the few that broke through the lines of the 164th, were wiped out later.

I don't know whether I mentioned it before, but all the boys in our outfit respected and admired Puller as an officer and leader who stayed right in the thick of it with his men. As an example of the kind of a right guy he was, I recall that during our final drive he was wounded in the leg, not once, but three times by shrapnel. When the doctor pinned a casualty tag on hm and ordered his evacuation from the field, the Colonel became highly insulted. "Evacuate me hell," he said, "take that tag and label a bottle with it. I will remain in command." He remained and it was not until the next morning when his leg began to stiffen so much he could hardly walk that the doctor finally had his way.

It was now November 11th, and on November 12th more reinforcements poured in. Topside was taking no chances. We welcomed two more batalions of an Army infantry regiment our own Marine replacements. They, too, ran into the Japs' heavy artillery during their unloading at Kokum. Once more our destroyers laid down a heavy bombardment against the enemy's shore positions around the Kokumbona area.

We later heard that the enemy who had managed to escape the 164th Infantry by fleeing southward, were trapped and wiped out by the 2nd Raider Battalion which had landed at Aola.

News began to trickle in to us and we found out that our reinforcements that had landed on the 11th and 12th of November were rushed in just ahead of the Japs. Our intelligence had reported a heavy armada of Japanese warships and transports were laying off Buin apparently intended for Guadalcanal. This meant our naval forces were going to be in another major battle if the Japs were to be prevented from reinforcing their Guadalcanal invaders.

We did not resemble a crack fighting group. There was no such thing as any of us having a complete outfit. A bedraggled group if there ever was one. A combination of khaki and dungarees, so dirty and tattered, one would have thought us a group of beachcombers.

We tried as best we could to get the stench of sweat and dirt off of us.

After the October 24-25 battle, Basilone was in the field for eighteen days searching out remaining Japanese. Japanese Army losses sustained during the last week of October convinced Imperial Headquarters that the Solomons campaign would indeed be the decisive one so plans were made for yet another offensive. The Americans had fought tenaciously. But the Japanese were spurred on by their naval success at the Battle of the Santa Cruz Islands during that same week. Their warship losses were zero compared to the U.S. loss of four carriers and one battleship. And the Naval Battle of Guadalcanal would come in November. It would be Japan's most intense naval effort to date. Included in the massive force would be eleven transports carrying supplies for 30,000 men. Concurrent with Japan's assault force action, would be an American landing of more than 5500 men to reinforce the worn out Marine and Army defense units. Even though the Naval Battle of Guadalcanal caused losses to both sides, the U.S. gain was decisive. Admiral Turner landed the U.S. rinforcements with no loss, and the destruction of ten Japanese transports would finally tip the scales on Guadalcanal in favor of the Americans.

On November 8th Vice Adm.William "Bull" Halsey, Commander of the South Pacific Area and South Pacific Force, was deeply moved by the scene he beheld of sick, tired and ill Marines. He quickly put into action the mechanism for the Army's 182nd Infantry Regiment's relief of forces on Guadalcanal. 1st Division was done at Guadalcanal. Battle fatigue, malaria and the limited rations had taken their toll. They were no longer an effective fighting force. It was time for rest.

On November 14th the eleven Japanese Navy transports were spotted enroute to Guadalcanal. 12,000 troops on board were to be the final force in a

116

last desperate gamble to re-take the island. Marine and Navy aircraft decimated the convoy causing the loss of all but 5000 of the Imperial Army reinforcements. Further naval and air combat finished off most of the remaining force. The last desperate gamble had failed. Things were looking up. The 1st Division along with its Army and Navy brethren had saved Guadalcanal. It is no doubt that John Basilone and his men had contributed decisively. They had held.

The 1st Division had lost 1242 men on Guadalcanal. The wounded numbered 2655. Thirty-one Marines would be missing forever, their fate never to be known. The Marines were spent. Nearly all were suffering from illnesses of one kind or another—malaria, dengue fever, dysentery, and infections from fungus. Many had to be carried aboard the transports that would take them to Australia for rest and recovery. John Leckie, from his *Challenge for the Pacific*:

> They were shadow troops. Three months of uninterrupted ordeal such as no American troops had ever sustained, before or since, such as few soldiers in history have experienced, made them walking skeletons of parchment flesh and quivering nerve. They were the young ancients, the old-young, staring with a fixed thousand-yard stare out of eyes that were red-rimmed and sunken. Their bodies were taut rags of flesh stretched over sticks of bone. They had come to Guadalcanal muscular and high-spirited young men, but now each had lost at least twenty pounds, some had lost fifty, and their high fervor had ebbed and nearly flowed away. They were hanging on by habit only, fighting out of the rut of an old valor.

But the Japanese had lost many more on what would be known to them as the Island of Death. Fifty thousand of them were dead from combat on the island or from transport sinkings by the Americans. Thirteen thousand were rescued during the evacuation the following February and approximately 9000 died of malaria, dengue fever and other illnesses from the infectious "Canal"

The Marine Corps' Seventh Regiment led the pack with thirty-seven medals won, and John Basilone would be the recipient of his nation's highest award for galantry, as would Mitchel Paige.* Additionally, nineteen commendations would go to the 7th. Twenty-eight of the medals and fifteen of the commendations would go to John Basilone's1st Battalion.

William J. Owens from *Green Hell*:

---

* Sgt. Mitchell Paige of F Company withstood two Japanese charges as they pushed through to his gun positions. He too managed to get a disabled machine gun back into action. After losing all of his gunners he found two others who helped him position another one. Like Basilone he moved from position to position avoiding enemy fire killing a number of Japanese in the process.

The exhausted Marines, long overdue for relief, had existed in close proximity to deprivation and destruction for four long months. They had held onto Guadalcanal when few in the world felt they could. For agonizing months there simply hadn't been any replacements available for this battered corps..."

"Those first few months in the jungles of Guadalcanal experienced by the relative handful of men of the 1st Marine Division and associated forces have few parallels in the history of American warfare—indeed, in world military history. The extended Australian fight for the Kokoda Trail on Papua, New Guinea—the same kind of fight in much the same conditions at about the same time—may be the only similar battle fought in WWII. Both allied forces were pitifully undermanned, and woefully supplied, equipped, and supported—in contrast to the experienced, tenacious, and courageous Japanese troops facing them.

By November 26th the situation was desperate for the Japanese on Guadalcanal. No longer on the offensive, they were on the defensive. Major Nishiyama, acting commander of the 228th Infantry quoted one of his officers in his diary:

Rice, I really want rice. I want to give my men as much as they want. That is the only wish I have. Even when mortars are falling like a squall or the land is reshaped by bombs I don't worry. But I can't stand looking at my men become pale and thin.

The fight for Guadalcanal continued, with no major action, to February 9, 1943. The Japanese were defeated, because they were defeated on land by the Marines at Bloody Ridge, and they were defeated by the Marines and the U.S Army Guardsmen south of Henderson Field at Lunga Ridge on that fateful night of October 24th.

Although the Battle of Midway in June 1942 had put some finality to Japanese naval power in the Pacific confining them to the Pacific area west of Midway, it had not terminated their offensive moves against America and her allies. Japan's naval power was by no means shut down, nor was their fighting potential on the ground. Her Navy was still extremely powerful and her conquests in the Pacific still very much intact. Guadalcanal was truly the turning point in the war. It had reversed the situation in the Pacific, placing Japan on a defensive posture. The allies were now ready to move to the offensive. And John Basilone's Company C had made the difference. They had taken the brunt of Japan's last real all out combat effort to re-take Henderson Field. If the Japanese Army had succeeded, there is no comprehension of how far back America's battle to break Japan's hold on the area, and the war, would have been set.

By the end of December 1942, the agonizing fighting on Guadalcanal had decisively shifted control of the island to the Amercians. Henderson field had been secured and supplies and fresh troops were now arriving. The 2nd Marine Division along with Army units of the 132nd Regimental Combat Team were put in place and made ready to take on offensive operations.

Basilone was promoted to Platoon Sergeant on November 23, 1942.*

---

* Basilone's assignment tags designate the promotion to Sergeant on January 23,1942, evidently stemming from his Army training and experiences, and from the early Marine Corps recognition of his leadership skills. He was apparently already carrying the responsibilites of a Platoon Sergeant from available information regarding his activities in the field with Chesty Puller. Puller noted his performance and came through with John's Platoon Sergeant promotion on November 23rd. As can be seen by his assignment tags again, Basilone's promotion to the rank of Gunnery Sergeant comes on March 8, 1944. Some clarification here is in order: The evolution of the Gunnery Sergeant rank had to do with the Navy's very early internal conflict over whether the Marines would stay aboard as part of the ship's crew or switch to a land-based force. Gradually, by 1914, only about five percent remained onboard a vessel, and by World War I, a Marine gaining rank of Gunnery Sergeant ('gunny'), created in 1898, was being used by the Marine Corps as a Platoon Sergeant. The Corps still, however, retained the official rank of Platoon Sergeant. So to clarify, or confuse further, the Platoon Sergeant became any NCO holding responsibility for a platoon even though he might not have been officially promoted to the Platoon Sergeant rank. Today the situation is a bit different; the Platoon Sergeant rank does not exist. Instead, a platoon leader is known as a "Platoon Commander" and may be, in reality, any NCO, from Staff Sergeant to Corporal to Gunnery Sergeant.

CHAPTER 25

On January 2, 1943 John Basilone and the 1st Division set sail from the island of Guadalcanal. The 1st Division had given more than could ever be expected of them. Chesty Puller would never forget their courage. He would talk of them later many times when he appeared before green troops at places like Ft. Sill, Ft. Benning, Ft. Ord, Ft. Riley and Ft. Levenworth to mention a few. And he would talk of John Basilone at those places. He told them of his courage under fire. He told them of Basilone's struggle to knock down the mounting bodies of Japanese soldiers piled in front of his guns and of his harrowing trips to the ammunition dumps.

Basilone was not in much better shape than the other Marines bound for Australia. He remembered the films they had seen in boot camp that told of the miseries of combat fatigue. But those films did not talk of the malaria and dysentery, and of the gradual wasting away that prolonged combat brought on.

Looking about me during the long trip to Australia, the change in the men was heart-rending. Where only a few short months ago most of them were boys in thir teens now they appeared old, far beyond their years. Their sunken eyes reflected the pain and misery they had been subjected to. I was no different. My family on seeing me at this moment wouldn't even recognize me.

The only thing that kept us from just collapsing on the deck and retiring into a shell was the gratifying thought that at last we had met the feared enemy, defeated him on his own ground and poured the flower of his troops back into the earth and sea.

Hopes of a pleasurable rest in Australia were soon dashed when the Marines saw their accomodations—swampland in Brisbane. Basilone and his men were sickened at the sight of what was once a former Australian Army barracks centered in malaria-carrying mosquito country. Worst of all, since MacArthur was the commander of the South West Pacific Area, the Marines were technically under his command—US Army command. This did not sit well with the worndown Marines, now told that they were to construct beach defenses. However, most Army orders were ignored, with the Marines almost totally disconnecting themselves from the Army staff.

Coming all that distance cramped in transports, we could hardly believe our eyes when we finally marched and were carried into our rest camp. If we bitched about "Tent City" we were sorry. This was worse. Guadalcanal was paradise compared to this swamp. Gooney birds and mosquitos made sleep impossible.

Vandegrift complained to MacArthur, who was in command of the area, and finally got the Marines better quarters in Melbourne. But MacArthur advised that transportation for the Marines was not possible. The Marines would thereafter refer to him as "Dugout Doug." After more haggling and consultation between MacArthur and Halsey, it was Halsey who provided transport ships. The men were shipped out to Melbourne on the *West Point*, which was, before the war, the passenger liner *America*. When Halsy came through, he really came through.

The Marines entered Melbourne with a bang. They could not believe the sight from the transport ships. There at the dock stood hundreds of Australians to greet them. The streets were lined with cheering crowds who now realized that the US Marines had truly saved them. The Aussies came to see the now rag-tag men of the 1/7 marching down mainstreet Melbourne behind the 1st Division Band.

The men were set up in a camp called Frankstown, about 40 miles outside of Melbourne. In Melbourne was an arena where the Australians played cricket. Tents were placed near the arena for those Marines still suffering from malaria. Marines were also treated at the hospital at Melbourne if the sickness did not improve at the camp.

Melbourne was the polar opposite of Brisbane. The Marines loved it. It was an old Victorian town with department stores and hotels and considerate people. Trollies toddled along adding to the charm of the place. Basilone's eyes teared as he gazed upon the city from the ship. It was almost like coming home.

During our march through the city our eyes drank in the sights. We had forgotten what a simple thing like a wide city street looked like.

The street lights, after the dark, blacked-out nights on Guadalcanal looked like beacons.

William Whyte said from his *A Time of War*:

> Melbourne was great duty, and no veteran will ever forget the time we spent there...Melbourne seemed to take us to its municipal heart—a local paper called us 'The Saviors of Australia'—because it hadn't seen many servicemen or much wartime activity at that time. We did everything we could to change all that—even affecting swagger sticks, in the British imperial tradition.

To John Basilone it was paradise. The city's suburbs were much like home in Raritan with asphalt roads and beautifully kept yards and gardens. And for John there were the golf courses. It was the Raritan Country Club all over again. There were lush countrysides with sheep farms and cattle ranches and fine horses. They roamed the countryside and city taking in the sights to their hearts' content. The people loved them, and they reveled in it as they rode the streetcars and taxis taking it all in. They regularly went into the town of Adelaide and danced at the USO Club there. From camp they traveled to Melbourne leaving at noon and returning by six o'clock the following morning. Soon that schedule would change as the hectic pace wore them down. But they were getting stronger; the cold sweats from malaria and dengue fever decreased in intensity. They were coming alive again. They caroused and found the women, and John admits that he found plenty himself.

Some of the boys fell in love, some lived with families, others went out to the farms, especially the boys from the "Mid-West" and they really had a ball. They did all the farm chores and while exhausted, they enjoyed it.

All was going well for the Marines until the Australian 9th Infantry Division arrived on furlough. These were the famed "Desert Rats." The expected confrontation occurred shortly thereafter. The Marines were there dancing with their women and spending an almost endless supply of money on them. Fights between the two services became commonplace at the pubs. Basilone was quick to learn that the Aussies were tough fighters and very seldom gave ground as they fought gang style.

One night I got involved over a gal. I tried hard not to lose my temper; after all I held the boxing championship in my division and did not want to take advantage of my boxing knowledge as I was always afraid I might hurt someone in a fist fight.

The Aussie did not back off and Basilone hit him with a "straight left." After falling to the floor the Aussie lunged at John. Immediately the Aussie's buddies came at Basilone, too. The melee started with Basilone taking them all on using whatever skills he could. His Marine buddies dove into the brawl. Then came the MP's in an attempt to quell the riot.

The fights continued to the point where the Marines traveled in groups for fear of getting caught alone against a group of the Aussies. Things escalated to a fever pitch, so much so that General Rupertus had to intervene. He had to be very creative if calm was to return to Melbourne. Consulting with Captain Leon Brusiloff, leader of the 1st Division Band, he came up with the idea that saved the day for all concerned. He told the Marines to throw a party for the Aussies. It was brilliant. He took the greater chance by sticking his neck out very far. He allowed further that no MP's would be in attendance, trusting his Marines. The beer, however, was to be served in paper cups.

Forty-five hundred Marines showed up for the party at the cricket grounds, as did an equal number of Aussies. It did the trick.

For the occasion the Melbourne cricket grounds were turned over to both armies. We got to know the Aussies better and believe it or not the fights in the pubs stopped. Things once more returned to normal. Shortly after the "Peace Conference," the Aussies Ninth was pulled out and sent to New Guinea. With all the fuss and fights we were sorry to see them go. Our money was getting low and the Aussies were good for a beer or two.

It was early May 1943 when the rumor mill had it that Puller and Captain Rogers were going to recommend that Basilone receive the Medal of Honor, but he dismissed it believing that he had done nothing more than his buddies who fought along side him. Soon, however, word around the camp said that General Douglas McArthur himself would be visiting Melbourne and a large parade was in the making. The rumor soon became fact and preparations were made for the big day. It had been said that McArthur was now to keep his word about return-ing to the Philippines to re-take the islands. But the parade was not for McArthur.

The sun on the morning of May 31, 1943 was bright and warmed the Melbourne sky. Basilone wondered why he had not heard more of the parade's planning. He wondered while last minute preparations were being made throughout the camp as men rushed from place to place. And he was not on the day's duty roster. It was to be just another easy day for John, he thought, with liberty that evening after the parade.

I thought it peculiar that I was left out of any details and wondered could it be true? Was I really going to be honored? I trembled at the thought. The import of such an honor, authorized by the President of the United States and Congress. It hit me like a bullet. My God, I thought, if this is true, the folks back home must know it by now. I wondered what Mom and Pop thought.

John donned dress uniform with the other men and went with the routine of parade preparation falling into formation at the order from Captain Rogers. Then, another command. Flanked by the honor guard his captain snapped the order, "Sergeant, fall in." Basilone in stunned silence came forward as Rogers motioned to the position between the colors. After Sgt. Mitchell Paige fell in next to him the march progressed to the parade ground and on to the reviewing stand with the band playing behind them.

There was General Vandegrift and Colonel "Red Mike" Edson. He saw them gaze in his direction. It began immediately. The advance color guard was already passing with their salutes to the reviewing stand.

Then a sight unfurled before my eyes that tore my insides. As each compa-ny passed in review they smartly eyed right in a salute and continued on to their position on the vast parade grounds.

Now he knew. He became filled with their love and admiration. Their warmth filled him as he struggled to keep from breaking down. After the last unit passed by he and Paige were lead by the arm to the center of the parade ground.

Vandegrift was smiling, holding a document. He first read Mitchell Paige's citation outlining his combat action at the Nose, near the Matanikau River. Vandegrift then placed the Medal of Honor around his neck and saluted. Vandegrift then moved to Basilone and turned to face him. Basilone saluted. The General returned the salute and read the citation:

The President of the United States takes pleasure in presenting the

CONGRESSIONAL MEDAL OF HONOR

TO

SERGEANT JOHN BASILONE, UNITED STATES MARINE CORPS,

for service as set forth in the following

CITATION:

"For extraordinary heroism and conspicuous gallantry in action against enemy Japanese forces, above and beyond the call of duty, while serving with the First Battalion, Seventh Marines, First Marine Division, in the Lunga Area, Guadalcanal, Solomon Islands, on October 24 and 25, 1942. While the enemy was hammering at the Marines' defensive positions, Sergeant Basilone, in charge of two sections of heavy machne guns, fought valiantly to check the savage assault. In a fierce frontal attack with the Japanese blasting his guns with grenades and mortar fire, one of Sergeant Basilone's sections, with its gun crews, was put out of action, leaving only two men able to carry on. Moving an extra gun into position, he placed it in action, then, under continual fire, repaired another and personally manned it, gallantly holding his line until replacements arrived. A little later, with ammunition critically low and the supply lines cut off, Sergeant Basilone, at great risk of his life and in the face of continued enemy attack, battled his way through hostile lines with urgently needed shells for his gunners, thereby contributing in a large measure to the virtual annihilation of a Japanese regiment. His great personal valor and courageous initiative were in keeping with the highest traditions of the United States Naval Service."

Franklin D. Roosevelt
President, United States.

125

As Basilone's eyes filled General Vandegrift, holding each end of the medal's ribbon reached around the neck of Sergeant John Basilone and fastened the medal to him. "I am proud of you, Sergeant," he said calmly while shaking the Gunny's hand. "It is a pleasure to deliver this medal to you in the name of the President of the United States."

The kid from Raritan had done well. He had fulfilled his father's request. Those words that had gone with him the day he left Raritan for the Army. "You do good. Remember, Basilone is a good name." Yes, Basilone was a good name.

In June his family heard from him again. It was the first message home since his one-line note they received following his landing on Guadalacanal. John simply scribbled another quick note:

> "I am very happy for the other day I received the Congressional Medal of Honor, the highest award you can receive in the armed forces. Tell Pop his son is still tough. Tell Don thanks for the prayer they say in school."

I was proud, fiercely proud, yet humble, joyful and sad as I thought of my dead buddies who had helped put this wonderful possession around my neck.

John Basilone had taken his place among the immortal group of Marine Medal of Honor recipients who had gone before him. He now stood with his own hero of World War I, Marine Sergeant Major Daniel "Dan" Daly whose combat actions during China's Boxer Rebellion, Haitian insurrection and Belleau Wood yielded him two Medals of Honor and the Navy Cross among others. Daly was Basilone's Marine Corps inspiration. He read everything he could get his hands on regarding Daly's Corps career. Basilone would say, "If I can be just half as good a Marine as he was, I'll be satisfied."

With the ceremonies closed, John went hurriedly through the throngs of Marines quickly surrounding him. They loved him and he knew it, but his feelings were a mix of humility, pride and embarassment. But, like it or not, he was their hero. This was especially so to the newer, younger Marines who sought him out both to hear him talk of that raging night of October 24th and to see and feel the medal.

Now he was going home. He was going on leave to the States and would be briefed on his next assignment at Marine Headquarters in New York City. He was told nothing else. It was in late July 1943 when his departure day arrived. Lined up on either side of the street at the company camp his fellow Marines cheered and wished him well as he passed between the men while shaking hands. Leaving them now and feeling the warmth of their admiration caused him to finally break down.

To top it off they had given him two hundred dollars to buy a watch. They, too, yearned to go home and he knew it. He could see it in their eyes. His earlier emotional encounter with Bob Powell was tough enough. He had told Powell that he was leaving for home and could feel Powell's pain at being left behind with thoughts of going home.

John said to them, "I'll be back," as he jumped into the jeep, but he knew they didn't believe him. But John would not return to the 1st Division.*

---

* The 1st Division's 1st, 5th and 7th Marines landed on Peleliu on September 15, 1944. The 1st Division would experience sixty-percent casualties on Peleliu with 1,124 Marines killed. 1st Marines' casualties would be the highest in Marine regiment history. The horrific 1st Division losses at Peleliu would cause a re-evaluation of island combat tactics and bring the introduction of the flamethrower to extract the Japanese from tunnels and caves during later island campaigns.

CHAPTER 26

In late August 1943 Manila John, along with one hundred fellow Marines arrived at Roosevelt Base, Terminal Island, California to a rousing welcome. He was America's Hero of Guadalcanal. The press was filled with stories about him and the public loved it. They sought his autograph everywhere he appeared. But John Basilone was a shy man not taken with the bright lights of fame. He would have preferred to be home in Raritan with his family, but the hero days were just beginning. He felt the pressure of it right from the start and a real fear of it all set in. One children's magazine called him "Johnny the Jap Killer."

He told his superiors that he wanted to go back, and denied the commission they offered. They said no. He was in the states to stay and was to be the feature attraction in a pending bond tour. This he agreed to, but he did not want the instructor position at Pendleton they offerred to him; he termed that a "soft berth." His buddies thought he was crazy for wanting a return to combat in the jungle. They called him "Jungle-Happy." But they did not know John Basilone. John Basilone was a Marine, first and always.

Why had Chesty Puller gone back so many times? Or others of the "Old Breed?" It is not hard to understand when one ponders the Marine Corps spirit of commradeship and Corps unity. Marine Corps tradition was built upon the dedication to duty exemplified by Marines like John Basilone, Chesty Puller and Dan Daly. Marines don't leave their dead or wounded behind. They go back.

While at Terminal Island, John went to see his brother George who was a Marine now at Camp Pendleton. John was eager to see how he was and to find out how things were going at home. Basilone's popularity had become known everywhere, and Pendleton was no exception. He was greeted with the same reception as he had at Terminal Island. His commanding officer wasted no time in having John's brother George relieved of duty so the two could spend time together. Talking in the canteen George brought John up to date telling him that he was a national hero. There was going to be a parade in Raritan in John's honor, the largest ever to be held in New Jersey. He told John that he was a hero to everyone in the country; everyone knew who John Basilone was. He was becoming a Marine Corps icon.

John asked his brother to come to Raritan with him; he was sure he could arrange it through his own CO, but George declined. He would not feel right about leaving when his buddies could not have the same privilege, especially after he had just returned from a fourteen-day leave back home himself..

As always in the military of any branch there was the waiting. Basilone was told to respond and do whatever he was told regarding his combat action on

Guadalcanal—no matter who was doing the asking—press officer, reporter, radio announcer, anyone. The time in between was a waste to him. So he and the servicemen who were to tour with him sat in the barracks and waited, and boiled with frustration at the screw ups associated with the tour's logistics. Tempers soon flared so Basilone and the servicemen with him became rebellious to it all and sought out fun in Long Beach whenever they could. They hit the bars and cursed the Brass. This interval of time before the tour began when he was doing nothing, contributing nothing, was the hardest time for him and he let anyone who would listen know it.

But John did not have to wait long. He was soon on his way to New York and, shortly after arriving, was seated before a Colonel at 90 Church Street. Not being used to all the attention and incessant interviews he complained that he felt like a "museum piece." The Colonel calmed him down advising that he just be himself.

On the morning of September 4th he faced the many reporters who had been seeking him out and who were now gathered in the Corps Press Room. And he told his story, the story of that horror filled night of Octorber 24th. With sweat pouring from his forehead he told them of the right flank gun going down with only two Marines still alive at that position and of his dash to get ammuniton and water. The room, jam-packed with reporters and cameramen, was hushed as he recounted events of that horrific night on Guadalcanal.

At noon John was taken to City Hall to meet Mayor Fiorello LaGuardia, the "Little Flower" himself, who extended to Basilone the official welcome to New York City. "I know you must be good," said the Mayor excitedly, "I know you have plenty of guts, because that medal is not awarded lightly." There with the flashbulbs going off and the ever present reporters he talked with the mayor about the war.

The the Mayor asked me, "Sergeant, where did your old man come from?" I told him, "Naples." "Mine came from Foggia," he replied, but we are Americans." I laughed and said, "You bet we are." "Sergeant," he asked, "I guess the Japs are glad to hear you left Guadalcanal." "I don't know about that," I replied, "but I can't wait to get back." "Well, son," he said, "if you don't get back, you at least have the satisfaction of knowing you've done more than your share."

They discussed the bond tour, the Third War Loan Drive, which would kick off on Wednesday of that week. It would carry Basilone on a whirlwind tour of ten Eastern cities.

After their discussion the photographers cornered them for a photo of the hero and the Mayor shaking hands. Filled with pride at having met the Mayor of the City of New York John was swept up and taken to get ready for his trip to Washington, DC. It would be the Navy Department Press Room next. There were more reporters and more flashbulbs.

John was tired of it all—the reporters, the cameras, the incessant questions, the lime light, the phoniness of it all. He had to have a break from it before he went crazy. He asked for and was granted a weekend pass to see his family. It was no different in Raritan though as the people found out that he was coming home. They waited for him. There he was stepping from the trolley. They were all over him. Everyone he knew from his childhood was there waiting to shake his hand, to see their hometown hero. He loved them all, but his focus was on the peaceful quiet of home and family. There was his brother Carlo. John reached out for him as Carlo pulled him away from the arms reaching out for him. With a wave he and Carlo trotted off to 1st Avenue and home.

But the town folks were there, too. Finally, there was Mom and Pop and all of the family. They hugged. Tears of joy flowed with the kisses. The friends came and went. He was home with those he loved the most. Of course he had to rehash the story all again for them, but somehow it was different. He didn't have to perform. He could be himself and be comforted by them in his pain of losing his buddies on Guadalcanal. And finally he was sleeping in his own bed.

He was the center of activity in Washington. He told his story again going back to his own world of the jungle, not even aware of the reporters around him. He would re-live it again and again with all the horror of it, and there would be a nightmarish quaking in him each time. And they would listen as those before them had, in rapt attention, mesmerized by it. After he was finished there was only silence. Stunned by his story they asked, "Sergeant, we'd like to shake your hand."

Bond Tours consisted of various troops of celebrities during World War II known as "Airmadas." John was assigned to Flight No. 5 of the War Veterans Airmada. Traveling with him would be the Army's Sergeant Schiller Cohen, the Navy's Bosun's Mate 2c, Ward L. Gemmer, and Machinist Mate 1c, Robert J. Creak, Army Air Corps. Accompanying them were movie stars, Virginia Grey, Martha Scott, Eddie Bracken, John Garfield and Gene Lockhart. Basilone's group would cover the Northeast with trips to Newark, New Jersey; New Haven, Connecticut; Providence, Rhode Island; Pawtucket, Rhode Island; Manchester, New Hampshire; Worcester, Massachusetts; Albany, New York; Utica, New York; Rochester, New York, and Allentown, Pennsylvania.

The tour kicked off in Newark, New Jersey. Basilone was at first reluctant to take part in the tour knowing that he would have to appear before crowds of people. He heeded the advice and counsel of his Colonel and went along know-ing that he would be contributing to the welfare of his buddies back on the "Canal" by helping to raise money for much needed supplies and equipment.

With a Navy blimp flying overhead dropping paper bombs, Virginia Grey, Gene Lockhart and John Garfield released carrier pigeons from Lincoln Park with messages to Ft. Monmouth's commanding officer—the three messages, "One down," "Two to Go," "For Victory."* After speeches by Mayor Murphy and oth-

---

* Which meant: Guadalcanal—one, Tokyo and Berlin—two to go.

131

ers there followed later, dinner and a showing of "Mr. Lucky" at Proctor's Theater. After an introduction to the audience by Virginia Grey, John Garfield and Eddie Bracken the service men spoke urging the people to "Back the Attack."

Arriving in Jersey City at about 11:30 AM after a ride with police escort over the Pulaski Skyway, the troop was greeted by city officials at City Hall. A collection of politicians and others totaling about three hundred gathered at the Plaza Hotel. Speeches there were kept short. The crowd at Journal Square was immense with people coming from all over the city. It was awe inspiring and touching to Basilone.

It was at Jersey that John began to have deeper feelings for Virginia Grey. He was intrigued by her. They walked and talked together during the evening off-hours. She was sincere and caring, but his infatuation was to go nowhere. From Prosner:

> I hadn't been with one woman in years and wasn't sure if I was one-woman material anymore. It was always love 'em and leave 'em, have a few laughs and then ship out or make it back to base. Now I was in a whole new ballgame with Virginia, but I couldn't tell her. It would have only made her feel bad.

From Jersey City the troop went to Plainfield, New Jersey, where the reception was much the same. John was amazed at the story told there by Seaman 1c Elmer Cornwell who had been adrift for thirty-six days alone in a lifeboat.

Commissioner Potterton was the toastmaster and thanks to him the speeches were held down to three minutes each. "After all," he said, "The big rally starts at three o'clock in Journal Square Plaza and we want to really put it over big."

It's amazing how much the human body can take, although I feel there must be a guardian angel that watches over us in times of great stress. How else can you account for any of us being on this platform, instead of being in a lonely grave thousands of miles from home and our loved ones.

A flight from Newark Airport brought the troop to New Haven, Connecticut, where they led a parade of over five thousand participants. After a brief rest at their hotel the group was featured at the New Haven Arena. There, following the National Anthem sung by Hollywood star Edith Fellows and an introduction by Mayor Murphy and Governor Baldwin, Basilone along with his brother service men were introduced by the celebrities. They each spoke briefly to the crowd that gave them a standing ovation at the conclusion of the program.

In Rochester, John was anxious to visit the family of his dear friend Bob Powell who had backed him up so effectively on Guadalcanal. The two had trained together in Cuba and before at Parris Island. After the scheduled stop at the Red Wing Stadium John was able to get away to see Powell's mother and twenty-two year-old sister Peggy at 98 Garfield Street. He told them of his closeness to Bob and saw Powell's sister intently taking in every word about her brother's heroic combat action at Basilone's side. He could feel how proud Peggy was of her brother, especially knowing that he had contributed to John's medal.

After a pleasant visit, the memory of which I shall always cherish, I regretfully took my leave. They were a nice family. I wasn't surprised because Bob is quite a fellow.

In Albany, John did the same by visiting the mother of another buddy on Guadalcanal, Jackie Schoenecker. He put her fears to rest by letting her know that Jackie had not been wounded and that his malaria, as her son had made her aware of in his letters, was nothing to be concerned about. John told her that he, too, had come down with the illness and "was walking around with it." There was another stop John made in Albany.

In all that this author has reviewed about John Basilone there is not much talk about his budding relationship with Helen Helstowski, Peter Helststowki's twenty-six year old sister. Even in his own recollections Basilone does not mention her. Pete Helstowski was with him at Guadalcanal and for many a night they had shared the same foxhole and watched each other's back. Helstowski was wounded, however, and sent back to the States.

Through the loneliness and isolation that was Guadalcanal, letters from loved ones were, of course, treasured, but with the exception of family and friends Basilone had no "girl back home." Helstoski noticed that and felt sorry for him so he arranged for Helen to write to John. At first John did not think much of the correspondence between them, but soon began to look forward to Helen's letters and looked forward to meeting her. Now back home she was on his priority list of people to see. After their meeting Basilone seemed to be a changed man and had fallen in love with her. Apparently it was a one-sided affair, for she did not express the same feelings to John, so the relationship eventually faded.

By this time Basilone began to tire of the notoriety and acclaim. Although he appreciated the citizens' adulation and sincere praise, he desired only to return to combat and the company of his buddies. And that public admiration continued unbounded during visits to cities remaining on the itinerary. When we read Baslilone's own words we can get a sense of his growing frustration—and perhaps there was a feeling of guilt. He was a Marine first. And although he was with the Hollywood stars, he was not cut out for showtime. Basilone knew that his time was running short. The furlough was winding down and he was looking forward to being with his family again.

In addition, no matter where I went, there was always some guy who would ask a million questions about the Japs and outside of the job I was now assigned to, I didn't feel like talking about them. Too many of my buddies were still dying in the stinking jungles, which, when I looked around, seemed like a million miles away. Still, they were fighting, praying and dying.

How much longer could I continue feeling like I did?

On the morning of September 19th he left New York and in a short time was at last home, in Raritan, New Jersey, with family and friends. Mayor Peter Mencaroni and Township Committee Chairman William Slattery were the first to meet him. He was both in awe and moved by the hometown crowd that welcomed him. As his car moved through town throngs shouted and waved, pressing hard against his car.

At St. Ann's Church, the first stop, neighbor and friend John Fasoli was there to greet John and his family. Fasoli was now a major in the U.S. Army. At John's request a mass was to be celebrated for his buddies back fighting on the islands in the South Pacific. Father Russo along with Father Graham concelebrated the mass as loudspeakers rang out the Latin to the crowds outside.

John prayed that he might continue to keep in mind the strength of character and humility required of one who has received his nations highest honor. Four hundred of his St. Ann's Parish friends now served their country as was listed in the Parish Honor Roll. Basilone would dedicate that honor roll following mass. As Basilone prayed he heard the words of Father Graham who assured the congregation that God had saved John for "some big work" The nation's youth would be influenced by his life. Most of all, he prayed. He prayed for his buddies—those he left behind on Guadalcanal; those who fell and bled, and died, so that he could be there now alive and well. It was as if he had been propelled forward by some unseen hand to this very moment. Now, in the warmth of those who loved him, he wondered at it.

A long time ago, it seemed ages. I had knelt in this very church and prayed the good Lord to help and guide me. Now, I was back again feeling very small and humble as I realized that God in his wondrous way had heard my prayers. Not only did I fulfill my promise to Pop to keep his name high, but God had seen fit to touch me with this magic, lifting me up for the whole world to see.

I had become a national hero, kids worshipped me, my buddies would give up their lives for me and actually did. I was featured in magazines and comic books. Newspapers had endless articles about my exploits and the bright intense light of publicity shown upon me day and night. To cap the whole incredible drama, the president of these great United States of America had seen fit to bestow upon me the greatest honor this country could give.

After mass John and his family were taken to The Raritan Valley Country Club where lunch was served. He could see the love in his mother's eyes as he gazed across the table at her. His father was "so proud, he just sat and beamed." His mind roamed as he sat listening to the speeches and the talk of what was to follow. The caddying days of his youth seemed so long ago, those days of restlessness and frustration, and the yearning for a place of comfort that would fulfill him.

It was on to Somerville, only a mile away, where the parade was to begin.

It would be the grandest and largest parade ever held in the area and would include twelve marching bands. It would progress from the east end of Somerville's Main Street to Main Street Raritan. They came to welcome their hometown hero, thousands of them, with flags and cheers. Huge photos of him were everywhere. Large signs read, "Welcome home Sergeant Basilone." He had come a long way to this, the first of many "Basilone Days" that Raritan would celebrate. They would continue to the present day.

Sitting up high above the rear seat between his parents he smiled and waved at the crowd. His best buddy, Pfc Peter Helstowski, sat in front. Although he suspected as much from what he had been told and from what he had witnessed in the cities, he was now there, among his hometown people.

A grandstand had been set up on the Duke Estate owned by Doris Duke, daughter of John Buchanan Duke, the tobacco baron and founder of Duke University. The crowd would number more than 20,000 as the newsreel cameras rolled recording it all. The National Anthem was sung by Catherine Mastice, a Raritan lady.

Basilone, perspired. There was the Congressional Medal of Honor with its bright blue ribbon placed around his neck close to his throat. He sat in the front row with his parents just behind him. Included on the grandstand were 250 people from state government and the military. Actresses Virginia O'Brien and Louise Allbritton were there along with stars Danny Thomas, Bob Morris and Maurice Rocco.

He spotted some of his closest friends, those from his childhood days, and he was deeply moved. He could see Tony Orlando and Alphonse Capetta. He hoped Sister Mary Cordula, his grammar school teacher, was there. He drifted back, back to those days of innocence at St. Bernard's School.

Introduced that day by Harry Hershfield of New York were New Jersey Senator Henry Frelinghuysen, former New Jersey Governor A. Harry Moore, Newark Judge Nicholas V. Albano, John Marshall Law School Dean and Past President of the Marine Corps League, Alexander Ormsby, Representatives from each New Jersey County, Raritan resident Colonel Carlo A. Pivarotto, and Marine Corps Adjutant General James I. Bowers.

Frelinghuysen's son was at that very moment in a Japanese prison camp somewhere in the Pacific.

Perhaps the most notable present was Jimmy Walker, former Mayor of New York. From his speech that day:

> I used to think I came from an important and rather significant place, but I had to come out to Raritan, a little place with a normal population of 6000, to see real enthusiasm and the biggest crowd I've seen in ten years. Reflecting on why this country with its comparatively short history has grown into such importance in the world, it is due to the many races which make up the American people. When they came to this country they had a wider opportunity and liberty and freedom that

compelled each to give this country what they were denied the opportunity of giving the countries of their birth. A casual reading of American casualties shows an amazing list of Italian names. The Italian-American and the Italian soldier are as valiant as exist when they've got somethig to fight for. Sergeant Basilone is an inspiration, not only to other Italian-Americans but to all Americans. We can learn from him what a precious privilege you and I have to be citizens of this great country.

From Henry Frelinghuysen:

Today on the far-flunged battle fronts of the world, some six hundred brave lads from Raritan have answered the drum beat of war, and you, John, are living witness that they fight valiantly and not in vain.

We had feared that the easeful ways of modern peace might have destroyed the courage of our people, but we know now that our young men still wear the red badge of courage, that Guadalcanal answers Gettysburg, to Belleau Wood, and the dogged devotion of Bataan and Corregidor to the bleak fortitude of Valley Forge. John Paul Jones fights anew in the Pacific, and the Battle of Lake Erie is now the Battle of the Coral Sea.

Sergeant Basilone, your deeds of heroism have been recited over and over again, and that is right. But may I express personally to you the feeling of respect and admiration I have for the fine honor you displayed when in recounting your experiences you said so modestly, "I think only part of this medal belongs to me, pieces of it belong to the boys who fought by my side."

Nothing could be more noble than your unselfish thought of your fellow comrades in your hour of glory. To you, John, it has been given, in defense of your country, to perform a brave and shining deed which after the dark days of war have passed away will still glow in the annals of American heroism.

The ovation from the crowd was soul stirring and as I meditated I found a small hand tugging at my sleeve. Looking down I found my niece, Janice, my brother Angelo's little daughter, one of my favorites, She had, during the senator's speech, found her way to the stand. Waving off my brother Angelo, I sat her in my lap where she remained for the balance of the program. The crowd roared its pleasure.

Catherine Mastice reurned to the microphone and sang, "Manila John," written by Joe Memoli, the organist at St. Ann's Church. The program was coming to a close.

Basilone rose and went to the microphone. Now in the intensity of the moment he fought back the tears. But regaining his composure he spoke to them.

I want to thank you good home folks for this wonderful gift. Today is like a dream to me. But there is one thing I do want to say for all my buddies overseas in the front lines and that is that they really appreciate what you are doing for them and how you are backing the attack. Thank you for everything from the bottom of my heart.

The crowd responded with thunderous applause. He choked up and could say no more as John's friend Judge George Allgair then presented him with a $5000.00 dollar bond.

Basilone's parents spoke briefly as he looked on at them. "Look at Pop," he thought, "right up there with the big fellows."

After a weekend return to New York City, John was back in New Jersey visiting the Somerset County Bar Association along with manufacturing facilities there—Calco at Bound Brook and Johns-Manville at Manville. He sat quietly in the car on the return to New York after the homecoming celebration allowing the magnitude of it all to settle in. He knew Pete Helstowski sitting upfront could feel the solitude of the moment, too. Pete understood all of it. Pete had been with him through it all.

Then it was on to Pittsburgh and the steel plant and the rest of the stops all along the northeast. The tour had indeed been fruitful; the troop had raised $19 billion in bonds before it was over on October 2, 1943.

The stardom had not been easy for the shy Marine. This was not John Basilone's world.

He was out of his element and longed to be back in combat, out of the limelight. He was, after all, a Marine, and his world was the Marine Corps. The celebrating had warmed him, but he had to make all of it temporary. Maybe it was not understandable even to him when asked for a return to combat. But, to his request, the Brass responded with a firm "No." He was the hero his country needed now. There were airplanes to build and ammunition to make and he was needed on the home front to help make it happen.

CHAPTER 27

Finally he was back home, in Raritan, in the comfort and warmth of his family enjoying the thirty-day leave promised him. He rested and allowed the home fires to engulf him into peace. But that peace became shattered at times as he was haunted by the sullen images of his brother Marines he left back on Guadalcanal. They were locked into his mind's eye. He could feel their fear, their anguish. He could see the Japanese grimacing and screaming as they charged, "Maline, you die," their mortar fire preceding them—the grenades coming in. The angry fire of their nambu guns in the distance and the smell of cordite. When would they stop coming at them? For an instant he was back there with them. Dead Marines were all around him.

He drank some of the tenseness off at Tony Orlando's bar. He was a celebrity at Tony's, too. There were no drinks to buy, not at Tony's place. Tony would not hear of it. Mr. Anthony Orlando was a gentleman's gentleman. He was just that—a very gentle man. Throughout the war Tony sent letters and goodies to every serviceman from Raritan. Their photos adorned the mirror and walls of his tavern. He loved them.

More appearances were to be made; Ed Sullivan,* writing for the Daily News, and Toots Shor pulled him into New York. He did quick bond rally appearances, a special one on Broadway at the Capitol Theater. After being introduced by Sullivan he told the audience of that night on Guadalcanal. And they were mezmerized by it as they listened, still standing after the opening applause. When he had finished, the applause thundered again and continued for fifteen minutes. He had told about the horrors of Guadalcanal like he had not at earlier appearances. It had been building inside of him for weeks now so he told of the blood and death, and of his buddies, and of the malaria and combat fatigue.

When it was over he nearly collapsed. Sullivan came to him as he rested and said that it was the longest ovation he had ever experienced.

In time his orders came through. He would be going to the Washington Navy Yard and guard duty, and a desk there. He was beginning to believe that there would be no end to it, what he referred to many times as his days of being a "museum piece."

Frustrated at the desk job he was being forced to take, John became so depressed that the family began to notice. After a tirade with a reporter, one of many reporters that showed up at the family home, Carlo pulled him aside. He was closest to Carlo; Carlo always seemed to know what to say ever since they

---

* Of television's famed 1950's "The Ed Sullivan Show."

were kids. But John wasn't in the mood to listen. He knew what Carlo was going to say after hearing that John wanted to go back to hs men. "John," Carlo said, "you don't have to go. You've done more than anybody can do, and you can be anything you want to be now. Stay home."

They walked to Angelo's tailor shop and talked there. Angelo was the calm one who looked at things as they were. He would make sense of it all. But John wasn't ready for the pat answers—staying in Raritan, having a family and starting a business as Angelo suggested. Start life fresh now? While his boys were still fighing? Only a Marine could understand.

He would have none of it. And somehow, in his gut, Carlo knew it. John was different. He had always been different. He had been places and experienced things that no one else had, more than any other in his family. He had another family out there, waiting.

Shortly before he left for Washington, Basilone walked into the Raritan Candy Kitchen where he had hung out as a kid. It was there that he had eaten penny candies in his childhood and discovered the opposite sex.

"Hi Len," he said to young Leonard Grasso behind the counter. Grasso gave Basilone a coke as they talked of better days to come when Raritan would be a happier place with the war over. "I'm going to Washington, Len. I don't know what will happen after that, but I have to get back to the action. I know the family will miss me, but it's something I have to do." Years would go by and, in 1995, Leonard Grasso and his wife Margaret would sing "America the Beautiful" and the "National Anthem" at the Basilone Monument after the parade in his honor.

A letter arrived at the Basilone home from his beloved Sister Mary Cordula.

> Dear John,
> Before me is a picture of your own big self talking through a microphone. I can't help but smile and think back to days at St.Bernard's when on Friday afternoons you and the rest of the class did the same thing—only it wasn't into a real "mike" not before such a large audience. Remember? At that time you never realized that such prayer was a preparation for later years. I still have the picture of your memorable class and I show it withgreat pride whenever I can. Occasionally I hear from one or the other. Now that I am with Sr. Florida Coeli, I have her to help me along in singing the praises of dear Raritan and its many good people. I hope some day, please God, to visit my good friends and pupils there.
> What pleased me most, John, in the great work you've been doing, is your deep faith and trust in God. May it always be that way. The world today is fighting because its leaders have forgotten God. When they enthrone God again in their hearts, will peace reign with them and the rest of the world.

No doubt you have been kept very busy bringing cheer and comfort to many these days. Your visit home, too, has brought untold joy to your dear mother, dad and family. This glory and honor which is yours now, will soon pass but you'll still have your mother and dad, so while you're home give them all the pleasure you can.

I have told all the children here in the home about your bravery and loyalty to duty. Now, all the boys are going to be Marines when they grow up. As if the uniform makes the hero. If in your course of travels you get up this way be sure to visit us. When you have a spare moment pen a few lines about your own big self and be sure to include your correct address.

May God bless and keep you safe always, is my daily prayer. Pray for me.

Your Loving Teacher in Christ,
Sr. Mary Cordula

P.S. Permit me to bestow the enclosed medal on you. It's not for bravery but for safety.

His CO in Washington offered Basilone a commission. All he had to do was stay and continue the speechmaking and pose for the cameramen. Basilone said no to the commission. He would repeat what he had said many times before, "I'm a regular Marine and that's the way I want to stay." He would hammer the CO to let him go every time he got the chance. It was always no. The yearning for the return to battle intensified as he wearied of Washington. Then an unforeseen opportunity came his way; he was ordered to go to New York City and make an appearance at the Waldorf Astoria.

He was welcomed as guest of honor at the National Association of Manufacturers with General Vandegrift on the dais with him. The event marked the end of a six-month whirlwind grind for Basilone. But even there, among other celebrated guests, the ghosts of Guadalcanal possessed him.

Yet as I drained my toast, the bottom of the upturned glass became a mirror reflecting the green, stinking, steaming jungle of Guadalcanal, with Jap snipers in the tops of the palm trees. I could hear once more the ping of the sniper's bullet, the sickening sound of flesh split asunder under the impact and the piercing scream of the sniper as he plummeted to his death the victim of a revengeful Marine as he sprayed the top of the sniper's nest...

Yet deep down I began to feel the inactivity, nights became a succesion of flashbacks. The faces of my buddies, battle weary, haggard, eyes sunken with fatigue and fever would pass silently and I would vow to them that somehow I would get back.

The event did present an opportunity for Basilone to approach Vandegrift directly about getting back into combat. Here came the often quoted Basilone line, "Sir I want the fleet." Vandegrift made no promises saying only that he would look into it.

I felt out of things and wanted to get back to the machine guns. I'd done three years of duty in the Philippines and I wanted to be with the outfit that recaptured Manila. I could not bear the thought of Marines landing on Dewey Boulevard on the Manila waterfront and me not with them.*
The "Man" must have known what I was thinking, maybe he felt the same way, being tied down to a desk himself.

Vandegrift did come through. John was going to California.

He had some time home again before departing, and it was during this time that he began to have feelings of uncertainty about the future and what was to become of him. He could not see beyond the war. Yes, there would be an end to it, but he could not picture himself anywhere except in the Marine Corps. Or was there more? Would he be alive? Would the Marine Corps be the finality of it all? The doubts crept in. It was not the fear of dying that got hold of him, but rather it was the unknown; it was being out of place and out of time, in a twilight world, alone.

It was sure that the family had the same fear, as other families had all through the country. And like other families John's family would avoid even the thought of losing him. With John there would be the realization of it; he would probably not come home. No, there was more there. His spoke the dreaded words. To Phyllis and Carlo, on the porch in March of 1944, with the sweeness of lilacs in the evening air of spring, he could say the words, "I'm not coming back." Phyllis said, "No! Don't say that!" But Carlo knew; he said no, it wouldn't happen, but he knew.

But courageous men go; Marines go; heroes go, because somehow they know they must.

So within two weeks after his request to the "Man," John walked happily into his barracks at Camp Pendeton, San Diego, California. Now with the 27th Regiment, Fifth Marine Division,** B Company, he was among battle-seasoned

---

* The Marine 1st Division was now serving under Army General Douglas MacArthur whose forces had come up the New Guinea coast on their way to the re-capture of the Philippines.

** The 5th Marine Division was created during World War II for the Battle of Iwo Jima and the planned invasion of the Japanese home islands. It was activated on Armistice Day, November 11, 1943 with Division Headquarters beginning operations at Camp Pendleton on December 1st, at which time, men and equipment began streaming in. The official activation date was January 21, 1944. The Fifth was deactivated on February 5, 1946 and reactivated for service in the Vietnam War.

veterans and became a heavy machine gun platoon leader immediately. Seeing the heavy guns lined up between the bunks he carressed them gently as a man would a woman, knowing that they stood between life and death in combat.

John was promoted to the rank of Gunnery Sergeant on March 8, 1944, and transferred to C Company since B Company already had in service Gunnery Sergeant Stanley Kavota.

He was a celebrity at Pendleton, too. He knew he would be, but this was different. He was with his beloved Marines. Although a hero there, in shy embarassment he could handle their adulation. Now, at twenty-eight, he was becoming an "old man" in the Corps, so the younger men were in awe of him and he was very protective of them.

The boys in my platoon were all youngsters and looked to me for guidance. They were fresh, eager kids and had no conception of what they were in for.

I resolved I would do anything I could to insure their chances of coming back.

Tony Cirello, a Marine and friend from Raritan, met Basilone on base one day:

> He was like a god to his men. He had them setting up a machine gun in nothing flat. I was there with them once and he said, "Tony, you want to see something?" Then he shouted, 'Set em up!' And you should have seen those men hop. There was some talk about John's being transferred; the men almost mutinied.

Keith Rasmussen, a Marine and Iwo Jima veteran remembered well an incident when he and a trainload of other Marines were returning to Camp Pendleton after leave in Los Angeles. A group of Marines was having a great time in one of the cars.

> There he was, broad-shouldered, good-looking Italian guy raising hell. I knew Manila John was around, but I didn't realize it was him. He was raising up a storm. He wasn't wearing his blouse, sweating profusely, really having a good time. This lieutenant comes down the aisle, walks up to him and says, 'Marine, act the part.'
>
> John reaches over the train seat, picks up his blouse. He only wore one medal on it, the Medal of Honor, powder blue with stars. He shows it to the lieutenant and says, 'My name's Basilone. What's yours?' The lieutenant salutes him, spins around, and walks right back down the aisle out of the car. And everyone just roared. It was great. He was an inspiration to us all.

At Pendleton Basilone would serve with Marine veteran sergeants, Ray Windle and Biz Bisonette. With them Basilone now trained the new young Marines in machine gun operations and in the art of fighting as required in jungle warfare. He saw in these youngsters that green, ego-inflated, new Marine invincibility. He would tame all of that. He would take them through the paces as Puller had done with him and as Dan Daly had done before him. They marched and slogged along lugging their machine guns. Immaculate uniforms became stained and torn with training in hand-to-hand fighting and the "snapping in," (into action) of their heavy guns down in the dirt and mud.

The Marines trained in amphibious operations and, most importantly, the assaulting of pillboxes and other fortified defenses, in keeping with the designated role of the Fifth Division: to locate, close with, and destroy the enemy by fire and maneuver. As their insignia displayed, they would be known as the "Spearhead." Doing the assault with precision, by the book, was the order of the day. Over and over again, they practiced it—positioning the guns for effective covering of the demolition man, timing of machine gun fire, covering of the demolition man's withdrawl and follow-up final destruction of the enemy within the fortification using their newest weapon, the flamethrower.

Basilone pushed them harder and harder, drilling them again and again. Save as many of them as I can, he thought. They have to have the best chance of survival.

The inauguration of the 5th Division brought celebration to the 26th, 27th, 28th Regiments. Regimental battle flags were unfurled, and it was party time with actors Edmond O'Brien and Ann Blyth giving glamour to the celbrating.

For John Basilone it was lady time again, but this time it would be serious. He had met her a few days before the inauguration when they only exchanged glances. Wasting no time, when he saw her in the mess he asked her to go out with him to the movies after the celebration.

She was different, not giddy, maybe a bit shy, certainly not standoffish, but she was not one to fall all over a Marine—even Medal of Honor recipient John Basilone.

CHAPTER 28

It was spring in San Diego and for John Basilone love would blossom there. She was a young brown-eyed woman Marine mess sergeant. It happened quickly for him. Lena Mae Riggi, John's equal in age and living in Oakland, California, at the time, was a tough dark-haired Italian-American farm girl from Oregon.

It took a lot to impress Lena Riggi. "I'm a woman before my time," she had told her longtime friend and roommate, Barbara Garner. "I can do anything they [men] could do." To this writer she said, "I remember one of my friends saying that John Basilone wanted to meet me. I said, 'Who is John Basilone?'" Though she maintained her distance from him initially, she eventually gave in. Soon they were dating regularly from February through March,1944, and as summer approached they planned to get married. As the war raged on with events of the day uncertain, engagements were short.

On Monday, July 10, 1944, at 6:30 p.m. at St. Mary's Catholic Church in Oceanside, California, John and Lena were married. Chaplain Paul F. Bradley of Brooklyn, New York, performed the ceremony. Corporal Virginia Payne sang the "Ave Maria." The wedding party was all Marine. John, his best man, Clinton Watters, and ushers, in regulation uniform green contrasted smartly with the white summer reserves worn by the women. The women's spruce green hats and the bride's bright white taffeta brought it all together.

Their twenty-five guests included Colonel Louis Plain, his Executive Officer, and CO Colonel Duryea. Giving Lena away was NCO, Sgt. Frank Budemy. Her maid of honor was her Marine friend Ruby Matalon.

After the ceremony and reception at the Carlsbad Hotel in Carlsbad, California the couple went on their fifteen-day furlough-honeymoon to Salem, Oregon. John was on his way to having his three most wished-for dreams come true—getting married, having kids, and, after the war, opening a restaurant. Lena reminisced to this writer, "He always talked about having a house with lots of rooms and a picket fence."

From a Tatum interview of Marine William Weber who attended John and Lena's wedding:

> As far as I could tell, they were about the same age, maybe a year two different. Not much. The new Mrs. Basilone was an attractive woman. They looked like they were in love to me."
> When they returned from their honeymoon in Salem, Oregon, Weber asked Basilone, " What did you think of Oregon?" The

sergeant laughed and said, "I never saw so many fucking onions in my life.

Back in Raritan, the Basilone family was not happy. They had not even met Lena, and they had known for a while how much John loved California. Would he stay there even after the war? Italian families usually stayed close together. They hadn't had that much time with John. So, they asked, who was this girl? It is not hard to assume that they were hurt at being left out of John's marriage celebration. It is not hard to assume, too, that Dora Basilone could picture in her mind the grand St. Ann's Church wedding that would take place upon John's discharge. As a consequence Lena suffered the brunt of the family's feelings of rejection, feelings that time would not heal, and she would become embittered by the situation. She did, however, have a warm relationship with Ann, the wife of John's brother, Carlo.

Finding a place to live was not easy even with the couple's combined income. Not wanting to "trade" his Medal of Honor for special treatment when searching for an apartment John and Lena continued to live separately in their barracks. They did have time together though; on one trip they escaped the routine of base life by taking the train to Los Angeles and went to Slapsie Maxie's,* a club on Beverly Boulevard. The line to get in was long with sailors and Marines trying to crowd in. After recognizing the Medal of Honor winner, one of the men in line tried to pull John and Lena to the front of the line. John said no; he would not accept special treatment. They never returned to Maxie's. On a 72-hour pass they went instead to the Trocadero on Sunset Boulevard where comic Joe E. Lewis performed. He spotted John in the crowd at the club and John was, once again, in the limelight. John stood and bowed politely. The couple had a grand time there and became Lewis' close friends. Lewis was a lover of servicemen and did USO shows regularly out on the Island bases. That weekend was to become the most memorable to John and Lena.

Lena recalled going to dinner with friends at the Brown Derby in Oceanside. There would always be a crowd and it was a bit difficult to get a table. Again, John, not wanting to flaunt his medal, would not mention it for special treatment. So without telling him they would advise the hostess that her husband was "John Basilone." There was not a problem with getting a table after that. But time was running short.

While Basilone was out of the action, in the Pacific the war raged on. At the end of 1943, McArthur and his U.S. Army forces hedgehopped up the New Guinea coast while "Bull" Halsey kept pace with him driving the Marines up the Solomons chain taking first the Russell Islands nearest Guadalcanal. Then, at the end of October, shortly after John left Guadalcanal, Halsey hit Bougainville. Then came New Georgia. Both islands claimed Marine lives with no pity.

---

* New York boxer Max "Slapsie Maxie" Rosenbloom.

McArthur's forces jumped from New Guinea to New Britain. Rabaul was within their grasp. Halsey and McArthur closed the trap around Rabaul in what was named Operation Cartwheel. It was the grinding merciless drive toward the home islands of Japan with the Japanese giving no ground easily.

New battleships came on line by the middle of 1943 with which the U.S. Navy would do pre-amphibious bombardment of islands in the Gilbert, Marshall, Caroline and Mariana chains. Selected islands would be taken in succession during the north and westward advance toward the Philippines. The vastness of the total operation was enormous in scope and would be a first in all of naval history. Newly built fast carrier task forces deploying hundreds of aircraft advanced in support of new and faster battleships. But the amphibious landings would cost Army and Marine lives numbering in the thousands.

On November 21, 1943, as Basilone ventured forth on his bond tour, Makin and Tarawa Islands in the Gilberts, the first of the island chains to be stormed by Marines of Task Force 30 would claim the lives of 1500 Marines. Many more would be wounded.

The Japanese emplacements were many and formidable. Direct hits from battleships on these fortified enemy emplacements would many times cause little or no damage, and terrible losses were endured as each pillbox and fortified gun position was taken one at a time. Japanese resistance was suicidal. Surrender was not an option.

Kwajalein was taken on February 1, 1944, with terrible loss to the U.S. Army's 7th Division. From the successes in the Gilberts and Marshalls, the Marianas were next with hard fighting there on Guam and Saipan. McArthur kept pace as he jumped 580 miles to Hollandia located midway up the coast of New Guinea.

As the Americans came closer to the Japanese home islands with each landing, the Japanese endeavored to stage the "decisive battle" during which, it was hoped, they would finally defeat the American Navy in the Pacific. As Basilone followed news of the action in the Pacific, on June 5, 1944, 20,000 U.S. Marines and Army troops landed on Saipan, the greatest force to mount an amphibious landing to that date. Two Marine divisions along with the U.S. Army's 27th Division met an island defensive force of 32,000 Japanese. Bombardment of 2400 16-inch shells from battleship guns continued right into the landings. On July 9th, the day before John's wedding, Saipan was finally secured. U.S. losses were more than 3000. As usual Japanese losses were horrendously more. Surviving Japanese soldiers, along with thousands of civilian inhabitants, committed suicide. From James Stokesbury's *A Short History of World War II*:

> Napoleon once remarked that a victory was no victory without
> prisoners—But he never fought the Japanese.

The Japanese defeat in the Marianas gave Americans a jump-off point 1500 miles from Tokyo, well within the range of U.S. Army Air Force B-29's. July 10th saw the first of the long-range raids on the Japanese homeland. It would be a surprise to Imperial Headquarters as they believed the Americans would first make landings on China's western coast. The Japanese home islands of northern Honshu and Hokkaido were bombed next in addition to airfields near the industrial centers of Hakodate, Muroran and Otaru.

The problem for B-29 pilots with shot-up engines and wounded aboard is that many times they could not make it back to Saipan in the Marianas. It was just a bit too far. They needed an emergency base closer to Japan. That ideal base would be Iwo Jima, an eight-square mile atoll lying alone along a straight line almost half way between the Marianas and Japan. From their base on Iwo Jima, harassing Japanese fighters came up to greet the American flyers causing general havoc. They ventured on to Saipan to continuously strafe American airfields there. Warnings from Iwo went out to the home islands advising them of the U.S. bomber formations headed their way.

Iwo Jima would not be taken easily. General Kuribayashi and 23,000 of his soldiers would see to that.

In the European Theater of Operations, on June 6, 1944, the Allies landed at Normandy. The G.I.'s were on the move across France to liberate the European continent. Then, in East Prussia, ten days after John and Lena were married, a bomb went off in a wooden barracks building at Hitler's Wolf's Lair in a daring attempt at assassinating Adolf Hitler. Count von Stauffenberg, a much-decorated soldier in Hitler's army, and leader of the attempted coup, along with the conspirators, suffered the consequences.

CHAPTER 29

Iwo Jima, island of volcanic ash and sulphuric sand. A Japanese soldier referred to Iwo Jima as "an island of sulfur, no water, no sparrow, no swallow." To the Japanese it was just another Nanpo Shoto, or "Volcano Island." With Mt. Suribachi ("cone-shaped mountain") standing as sentinel at almost 600 feet, Iwo Jima, having virtually no vegetation, was a veritable wasteland. Iwo Jima, Japanese for "Sulfur Island" and coined by English explorer Gore in 1673 because the island's air was saturated by the stuff, was 8 square miles in size, a mere flyspeck. But it lay only 660 miles from the Japanese home islands, in a virtual straight line, to the Mariana Island chain. Before World War II no one cared about its existence so it languished in insignificance. The Japanese ignored it. It just sat there for about four hundred years—waiting to display death and agony. Iwo Jima and its two tiny sisters, Haha Jima and Chichi Jima, known as the Bonin Islands, were first happened upon in 1543 by the Spanish sea captain, Bernard de Torres.

Although Commodore Perry attempted to claim the island chain for America in 1853 congress declined and the island sat occupied for a time by a mix of people from different lands. Japan took final occupation in 1861 as the earlier settlers thereafter trickled away. From that time on the Japanese would consider the chain theirs and would work to turn it into a defensive outpost right to the beginning of World War II. From Bill D. Ross's *Iwo Jima, Legacy of Valor*:

> So security-minded were the Japanese that in 1937 a large sign was posted in Japanese and English at Iwo's East Boat Basin, the only place on the island where people and supplies could be landed. It read: 'Trespassing, surveying, photographing, sketching, modeling, etc., upon or of these premises without previous official permission are prohibited by the Military Secrets Protection Law. Any offender in this regard will be punished with the full extent of the law.'

Work on the first of three airfields (Chidori) on Iwo began after the Pearl Harbor attack with 1400 Japanese troops supporting the construction activity from Chichi Jima. The airstrip effort built up steam after the Americans took Kwajalein and Eniwetok in February 1943. Through the logical conclusion that Iwo would be Japan's last hope to halt the American advance to the home islands, Emperor Herohito ordered that the island become an impenetrable defensive fortress. So in 1943 he appointed General Tadamichi Kuribayashi to direct the construction of the fortifications.

Kuribayashi, having been a commander in Manchuria and China, was the ideal choice. He had spent time in the United States as a military attache and had come to know the American people well. From Iwo Jima, *Legacy of Valor*, he stated:

> The United States is the last country in the world Japan should fight. Its industrial potential is huge and fabulous, and the people are energetic and versatile. One must never underestimate the Americans' fighting potential.

At Kuribayashi's direction, impressed Korean laborers dug miles of tunnels that twisted and turned connecting well-sighted artillery emplacements and pillboxes. The machine guns and other smaller weapons readied for action numbered just under 5000. By the end of 1943 Iwo Jima had become the model of what an island fortress should be. Imperial Headquarters, however, did have some doubts as to American intentions. There was some suggestion that the Americans would first make landings on China's western coast and advance to Japan via that route.

As the Americans came closer to the Japanese home islands with each landing prior to that of the Marianas, the Japanese endeavored to stage the "decisive battle" during which, it was hoped, they would finally defeat the American Navy in the Pacific. A defeat in the Marianas would delay the decisive battle and bring it to another island closer to Japan.

To the Americans, at this point in the Pacific War, location was everything. Iwo would give the Army Air Corps B-29 bombers safe haven for emergency landings and there, too, they would be safe from enemy attack.

As Basilone hungered for a return to combat while languishing at Pendleton his heart sank when he heard of Marine and Army losses at Saipan, and his frustration mounted.

But the Japanese Navy's "decisive battle" was not to be. They had lost the Marianas— and knew of the impending threat after its fall—so the all-out effort to turn Iwo Jima into a formidable obstruction intensified as the number of Japanese troops stationed there increased dramatically. By 1945, 23,000 of Kuribayashi's men were ordered to hold out to the last man. Although admitting that a victory was not possible, all that could be done, would be done, to make the Marines pay dearly for the island's conquest.

From Richard Newcomb's *Iwo Jima*:

> General Kuribayashi was a warrior in the samurai tradition.
> Yet, given command of the defense of Iwo Jima, the general defied traditional Japanese military wisdom. He knew the island, the gateway to his beloved Japan, would fall. He hoped only to delay the process. He dug thousands of feet of tunnels. He built false gun emplacements. He buried tanks. He planned

to let the Americans establish their beachhead; but he would retreat slowly, make the Marines fight hard for every inch of Iwo Jima. The General did not look for glory. He knew he would die. He hoped only to fight valiantly and to die with honor.

With B-29 losses and casualties mounting, Chief of Staff George Marshall, in July of 1944, ordered the capture of Iwo Jima by the middle of January. Operation Detachment would be its code name. General Millard F. Harmon, the Army Air Corps' highest ranking commander in the Pacific knew, too, that the fastest way to end the Pacific War was to crush Japan through the bombing campaign as advocated by Nimitz and Marshall. He would be going against the wishes of General MacArthur whose plan proposed that the final attack be made via the Philippines and Formosa (Operation Causeway). MacArthur's plan was backed by the Joint Chiefs who advised that planning be started for his operation.

Admiral Ernest J. King, Chief of Naval Operations refereed a meeting between MacArthur, Nimitz, Marshall, Rear Admiral Raymond A. Spruance, Millard, Army General Bolivar Buckner and Navy Captain Forrest P. Sherman. Nimitz, though initially favoring MacArthur's plan, changed his mind. Iwo Jima would be taken as planned and as detailed by Spruance. According to Nimitz, Spruance had done "a masterful job that carried the day."

It was two weeks after John and Lena's enjoyable weekend at the Trocadero that word came down. John was to ship out. Lena's friend Ruby gave them her apartment in Ocanside for their last night together, but as it turned out the apartment was too far from the base; with a departing time of 4:00 AM, John would never make it back in time. So the couple spent their last night at the mess talking late into the evening about their future together.

"I'm coming back, Lena, he told her softly. She held back her tears and looked into his eyes saying, "I know."

John shipped out from California on the USS *Baxter* and arrived at Camp Tarawa, Hawaii, sailing into Hilo Bay on August 8, 1944.

The Marines camped on Maume Beach in the city park during their first few days on Hilo. It seemed that a Marine had come down with an unexplained illness causing the Marines to be quarantined at the beach area. But soon they were on flat cars on their way by rail through the Hawaiian jungle to Camp Tarawa. As the train squeaked along winding its way inland Basilone, was fascinated by the beauty of the place as he gazed at the multitude of color surounding him. There, beyond, were the volcanoes Mauna Loa and Mauna Lea, their snowcaps crested against the clear blue sky. Then Camp Tarawa. Known as the Dust Bowl, it was 50,000 acres of volcanic dust that permeated everything. There were no amenities at Camp Tarawa. Hilo was a tortuous twelve miles distance through the jungle from the town of Kamuela, and if one got there somehow, the reward journey's end would be a shack called the Aloha Sandwich Shop.

Basilone worked his men as he had done at Pendleton. Take the blockhouse by the book; cover the demolition man with carefully directed close-in machine gun fire; follow him away from the fortification before the satchel charge blew an opening in the concrete wall. Then transfer machine gun fire to cover the flamethrower man close-in again, just inches away from him, as he poured flame into the opening.

With Basilone was Cpl Robert Casey, Jr., a friend from home who had left Villanova University to join the Corps. He would be with John at Iwo Jima. Also with him was Private John Littlefield* who would remember Basilone with admiration: "John was cavalier, almost dashing," he would say, "like actor Victor Mature." At Camp Tarawa, Basilone would be like a father to him, remembering how John would give him money for bus fare back to the base when he was short of cash. Basilone, he said further, was deeply concerned about his men and did consider them "His men." Basilone's leadership style, he said, would emphasize teamwork.

After being with C Company for only a few days Littlefield was about to leave for San Diego to load the *USS Baxter* when Basilone asked him his name. He replied, "Private John W. Littlefield." Basilone retorted, "Well from now on you're "Little John" because I'm "Big John" and we can only have one "Big John." Littlefield remembered how C Company's machine gun platoon all shaved their heads for a reason he could not remember. Some years previous to the writing of this book Littlefield sent a letter to the editor of *Leatherneck* magazine.

> Dear Sir:
> As and avid reader of *Leatherneck* for the past 45 years, I read with great interest of the heroic life and death of GySgt. John Basilone. I can never forget him. He was my leader as I served with the machine gun crew, third squad, during the capture of Iwo Jima.
> John Basilone was an exceptional Marine. He was not only a talented man in his code of conduct, but he was an example of discipline and courtesy with those who served under his direction in the field or on liberty. Two months after I got out of boot camp (August 1944), I was assigned to his machine gun section, and I traveled with him to the big island of Hawaii. While at Camp Tarawa, we had an unexpected inspection. On our company street, we had to display our gear for the officers of Company "C," 1st Battalion, 27th Marines of the Fifth Division. We had just returned from the beach, and we were not prepared for this field type of inspection. I was in formation, in front of my tent, and all at once, the Colonel and Major were in front of me. Obviously, they recognized me as a raw recruit, and they gave me a series of questions. It was a sure fact they didn't like my answers.

---

* John Littlefield became a Minister in Louisiana.

But John Basilone was nearby, and he saw how nervous I was. The gunny approached the Colonel and said, "He's a new man, Sir. A boot.Leave him with me and my men in the machine gun section, and we'll teach him to be a good Marine."

The colonel's jaw tightened, and then relaxed. He and the Major turned on their heels and departed, and I was thankful that I was not going to the brig and thankful to be a member of Manila John Basilone's machine gun squad.

Chuck Tatum interviewed Marine William Weber who had attended Basilone's wedding. Weber was already in C Company at the time John arrived at Camp Tarawa. Tatum:

> Weber had a 'secret.' He was an accomplished typist and didn't want the Corps to know. He confided in Basilone that he 'joined the Corps to fight–not type.' The sergeant explained he could serve well being a typist. Weber told the platoon sergeant*, 'Well if you don't want me, I guess I have to go.....but I joined to fight.' Basilone said, 'Go over there and stand at ease.' Weber reported to company headquarters and 'hung around,' as Basilone suggested After seven days he had orders transferring him back to C Company. 'I guess Basilone had something to do with it. I never told anyone else. I was honored to be in his platoon.'

John wrote to Lena on August 21st, and almost every day thereafter.

My Darling Wife,

Honey we had a good trip across, most of the boys got seasick but I was pretty lucky I didn't. We are now on an island somewhere in the Pacific and it is very hot down here, but it is also a beautiful place. Honey tell Mary Lou her boy friend Van is also down here. I met him the other day. Watters, Johnston Martine and Wheeler all sleep in the same tent with me so when we got our sack squared away I said okay let's get our best girl picture and hang them up, so they all pulled the wedding pictures out, now I have you all around me honey. Gee but I miss you more than anything in the world, I have that color picture right by my side now and watching that lovely smile of yours. Honey did you get any letter from home yet if you do let me know. How do you like working for the officers

---

* Basilone had already been promoted to Gunnery Sergeant.

now okay? Mary isn't working you hard is she. If so tell her I'll be back with my machine guns. Also that Watters sends his best regards to her. Well kid it's pretty hard to write anything about this place as you know our letters are censored. Honey I am making out another allotment to you for $75 it may take a month or so to get through. You know coming across there was a rumor that there was two Bams* aboard ship and they said one was a sergeant, and everybody said that it was you kidding me about it. It was all a scuttlebutt. Well honey I'll close for now and hope to get a letter soon from you. Closing with lots of Love and Kisses (Regards to all)

Love Always

Johnny
Love and Kisses

A day or so later he writes:

My Darling Wife,

Here I am anxiously awaiting your letters which have not yet arrived. As our mail down here is a little fouled up, I guess I'll get your letters all at once. I'm sitting and gazing at our wedding picture, gee but you look so sweet smiling, it makes me want to hold you in my arms and just keep kissing you Darling. Well kid how are you feeling these days, okay, and is Mary working you hard. And how is your new job coming along. Honey you should see my platoon now they have bald heads, we had some pictures taken and as soon as we get them I'll send them to you, you'll get a big laugh out of it. We were calling Watters glamour boy so finally got him to cut his hair too. The boys are sure making our tent look more and more like home, there is still one thing we need down here Honey, and that is you Darling. We have adopted Watters as the mother of the tent. Honey the Sgt. Major was asking about you the other day. You should see him now. He looks like a rugged man and we don't have to shave down here. Well Honey it is chow time so I'll close for now Honey with Lots of Love and Kisses.

(Love you
Miss you)   *Love always*
                                     Johnny

---

* Slang for women Marines—"Broad Ass Marines."

Regards to all.

Excerpted from other letters:

Undated

> *...I just can't wait until the day I get back as we can start on our hut. I miss you more than anything in the world Darling. You know I have a new song now (Some day I'll meet you again). I look at our picture and sing and it always seems like you are real in the picture and you are answering me...*

Undated

> *...I was a lucky guy today got a letter from you and one from my kid brother who is in a rest camp. I don't think he is very far from me. I may get to see him...*

Undated

> *...the boys just now left for the movie. I didn't feel like going so I'm alone in the tent with your beautiful face in front of me...also I don't want ten kids I only want one...*

Undated

> *...Darling I love you so much that I feel like stealing a plane and fly right back into your arms, and hold you and kiss you. I can just see you now with that little curl always falling over your eye, I bet your hair is very pretty and don't let them cut it...*

Undated

> *...You know honey I miss you so much I think I'll re-marry you when I get back. I sure wish this war would be over soon so we can be together again Honey, and I'll never leave you for a minute just hold you and love you Darling. Blood and Sand.* You said in one of your letters about the moon light one night. Well Darling that same Moon I was looking at down here and I could see you sitting on it and smiling down at me and saying hurry home Darling, and I said "I'll be seeing you in all those familiar places"...***

---

* *"Blood and Sand"* was a 1941 re-make movie. Rudolph Valentino starred in the original version. In 1941 Tyrone Power inherited the role playing a famous matador whose fame and fortune are lost after his involvement with a sweetheart. Starring also were Rita Hayworth, Linda Darnell and Anthony Quinn.

** Popular WWII record by Tommy Dorsey and Frank Sinatra.

Undated

> *...I received a letter from my sister Mary, and she sure wishes that you would go to New Jersey. I told her that as soon as I get back we will go together. Gee kid I sure miss you, I don't know what I would do without the wedding picture in front of me. Honey I never in my life missed anyone as I miss you Darling. I have been away many a time, but Darling this time it really got me. Honey when I get back I'll never leave you for even a second. I heard our song the other day over the radio (I'll Get By).* It sure put me in a trance...*

Undated

> *...Don't worry none honey for this war will be over soon and you and I will be together again and start romancing again, for I'll be back. Blood and Sand...*

Undated

> *...Kid I sure miss you, wish this war would be over so as we can be together and get that white house with the blue shutters and the white fence, and honey I'll paint the fence every day...*

Undated

> *...Well Honey I have been very good, I haven't had a drink in a long time. (P.S. I can't get any.) The funny thing is I don't miss it. I'm going to church tomorrow and will write a letter right after mass...*

* Popular WWII record by Harry James and Dick Haymes.

CHAPTER 30

There would be no attempt to hold the beaches. Kuribayashi had placed his real firepower at Suribachi and at emplacements at the island's northern areas. He would use only his troops at the beach with their automatic weapons. Heavy fire would be held until the Marines made their landing. Then he would blast them as they stood pinned to the narrow constriction of the beach using mortars, rockets and artillery, destroying them there. Believing that the Americans would probably survive the onslaught he would then withdraw his troops slowly keeping up the pressure, taking as many American lives as possible. He had learned from Normandy and the success Marines had experienced during other island landings in the Pacific; if one did not destroy them on the beaches with concentrated fire they would break through the thin defensive crust. He would have to set up "defense in depth." Defensive fire from the beach as a primary deterrent would not work. It had been used in the Marianas and it had failed.

Kuribayashi drew harsh critcism from his superiors at Imperial Headquarters for his reasoning. But he gave no ground. He would wait until the enemy had landed and had advanced to 500 yards; Suribachi and the Motoyama area would supply artillery fire, and automatic weapons would spray fire from the Chidori airfield. As the Marines advanced, Chidori defenders would retreat north and would make the major stand from the tunneled and bunkered defenses there.

Japan's outpost island defenses were gone and the Marines were closing in—to Iwo Jima. The American attack force would be the most massive to date—more than 800 vessels in all. Pre-invasion bombardment would emanate from eight new battleships and fifteen cruisers. Sixteen carriers would send in fighters to bomb and strafe. Seventy-seven destroyers rounded out the armada along with landing craft, supply ships and other required vessels. The fleet would stretch beyond the horizon. 70,647 Marines would make the assault. Again from Newcomb's *Iwo Jima*:

> But this array of power deceived no one, least of all the Marines. After Tarawa, the Marianas, and Peleliu, there were no illusions left. Iwo Jima would be a return to war in primitive style. Naval gunfire, planes, and artillery would be of some assistance, but there would be no room for mass or maneuver. This would be a battle of man to man, a battle of caves and tunnels, of flame and satchel charges, knives and

bayonets, the rifle and the grenade....Iwo was different, and the difference was recognized. It had no jungles, no coral reefs, no mountains; it was nothing but a stone fortress set far out in sea. To an astute Marine eye, it was apparent at once that the battle would mean frontal assault.

On October 9, 1944, Marine General Holland Smith received orders from Nimitz to make plans for the invasion of Iwo Jima. Later, "Howlin Mad" Smith as he was known due to his flaring temper, would say, "I was not afraid of the outcome of the battle. I knew we would win. We always had. But contemplation of the cost in lives caused me many sleepless nights."

Organized as the Fifth Amphibious Corps the Marine force was organized as follows:

> Fifth Division with 26th, 27th (Basilone) and 28th Regiments landing on the extreme left (west), commanded by General Keller E. Rockey.

> Third Division with 9th and 21st Regiments at the middle, commanded by General Graves B Erskine.

> Fourth Division with 23rd, 24th, and 25th Regiments on the extreme right (east), commanded by General Clifton B. Cates.

The 3rd Division had just taken Guam and was now cleaning up the island of remaining Japanese troops in hiding. The 4th was on Maui.* They were well worn after four campaigns in 1944. The Fifth, untried as a unit force, as told above, was also in Hawaii on Hilo. The Fifth did have its share of combat veterans. In all, about forty percent had seen action. Although a new Marine Division, it included many old Marine Raider veterans along with experienced Marine paratroopers. Medal of Honor winner John Basilone and his cadre of tough fighting Marines would give new recruits assigned to the Fifth greater hope and courage as they faced the challenge before them.

October 20th
>...*Well Darling it's hard to say how long we will be here, you probably will know when we are gone*...

October 29th

>...*We got a radio playing and guess what was playing, no kid-*

---

* With the 4th on Maui was George Basilone.

ding, "I'll Get By" We got a couple of packages today. I got one from home with salami in it, boy did they go for that. In about 3 minutes flat there wasn't any left...

October 30th

...I had the most wonderful dream last night, there we were together just like when I was courting you and we were in the park at Oceanside making love and just when I was reaching to kiss you, and then I woke up, and it was a dream, so I jumped out of my sack and kissed your picture and made it real.

November 2nd

...I sure wish that this war would be over so as we can be together again for I love you more than anything in this world. You know when I was in Catholic school the Sister use to tell me if you pray every night that things would come out okay. So I'm the best prayer there is honey...

November 4th

...Paterson was just in here and he was telling me...you know he always calls me Uncle John. Well he said today that if he gets twins he is going to give me one, the boys always kid me about having a baby. You wait honey we'll surprise them when I get back...

November 12th

...Today honey I received a package from my sister Phylis, she is the one I showed you a picture of her two girls and now she has a baby boy. You know honey she looks almost like you, I bet if you were together people would think you were sisters. Honey I was talking to a kid the other day and he told me all about your Halloween Dance you people had, His girlfriend wrote and told him, I bet you were the life of the party as he said you were dressed like Carmen Mirranda and you had carrots in your hair...

November 15th

...Just got in from the field and there on my sack was a yellow sheet of paper telling me to go to the post office and get a package, Darling that was a wonderful gift, I felt like a kid again just receiving my first birthday present...I was talking to a couple of married men and they were talking about what they are going to do after the war, I told them you and I honey are going to Niagra Falls for a long honeymoon. Martini just came in

and he gave me a cigar, he said it was a birthday gift to me...Honey thank you very much for the [I.D.] *bracelet...*

November 26th

...Honey I was just talking to...you know Jackie's husband and he was asking me what I was going to do after the war, I told him that I didn't know that, after the war I would know then, I have no worry as long as I have you...

November 29th

....Honey today I was looking in my sea bag and I found a little pink heart with white lace around it and I pinned it right next to my heart, it was from your wedding dress...

The best of men that America had to offer would go to Iwo. They would go where the Corps sent them with no questions asked. No compromise would be at issue. The job had to be done and they were confident that no force could defeat them. Yesterday it was Guadalcanal. Now it would be Iwo Jima. Leading the young and inexperienced were those that had paid their dues.

From Bill D. Ross in his *Iwo Jima, Legacy of Valor*:

> These were the 'old salts,' the 'old breed' of noncommissioned and commissioned officers—the John Basilones and the Chandler Johnsons—whose home, career, and life were, by choice, the Marine Corps. They were the 'old pros,' most in their mid-twenties or early thirties, who had met and defeated the Japanese in earlier campaigns, some as many as four times, beginning at Guadalcanal. It was a rarity for any of them to have escaped being wounded at least once by the time they landed on Iwo Jima.

Like Basilone, others of the old breed regarded the Corps as their family and had joined when times were tough in America. Ross continues:

> Many of the senior noncoms on Iwo—the platoon, gunnery, and first sergeants—had joined up in the tag-end days of the 'Great Depression' when jobs were impossible to find. Now they knew no other life than the Marine Corps, and were devoted to it; to the sense of belonging it gave, to its traditions and comradeship.

December 1st

...Well Darling it's hard to say anymore, only that I love you so much that I pray every night that this war will soon be over so we can be together again. Honey the old Gunny just came

in and invited me to his mess for chow....you know honey he could go back anytime he wants to but he won't, he is always telling me one more landing and I'll go home...

December 7th

...I read that part in your last letter about house cleaning to the boys and Jack said we sure didn't have any luck in training me to clean up, but they know you will. Honey any time you want me to clean house it's okay with me, wish I could be right back there now cleaning our little white house with the blue shutters and the white fence....

December 10th

My Darling Wife,
Darling do you know we were married 5 months today and sure brings back some beautiful memories, Honey when I get back every 10th of the month you and I are going to celebrate our anniversary, I saw the priest the other day that married us, I was going to ask him for some pictures....I only wish I could be with you for Christmas, Man, I would be the happiest man in the world if I could have you in my arms and say Merry Christmas Darling...

December 15th

...I sure wish I could be with you for Christmas for I would be the happiest Marine in the world, Honey when we do have our Christmas together I'll make up for all we didn't have together...

December 17th

... I am going on liberty today for 3 days, and I won't be able to write for we can't write down in town for there is no one to censor our mail,...I'm taking our wedding picture with me so as I can have you near me always...

December 20th

...Darling gee Darling I would give anything in this world just to be with you for Christmas. Honey when this war is over we will make up for everything we missed.
Darling I'm glad you liked the Christmas present I had my sis get for you for me, Only I would like to have given it to you in person and tell you how much I love you...

December 22nd

...You know honey it is only 3 days from Christmas and they

say we are going to have turkey, that sure sounds good, I only hope and pray by next Christmas I'll be home with you Darling and that will be the best Christmas of all...

December 23rd

...We are going to have a big show tomorrow, 3 of my boys are going to sing, we tried to get Johnston to do us a dance but he won't do it. I am going to confession tomorrow and midnight mass, so you see I'm a good boy. Gee Darling I would give anything to be able to hold you in my arms and say Merry Christmas Darling and a Happy New Year...

December 25th

Hi Darling,

How are you today? Fine I hope. Today is Christmas and everything is fine, only you should be here with me to make it perfect....I also received a letter from my sis...that she is trying to move the family to Calif....

January 4th

...My kid brother came over to see me, he sure looks swell. All he talked about was you and he can't wait to see his new sister-in-law...I also may get to see [brother] Al soon. He sure will be surprised when he sees me...

Practice landings were made on the southeast coast of Maui and on the island of Kahoolawe by the Fourth and Fifth Divisions prior to shipping out. The rehearsals were considered a bust with some units not present due to bad weather while some taking part were missing equipment. Tanks and DUKWS (amphibious trucks or "Ducks") held back for fear of corroding ammunition due to the salt water. Tanks and artillery had to hold also due to choppy seas and imposing reefs.

On Christmas day the Fifth Division began loading transports. The Third Division would hold its debarkation for five weeks as they were almost fifteen hundred miles closer to Iwo Jima. The Fifth's first units boarded the transport *Athena* to the cheers of the crowds at the docks. By January 4th all were aboard. Vessels of this great armada constituted The Joint Expeditionary Force that now assembled off the island of Oahu. By early February the Third Division was loading on Guam.

January 2, 1945

...I received a letter from my sis the other day and she can't wait until she sees you. Honey when my family does see you I know they will all love you.

January 16th

> *...Gee honey when this war is over I'll never leave you out of my sight, I'll help you to cook and wash the dishes so as I can be near you Darling.*

January 21st

> *...Honey I just can't help but keep looking at the picture you had sent, you sure came beautiful in it. Darling I want you to know that I never was sorry that I married you, for I love you so much. Remember Honey when we were going togeth-er and we use to say that we can do anything because we love each other.*

At long last about the latter part of January 1945, we received orders to pack our gear and in jig time we were being ferried out to our transports at anchor in the deep waters just off shore. All sorts of rumors were flying, our des-tination, however, was top secret.

Under strictest of black-out instructions we slowly steamed away from our base. I had the strangest feeling at the time, wondering how many of us would ever see it again.

Much to our surprise in a short time we were dropping anchor off Pearl Harbor.

What lay before us was more than our eyes could take in. Another convoy had already weighed anchor off Pearl Harbor. Scanning the horizon the vast-ness of the coming operation began to penetrate. The ships, hundreds of them, were herded together by the largest task force I had ever seen. There were cruisers, destroyers, submarines, aircraft carriers and freighters. It was an impressive sight and just for a moment I allowed myself the luxury of thinking that perhaps we'd steam right into Tokyo Bay. Coming back to earth and know-ing the pattern of war we must wage, I knew it was impossible as long as the enemy had bases in the Pacific from which they could strike at our rear. There was no other way.

It had to be an island hopping assault, with a distressing number of casualties.

Looking around at the eager young faces in my crew, I knew I did the right thing in coming back.

Fishing around a bit, I learned that the other convoy had arrived from Maui Island with the Fourth Marines, my brother's outfit. * I got permission to pay him a visit and was soon climbing up the ladder to his transport. We spent the whole*

---

* George Basilone landed on Saipan on June 15, 1944 with the 4th Division, the month before John's marriage. Casualties were close to twenty-five percent with 3000 Marines killed and more than 13,000 wounded. At the time of his marriage John did not know if George had survived. After combat on Saipan, George landed with the 4th Division on Tinian.

day together.

He was with a good bunch, they liked him not only as a buddy, but also as a top-notch fighting Marine. George was never the type to talk about himself, but his pals filled me in on the Marshall Island, Saipan and Tinian invasions.* It seemed George did some pretty heroic things himself.

His commanding officer told me later that if there was any more of us home to make sure they joined the Marines. Even though you knew he was joking it felt good to hear. At the same time I thought of my youngest brother Donald. He had just joined, rather volunteered and was accepted by the Marine Corps. That made three of us in the Corps, and my brother Al with the tank units of General Patton.

I asked George's commanding officer if it could be arranged to have George visit me on my transport. He was pleased to do it and a few days later George joined me and met all my buddies. I know he was struck by their youth as he remarked to me later, "Johnny, I thought you said you had a lot of veterans aboard."

I said, "Sure we have, but we have them all assigned to groups; in that way the youngsters will have someone with experience to lead them.

George pleaded with me to ask for a transfer to his outfit. I knew he had in mind that his boys had been through three strikes and were seasoned vets. I told George that one of the main reasons I came back was to give the benefit of my experiences to the youngsters.

Knowing me, George dropped the matter.

All this time the job of refueling, supplies and provisions was taking place and we were fortunate enough to obtain shore leave.

I had heard through some friends that Dr. Fox, our old school principal from Raritan, was living on Hilo. George and I thought it would be nice to surprise him with a visit, besides, the thought of meeting an old hometown friend so many thousands of miles from home was exciting.

With three other buddies, George and I paid a visit to Dr. Fox, not telling him that we were coming. He was surprised and very pleased to see us. I shall always remember that day as one of the most pleasant in my life. We sat in his living room enjoying a few drinks, talking over old times, thinking all the time what a nice guy he was even if he was a school principal.

George and I had to wait for our boat to the transports and we sat on the pier stringpiece talking. I told George of my plans when this was all over. George thought it would be a good idea to invest the war bonds I had accumulated into a business I liked.

As we talked George told me of his plans and for the first time I can remember we both opened up. We talked about everything except the coming engagement, home, Mom, Pop, the rest of the folks, our friends, and how wonderful everyone had been to me.

George finally got around to asking why I had reqested the fleet.

"After all, John," he said, "you had it made, you could have called your shots. A commission or a soft berth at Camp Pendleton. Why come back to this rat race? You of all people should know what our chances of getting back alive are."

I had never seen George so serious. Picking my words carefully I replied, "George, when I left the theater of operations in Guadalcanal to come back stateside, I promised my buddies I would return and that promise I didn't make lightly. Furthermore my heart belongs back there. I left part of it on Guadalcanal. I won't be able to rest, much less look at myself if I sat on my ass back in the states on a soft berth, when so many of these boys need the help and experience I can give them."

George just shook his head and said, "Maybe what you say is true, on the other hand you did more than your share. You were lucky to get back alive. Why push your luck?"

"George," I answered, "the Marine Corps is my whole life. Without it the rest seems empty. This thing I have to do, something keeps pushing me. I know now what I want, if I don't make it, try and explain it to the folks. I know they always loved me, God knows I do them, but this is bigger than family and loved ones and I must do it."

George was silent, just then our boat pulled in to the dock and we separated for our ships. Leaving the dock my boat kept pace with George's, however as we neared the transports we veered off to port and I yelled over to George, "See you on the beach."

As I climbed the ladder to my transport I wondered if I had made myself clear to George. Deep inside of me I knew it was right, but I couldn't help but wonder if my own brother felt I was foolish in returning, what must all of the thousands of people who read about me think?

Basilone's last letters to his family are certainly not reflected verbatim in the following final monologue since his sister Phyllis undoubtedly compiled and edited them to present what would have been his last words and observations. This holds true for the monologue above on this page. But it is here, below, however that her edited presentation is most obvious, especially in the last paragraph, before his February 3rd letter to Lena.

Well, folks, for all to know, I sincerely felt I had to return. Sure I know I had it made. I had left a wonderful wife in California, one understood my feelings and the chances were that I would not return. What's the sense of kidding, the odds were a million to one that I would not return alive. Yet with all of this, my heart was clear. The uneasy feeling that had been with me since childhood had disappeared and I felt in my heart that God had pointed the way and I had but to follow.

It was as simple as that.

Everyone on board ship had sobered down and were busily writing home to their loved ones, as is the case before any major engagement. I had the feeling that this would be the biggest one we had ever been in.

We slowly slipped out of Pearl Harbor bound for some unknown island. Up on the forward deck of the ship where most of the men congregated shooting the bull, I could see my boys loading machine gun belts, joking and laughing in such high spirits. I wondered if they knew what faced them.

I had already forgotten how we had done the same thing on the way to the Canal for our first major action.

All this time the Marines were working on their weapons, cleaning and setting up their mortars and machine guns on deck. You could sense the almost tender way they carressed them, knowing their lives and those of their buddies depended on them being in perfect firing order. Other buckos were honing down their bayonets and huge bolo knives to razor sharpness.

All through the ship was feverish activity as if everything had been left to the last second. Actually every last minute detail that had been planned months ago was coming to a dramatic climax.

I gathered my men around me and went over the plans for the landing. I was worried as I felt sure we would be in the first wave. It seemed a crime as I looked around me and took in the young, eager faces, looking up to me for advice. What advice could I give them? They were trained down to fighting trim. The problem was in any assault to get your men off the beach and your guns set up.

Fully aware that the odds were against us heavily on account of being in the first wave, I only hoped and prayed we'd be spared. I knew for certainty there would be thousands of us dead and wounded before the beachhead could be secured. There was no doubt in my mind as I gazed at the the armada but that we would be successful.

February 3rd

My Darling Wife,

I am sorry I couldn't write to you sooner for it has been quite impossible until this time. I'm writing this letter out at sea, we are on our way into combat.

Well how is my little Darling these days, fine I hope. Everything with me is just fine.

Honey as I'm writing this letter I find myself thinking of your birthday. I sure wish I could be there with you Darling. I'm wishing you a very very happy birthday Darling.

It sure is hard writing as this ship is doing a lot of rocking and it is very hot. Watters and I sleep near each other and half of the time I find him in my sack when this ship starts rolling. Tell Dyer she should see Martini now with his mustache and beard. She sure would have a laugh. Right now Watters is giving a little school to the boys, they know I'm writing to you Darling and want me to give you their regards. We are having some fun with Johnston. He had 3 of his teeth pulled and can hardly talk only with his hand. Jack Wheeler hasn't received his bracelet yet, but I know he will receive it later.

Honey, Gunny Bald took sick before we left and he is going back to the states. He said he would stop in to see you when he did. I sure felt sorry for the old Gunny for he did want to make

one more combat before he would retire.
Darling I sure miss you. I love you more than anything in this
world. I'm hoping and praying that this war will be over soon
as we can be together for always Darling.
Well kid I'll close for now with lots of love and kisses to the
sweetest and loveliest wife in the world.

Love Always,

Regards to all,   *Johnny*
Love you, Miss you

During those last days before the landings thousands of Marines cooped in any spot they could find aboard ship to write their letters. They could say that they were at sea and could comment about the weather, but that was it as far their mission and whereabouts were concerned. On deck the Marines continually checked weapons and inspected ammunition. Bayonets were sharpened to finely honed sharpness. They read, played checkers and at times just sat on deck soaking up the sun. Plaster and rubber models and relief maps of Iwo Jima were made available to them for study. They now knew that "Island X" or "Workman Island," as it was referred to during training, was Iwo Jima. From Newcomb's *Iwo Jima*:

> In the *USS Cecil*, the Navajo teams had a final run-through. In a test over a circuit running from General Rockey's headquarters topside to a compartment below decks, four Indians beat four Marines in speed and accuracy of message transmission. In the Navajo language the Indians had an unbreakable code; no one outside the tribe had ever mastered Navajo.

Ever so slowly in groups, finally, the Fourth and Fifth arrived in the Marianas for their rendezvous with the Third. It was now mid-February as the Fourth and Fifth Division armada anchored off the coast of Saipan awaiting pre-departure consolidation of the naval force. The Marines wrote home, waited and wondered.

On February 15th, transports carrying the assault units departed Saipan leading the way to Iwo Jima. On the 16th, main body Fourth and Fifth Division transports then followed, Saipan disappearing below the horizon. The convoy included vessels required for every concern, from medical, to gasoline, to rations, cigarettes, everything. The strike force headed for Iwo Jima was the largest ever assembled to date. Iwo was now only three days away. From Richard Newcomb:

> The weather grew colder each day as the convoys moved north, and the sea was flat gray. But the nights were clear and

still, with a quarter moon and millions of stars. The universe seemed unlimited, and home was so far away it could no longer be imagined. The long lines of ships, their engines throbbing softly over the sea, moved steadily onward, never pausing, their wakes churning up a plume of phosphorescence in the halflight. No light or movement showed on the decks, but there was life inside.

By this time Iwo had been blasted for a total of seventy-two days by B-24 and B-25 bombers. From about six miles out Navy pre-invasion bombardment of the island began at 7:07 a.m. on the morning of the 17th. By reconnaissance the island had been gridded out into squares so that each gun on each ship had an assigned target. By February 1st, 696 targets had been plotted. They consisted of artillery emplacements, pillboxes, blockhouses and anti-aircraft and coastal defense guns. Major positions were ticked off as they were hit. All was going well until the rain moved in causing the bombardment to cease. The finely coordinated shelling intended to tear away sheltered emplacements did not happen. Only sporadic Navy fire re-commenced as the weather cleared intermittently.

John Basilone was confident. He had told Lena that he would return safely to her. He knew it. She had allowed him to regain his hope. Perhaps his intuition of impending death in combat expressed to Carlo had been wrong after all. Phyllis was right, he believed. He would return to Lena. She, too, believed he would come home to her. He yearned to be with her. That alone, he thought, would carry him through—and the people of Raritan were waiting and praying for him, too. He was right, they did wonder—why had he gone back? But, surely, he prayed, God would be good to him.

We had been at sea for some time now. The word was out, "Iwo Jima." The youngsters champed at the bit, the oldsters, including yours truly, paled at the name.

We had heard so many stories of the strong fortifications the Japs had constructed on this volcanic island, which by its very terrain was as obstructive as the Japs themselves.

A native planter came aboard and briefed our commanding officer. The information was all bad.

I sat down and wrote a letter to my wife, the ususal, not to worry, etc., then I wound up the letter telling her, we got a lot of green kids in this outfit and they're depending on me when things get tough. Now I know I did the right thing in coming back here, but don't worry, I'll be back. A few other letters, the last one to my sister Phyllis, and I had cleared my mind for the coming action.

The bombardment had done little damage. In fact it created a cratered landscape that gave even greater protection to the island's defenders. The first day's bombardment destroyed only a pitiful seventeen of the nearly 700 targets.

Bombardment from the *Tennessee, Idaho* and *Nevada* began at 8:40 a.m. on the 18th from about two miles out as *Pensacola* swept four miles further in to about 750 yards. She found that all was clear under water, but she was hit by a shore gun and sustained serious damage. She lost seventeen of her crew with many more wounded, Iwo's first casualties.

Next, the frogmen, in their small LCPR boats came in through a triangular wave of LCI gunboats that moved slowly and steadily forward ready to provide cover fire. The frogmen would check the shore for underwater demolition and other obstacles as had been found before other Pacific landings; there could be any kind of thing—barbed wire, spikes, just about anything. Then they would chart the sea floor and take sand samples from the beach. A line of destroyers laid back at about 2500 yards ready to cover as frogmen and gunboats alike passed between them.

But suddenly all hell broke loose as the Japanese opened up blasting the gunboats mercilessly. Every gunboat was hit by guns at the base of Suribachi and artillery fire from the northern area of the island. The determined crews held their battered vessels in the assigned area just a few hundred yards from shore. Finally, they pulled back as the frogmen completed their work. Destroyers assisted the gunboats with the wounded, causing the destroyer *Leutz* to be hit. Seven men died on the ship and 33 were wounded. The Gunboaters lost 43 men and counted 153 wounded.

Bombardment of the island resumed along with aircraft strafing and laying down of napalm. But after two days of shelling the island, on Saturday evening, the 17th, defenses were virtually intact. Even worse, the beach defenses had not been eliminated. So on Sunday morning, after a reevaluation of the situation, bombardment became even more selective. Rom Newcomb's *Iwo Jima*:

> Sunday morning visibility was only fair, with rain squalls, but battleships opened fire at 7:45A.M. from 2500 yards—a mile and a quarter—at sea.
> Working carefully and deliberately, The *Nevada* and *New York* began stripping the sand from the suspicious-looking hummocks behind the beach. This was done with single shells, to blow the sand away and reveal the concrete structures beneath the ground. Then a few rounds of 2000-pound, high-capacity shells, and another blockhouse was gone. As the Japanese scurried from their burrows, the 4-mm gunners followed them over the terraces and cut them down."
> "The deadly serious gunners of the *Tennessee* blasted cliffs for nearly five hours, carefully picking the coastal batteries out of the bluffs...The *Idaho*, concentrating on Suribachi, blasted away all day, steadily pulverizing the rock and concrete at the base of the mountain.

After a full day of shelling, many blockhouses, pillboxes and heavy guns were destroyed, but many, many more remained intact.

CHAPTER 31

It was coming together now. His hands moved along the textured form to feel for an unwanted furrow that he could not see, or maybe just to feel the life of his creation itself—the upper torso, the strong neck and muscular arms. He climbed down from the ladder and beheld it. It mustn't be over done. It must be lithe yet strong. The weapon must not weigh him down, it must rest there as if a part of him—an appendage. There was softness yet confidence and power, a relaxed intensity, triumphant. He had captured the child-man after battle.

On the morning of D-Day, February 19, 1945, the island stood before them, silent, forbidding. Morning pushed back the dawn and the sky became beautifully clear with only a sprinkling of clouds. It was a great day for an invasion.

To the left the mists gathered above Suribachi, the sentinel, obscuring its peak as it rose up menacingly before them. In front lay the flat black ash beaches with the steeply rising bluffs beyond. What most Marines remember is that Iwo Jima was different. It was not just another island that had to be taken. It was an alien place that God had somehow forgotten.

The armada that now gathered at sea was the greatest that had ever been assembled in all of history. Admiral Spruance arriving the evening before on his flagship *Indianapolis* prepared to direct the landing operation. A seven to eight knot breeze blew wisp-like at the admiral's flag.

John Basilone and his men had been up since 3:00 AM having been rudely awakened by the ship's gongs and blasting loudspeakers. Metal trays rattled with utensils as the men ate standing up in the crowded galleys. Some men couldn't eat the traditional steak and egg breakfast while others ate as if it was the last meal they would ever have. For some it would be. For many, breakfast did not sit well as their stomachs tightened. It was 6:30 AM and all was ready. Admiral Turner gave the official order to "Land the landing force!"

From here on in every event was carefully timed. The transport ships and LST's lumbered into position as sailors prepared them for the Marines' departure. Then at about 6:35 AM bombardment of the island commenced. It would be the most intense pre-landing shelling to date and would last for eighty minutes. Again they fired at pre-sighted assigned targets, each cruiser and battleship in turn, as the island was swept with their shelling. 16-inch battleship guns, cruiser fire and smaller caliber destroyer guns turned Iwo into a seething mass of dust and flying ash. The island and the sea shuddered from the concussions.

171

Higgins boats were lowered from davits on the transports and Marines clambered into amtracs (amphibious tractors) quartered deep within the holding decks of the LST's. Amtracs would lead the landings in the first three waves. John Basilone climbed into Lt. Roy L. Johnson's amtrac. He and his men would land in the third wave. The steel bow door of the LST housing Basilone's amtrac swung down. The machine creaked down and slid into the waiting sea. LTV's, 75-mm amphibious tanks and Marines in Higgins boats rendezvoused with them. The first three waves circled in the prescribed pattern awaiting the signal to go in. They waited to go into the meat grinder.

Chuck Tatum, in the first wave, recalls from his *Red Blood Black Sand*:

> As my amtrac bobbed and pitched offshore, the view I had of Iwo was at water level. Its dark silhouette filled the horizon making it look ugly and forboding. On the left was Mount Suribachi, a volcanic pimple on the ocean's surface. It rose 534 feet out of the Pacific Ocean, a true volcano, it was dormant in 1945. But its volcanic slopes were encrusted with Japanese gun emplacements. The cinder cone bowels had been hollowed out to provide living quarters for the Japs who were charged with defending Iwo to the death.
>
> Also contained there were a command post, hospital and communications center. It was an independent fortress from the rest of the island….We were two miles offshore and I could see three rocket firing ships (LCT-R's) steaming parallel to the beach, which was erupting in smoke and flames as their rockets blasted off. Iwo's pre-assault bombardment was in full swing. Battleship and cruiser guns added to the raging firestorm onshore…I looked at my watch. We had been circling in an assembly pattern for 22 minutes and were still two hours away from hitting the beach.

At 8:05 a.m. Marine pilots came in to slam the island with napalm first, then rockets. They carefully lined up and came in low from the south at the beaches in an effort to ignite every inch. They came in again crisscrossing, strafing with their 50-caliber guns. The Marines were ecstatic at the sight of it. Navy guns opened up again at 8:25 a.m. to pulverize the beaches even again.

Navy vessels off shore extended back ten miles. At two miles a departure line (LD) was set parallel to the beach by two ships, one at each end. Along the line smaller vessels were in place as lane markers for the assault boats. The time had come.

At 8:30 a.m. the pennant dropped for an instant on the signal vessel at the LD. The first wave began their run-in with shells still screaming into the beaches from the battleships and cruisers behind them. Six amtrac waves, each with 1360 Marines, would land in five minutes with 250 to 500 yards between each wave. Sixty-eight amtracs in the first wave, one carrying Chuck Tatum's gun crew, crossed the LD. It would be five minutes to the beach. Basilone, in the third wave, thought of the youngsters going in just ahead of him. He sensed it would not be a cakewalk for them. He would be hitting the beach behind many very young Marines. In all probability they would become confused if pinned down at the beach. They would attempt to dig in and become trapped and exposed there as the volcanic ash filled the holes as fast as they dug them.

Landing zones were set as follows: from left to right the beach designations for the first waves were "Green," "Red 1," "Red 2," "Blue 1," "Blue 2," "Yellow 1," "Yellow 2." Later waves would land on the opposite side of the island. The 27th (Basilone) and 28th Regiments would land left at the "Red" beaches closest to Suribachi at their left (south) and the intense fire to emenate from it.

The first wave came on, churning through the surf. At 400 yards out the bombardment moved inland and the Corsair fighters swept in fast and low for their last run. At exactly 8:59 a.m. the first LVT-A's, amtrac gun vehicles, hit Red 1 beach to provide cover for the oncoming Marines. In just three minutes most of the first wave was in, from Red 1 to Yellow 2. Marines landing at Blue 2 faced the steepest of the terraces and became bogged down. LVT's had to grind away at the terraces while firing north in order to provide a pathway for the Marines. Then the second wave came in.

By 9:06 a.m. Basilone, in the 1st Battalion, Company C of the 27th, was in at Red 2, in the third wave. In front of him were the 27th's Companies B, E and F. They had come in at Red 1 in the first wave and were taking heavy fire from Suribachi.

As they had planned, the Japanese held their fire during those first few minutes allowing the first waves their landing. The Marines ran for the terraces sloshing through the volcanic ash as if it was soft mud. They couldn't believe the landings had been so easy. If they could gain the higher ground above the terraces they could gain some traction there. Still Kuribayashi's men held their fire. He would let them get to the flat ground before ambushing them. Let them gain the beach with men and equipment, then let go with mortar and artillery fire.

Chuck Tatum, in Company B, immediately forward of Basilone, couldn't believe it. There was no enemy fire. He and the men in his machine gun platoon rushed for the terraces:

> The muffled exhaust of the third assault wave Amtrak's reverberated in the strange silence prevailing over the island. The offshore bombardment had ceased and we weren't shooting at anyone. The quiet was eerie and ominous. When the third wave hit the beach it would be jammed against hundreds of Marines clinging to the terraces.

The 27th's goal was to take Chidori Airfield (Airfield #1) to the north. The 28th would swing forward and left, both to seal off the south and take on Suribachi. But, unknown at the time to Tatum, even with the careful choregraphy of the landings, 27th's Company B, Tatum's, landed to the left of Company

C. Company A was positioned incorrectly as a consequence to landing in the position assigned to Company B. Tatum tried to evaluate his situation:

> I focused my attention on the back of a Marine four feet away. He had "C-1-27" stenciled on his gear. All around us were C Company troops! Steve [Evanson] and I were in the wrong place, or was C Company in the wrong place? We had to find our own people and ammo carriers.

Then, a little after 10:00 a.m., it started—from every direction and concealment. Mortar fire and artillery literally rained in at the Marines on the beach. Kuribayashi's anti-aircraft gun barrels had been lowered to almost point-blank position. Virtually every foot of the beach was sighted and blasted. The 27th and Marines at Red 1 and 2 took savage fire as Suribachi guns poured a hail of fire down on them and those of the 28th that had landed on Green Beach.

The Marines of every regiment tried to move forward, but the terraces were in some places thirty feet high. Marines huddled behind them looking back toward the beach in terror as the horrendous fire rained in on their comrades pinned down there. They frantically dug into the ash only to have it pour back down with every stroke.

Basilone saw them there, so many of them, in huddled fear and confusion. He turned and looked to the sea. The next wave was coming on. By 9:14 a.m. the fourth wave, too, was in. It was becoming a slaughter.

Chuck Tatum crawled forward with his assistant machine gunner. He looked back again at the beach and the Marines in the third and fourth waves, pinned flat down by the firestorm "hugging the deck."

> Among all the prone figures I noticed a lone Marine walking back and forth on the shore, kicking asses, shouting cuss words and demanding, 'move out and get your butts off this beach!' He gave the Marine Corps hand signal for 'follow me.' A group of men responded. Fascinated I wondered why he wasn't digging in like the rest of us. As he advanced I recognized the solitary Marine as Gunny John Basilone!...The 1st Battalion, 27th Regiment's living legend and Marine Corps icon was heading toward Steve and Me. The forward surge of Basilone's group carried into our position. On my left I could see Colonel Louis C. Plain, the 27th Marines' Executive Officer. He and Basilone were the only two men standing up and giving orders.

Tatum, unbelieveably, gives us a great mental photo of John Basilone at that very instant—in detail.

Basilone was kicking asses and prodding prone Marines to get up an get going, saying, 'Move out, get going, get off this beach or they'll kill you all.'

Gunney Basilone had a habit of not buckling his helmet strap and, sure enough, he didn't have it buckled on Iwo Jima. In fact, he had it at the same jaunty angle, pushed to the back of his head. I could see the cold black curly hair. And his ears, I wouldn't say the Gunney had big ears, but they were the same size as Clark Gable's. I don't believe the Gunney even had his sidearm, just a couple of hand grenades hooked to his cartridge belt. He had a carbine in his left hand, he had already ditched his cumbersome gas mask. He wore a light field pack and appeared as calm, as if this invasion was no more than a training maneuver.

The Colonel and the Gunney got the invasion under way....It was more by example than anything else that inspired the Marines to start the attack instead of digging in on the beach. The beach was a death trap, and the Colonel and the Gunney knew it...I couldn't see the lieutenants from B Company or any other officers. Only Basilone and Plain defied the firestorm raging around us. Kicking asses they screamed, 'Move out! Move out! Get the fuck off the beach you dumb sons of bitches!'

Even an hour and a half later on Yellow Beach the 23rd Marines' regimental headquarters would radio back to the fleet: "Taking heavy casualties and can't move for the moment. Mortars killing us."

But now, as the young Marines scrambled to Basilone's order, John scanned the terrain looking for a big gun that was sited to his section of the beach. He found it. Spotting Tatum, Basilone ran to him, slammed his helmet and pointed to the concrete blockhouse threatening them.

Tatum continues:

It probably housed a 75mm or larger cannon whose field of fire was directed down the beach to our right. It was a big bastard with incredible killing power, stalling the advance by killing men in the 4th Division. It may have been firing 'tree bursts.'

Steve whipped the 30-caliber machine gun into place as Tatum slammed the tripod down into the sand and chambered the first round from the belt. Nothing. To his horror he realized that the protective towel hadn't kept the grit from fouling the breach. Basilone kneeled beside them fighting the instinct to grab the gun himself in order to clear the jam, but Tatum pulled a tooth brush from his pack and swiped the breach clear of grit.

He was relieved when he fired the first burst even though it bounced harmlessly off the reinforced concrete blockhouse. Basilone tapped his right shoulder signaling him to move right. Basilone, with his two Marines in trail then ran to a spot about thirty –five feet to the right. Tatum quickly set the gun up and fired at the blockhouse aperture causing the Japanese inside to close it as Tatum's 30-caliber rounds came pouring in. As Tatum kept on firing to keep the port closed, as Basilone knew he would, John came back with Corporal Ralph Belt's demolition assault team. He instantly sent a Marine demolition man carrying a satchel charge toward the blockhouse. The Marine ran just three feet to the side of Tatum's tracer stream toward the steel blockhouse doors and, just as he got to the blockhouse, Basilone slapped Tatum's back to signal a cease-fire. As the demolition man approached the blockhouse he tossed the C-2 charge, turned and ran before the satchel hit the ground at the base of the doors. Tatum:

> We instinctively ducked for cover before the explosion splintered the blockhouse, blowing chunks of lethal concrete laced with steel around the perimeter. Basilone signaled for me to "commence firing" again and directed the flamethrower operator, Corporal William Pegg, a Marine of imposing size to repeat the precarious path taken by the demo man along our line of streaking bullets.

Corporal Pegg with his 70-pound flamethrower reached the blockhouse as Basilone again signaled Tatum to cease firing. Bill Pegg rammed the nozzle into the hole blasted from the blockhouse and sent an inferno of flame roaring into the hole. Chuck Tatum, with pride and admiration recalled:

> Sergeant Basilone directed this operation 'by the book,' just like we practiced it at Pendleton and Camp Tarawa. As I lay prone, ready to fire again, 'Manila John' stood astride my back, startling me. Bending over he grabbed the machine gun bail in one hand and with a practiced motion unlocked the tripod releasing the machine gun. Screaming in my ear, 'Get the belt and follow me!'

It was as it always was with John Basilone. He was not there to fool around. He was there on a mission and it would get done well, as a Marine was supposed to do it—no guesswork and no hesitation. It was like his father Salvatore believed and practiced when tailoring a suit. "Just do it well, John, it is what people expect of you." It was perhaps a kind of Marine Corps craftsmanship. So simple yet not so easy.

Tatum hung on to the ammo belt and followed Basilone closely up the embankment at the side to the rear of the blown-out blockhouse. Burning Japanese soldiers poured out the rear entrance down below them struggling to put out the flames engulfing their bodies from the gasoline jell. Basilone cut loose with the machine gun firing from the hip using the Basilone Bail* attached to the front of the gun. In seconds it was over.

Tatum:

> Basilone's eyes had a fury I had never seen before. Rigid, hard clinched jaw, sweat glistening on his forehead he was not an executioner, but a soldier performing his duty. For me and others like Pfc. Alvin C Dunlap who saw Sergeant Basilone's leadership and courage during our assault, his example was overwhelming....Rifleman Private lawrence "Cookie Hound" Alvino and Pfc. Steve Evanson also slaughtered the Japs as they exited the blockhouse. I counted nine Japanese dead, not including those incinerated inside that none of us could see. Our group suffered no casualties. But Private Alvino was bleeding from three bullet wounds in his leg from an earlier injury. Adrenaline kept him going.

The combat situation at this very moment was, no doubt, a confusing one, so it is necessary to include Corporal Ralph Belt's memory of the blockhouse destruction also. Although Belt's account is, in actuality, interwoven into Tatum's, it is necessary to include Belt's memory of the incident, although there is much missing from his account.

> Basilone and I were both in the 27th Regiment—he was with C Company, I was with B Company. We landed at Red Beach 2. Right after we landed, my squad ran into a Jap block-house firing canister shells at the 26th Marines, and doing a lot of damage, too. There was a Marine standing on top of this pill-box shouting for flamethrowers and demolition men. I was a demolition man, and my buddy right alongside, Pfc. Willim N Pegg, was a flame-thrower man.
> Before I had time to prepare demolition, Pegg moved to one side of the pill-box and knocked it out. He got a Silver Star. The Marine standing on top of the pill-box—shouting instructions, yelling for a machine gun, shaking his K-Bar knife at the Japs trying to get out—was Manila John."
> "He would turn his back on the Japs to yell at us—turn around toward them again—wave his knife and laugh right in their faces. I think Manila John was a great Marine. I am very proud to have served with him in the Marines and on Iwo Jima.

After giving the machine gun back to Tatum, Basilone signaled the men to

---

* See end of book.

follow him.

They headed north for the perimeter of the Motoyama Airfield #1. It was his assigned task and nothing would divert him from it. With succeeding waves landing behind them Basilone and his men were far ahead. They passed from a plateau near the runways to a dump area where smashed Zeros and Betty bombers had been bulldozed into piles, then climbed up to higher ground to the runways. Tatum looked at his watch—10:33. They had been in combat for an hour and a half. Almost immediately they came under heavy fire from Mt. Suribachi. Then mortar fire rained in from the north end of the runway. Jumping into a bomb crater Tatum knew they were now zeroed in.

Basilone, knowing it was the wrong place at the wrong time, bounded ahead pulling his men with him. He had cleared a main defensive Japanese position opening a path for advancing Marines. It would prove to be a major break-through in the earlier stages of the Iwo Jima campaign. At this critical time and position, Basilone alone was in command. Tatum:

> We had two Marines with Browning Automatic Rifles (BARS) with almost full magazines, and a group of riflemen. We had no officers. No one was in command except Basilone, and he was gone for reinforcements.
> It appeared to me we were the spearhead for the entire battal-ion...We hadn't spoken 20 words since hitting Iwo. During Basilone's charge from the beach, we were on 'automatic pilot' reacting the way we had been trained, running low to the ground. There was no time to talk and nothing to talk about.

Basilone, looking for more men to reinforce his forward position with Tatum, now spotted two or more tanks heading for a wooded area just beyond the beach. One of the tanks hit a mine and was on fire. One of the tankers was able to push the turret hatch open and as he was pulling himself free was shot by a Japanese sniper perched in a tree. Responding in kind Basilone shot the sniper down from the tree. Turning to the lead tank he motioned for them to follow as he lead them out of the mine field to the safety of the woods.

But Basilone and his men had been moving fast and they were now into the US Navy target area. Tatum recalled that "Corporal Ralph Belt, a veteran of other Pacific campaigns," yelled, "we're taking TOT ('time over target'—US Navy) hits!"

While Tatum and his fellow Marines were dug in, Basilone quickly found a group of Marines and was now leading them toward the airfield. Tatum looked back and could see them. His heart leaped knowing that reinforcements were on the way.

They were seventy-five yards from Tatum's position when the Japanese rounds hit the center of Basilone's group. Tatum heard them rain in. More than one explosion ripped the men apart:

Goddamn Sonovabitch! It was awful! It looked like Sergeant Basilone was down. Nobody was moving. The bombardment was creeping toward us and I ducked for cover. I felt the Japs were really trying to get all of us. The way I figured it we were a large group of Marines in the middle of their important airstrip with a perfect field of fire down the runway. We were an intolerable threat and they were trying to take us out.

CHAPTER 32

Tatum prayed that Basilone was still alive. But the terrible answer came that afternoon. How could it be? He shockingly questioned, "America's hero, dead. My own hero, killed? How could that be?" Yet it was. On only that first day of battle Gunnery Sergeant John Basilone, hero of Guadalcanal was gone. That sweet smiling, handsome curly-headed kid from Raritan, New Jersey, had died in combat at twenty-nine years of age.

John did not die instantly, but lay conscious for some time torn terribly at the chest and stomach. Corporal Ralph Belt* was with him for a short time:

> After we'd cut across the airfield, turned and began the advance toward the north end of the island, Pegg and I ran across a kid from our company by the name of Sorenson with a very bad shoulder wound. A few feet away, a corpsman was working on another wounded Marine. It was Manila John. "He'd been hit bad…As bad off as he was, he spoke to us and he wore that grand smile of his. I have thought about that many, many times since. He died soon afterward.

According to Chuck Tatum, Lieutenant John T. Casey, C Company's commanding officer, who led the company during the landing, was probably the last to talk with John before he died. He was advancing toward Motoyama Airfield behind Basilone and saw him there mortally wounded. Casey stayed with John for about twenty minutes before he finally succumbed to his wounds. Many years after the war, during an interview by Tatum Casey had this to say:

> He was still alive when I spoke to him and he knew he was a goner. I couldn't stay with him as the assault was proceeding and I had to lead my company. Several of my men had been killed by the same shell that got Basilone. [He paused before continuing] 'I will never reveal what Basilone said to me as he lay dying.'

For his PBS Documentary "Red Blood, Black Sand," Chuck Tatum interviewed Chief Warrant Officer John A. Daniels, not knowing at the time that Daniels was the 5th Division's burial officer and a close friend of Basilone. Quoting Daniels:

---

* Corporal Belt has since passed.

181

At about 1200 hours, Major Amadeo Rea, the Executive
Officer of the 2nd Battalion, 26th Marines reported to the battalion command post (on the front lines) and said to me,
'Gunnery Sergeant Basilone is laying [sic] dead on then end
of the forst airstrip.

Daniels found John late on D-Day afternoon where he fell at the south end
of Motoyama 1 runway. John had fallen with a number of other Marines during
the same explosion. The names of those Marines are unknown, but Tatum
believes that they most likely were two sergeants and a few other men from
Casey's C Company, lst Bn 27th. Daniels confirmed to Tatum: "John Basilone
suffered fatal injuries from mortar explosion or large shell fire." He had faithfully lived out those tattooed words now plainly visible on his out-stretched left
arm, "Death before Dishonor." Even with mortar fire coming in Daniels
removed John's body from the field along with others of C Company who fell
with him. Ninety Marines were removed from the area.

Three days after his death John was buried on Iwo Jima. The 5th Marine
Division Cemetery on Iwo Jima was formally dedicated on March 21, 1945.
Following opening prayers lead by the chaplains, Major General Keller E.
Rockey spoke along with the 5th Division Chapain, Lieutenant Roland B.
Gittelsohn. Gittelsohn talked of the extreme sacrifices made at Iwo Jima as the
"ghastly price of freedom." The flag was raised, then lowered as the somber
notes of taps played out over the ashen blood-soaked island.

For his combat action on Iwo Jima Basilone would receive the Navy Cross
and Purple Heart. Colonel Justin Gates Duryea, multi-decorated himself and
wounded at Iwo Jima, recommended that John receive a second Medal of Honor
for his heroism at Iwo Jima.

On March 7, 1945 Lena was notified of John's death. She was 32 years old
on that very day. On March 8th, Mayor James J. Del Monte, Rev. Amedeo Russo
and Dr. D. T. Russo arrived at the Basilone family home at 113 First Avenue,
where they told Dora of her son's death. Unfortunately reporters had inadver-
tently brought the news to her just before their arrival. With the confirmation by
Mayor Del Monte, Dora fainted.

The town of Raritan now went into mourning as the news spread quickly
through the small town. Flags were hung at half-mast at the schools and throughout the area. Judge George W. Allgair remembered that General Vandegrift had
promised Basilone that he would be among the Marines finally landing in Tokyo:

It has come as a complete shock. The boys in Raritan all idol-
ized John Basilone and his death seems unreal. The death of
any boy is a loss to his family and his community, but the high
honor which had come to him had set him apart and we have a
very deep sense of loss. It was not in John Basilone to remain

inactive in this country. After he had come home on furlough, he had to go back and see action.

Undersheriff Joseph Navatto, former mayor, who knew John well, said: The death of Johnny Basilone was a great shock to all his friends. He brought honor to his family, Raritan and to the Marines. On his last visit here he said he couldn't take it easy while his friends fought on—he had to get back in the fight. If his number came up—that was part of the game, and he wanted to be there with his friends when it happened. He hoped he could stay in the fight to the end. He was a tribute to this great country of ours, an American, a Marine, a hero who gave his life for his country. All of us grieve with Mr. and Mrs. Basilone and all his kinfolk. We share their suffering now as we shared their joy a short time ago. All of their friends in Raritan join me in offering our deepest sympathy; we know his sacrifice has not been in vain, and he will live forever in our hearts.

A Memorial Mass was said at St Ann's Church on March 10th. A letter had come from Dr. John F. Fox, John's school principal friend, now principal of a school in Honolulu. Dr. Fox related that John and his brother George had indeed visited him the night before they shipped out for what they termed the "big push." Dr. Fox related that they shook hands and George left first, with John saying to his brother, "So long, see you on the beach." Later, as John was leaving to catch his bus back to the dock, he said, "That is the last time I will see my kid brother until I meet him on the beach." The family knew, from Dr. Fox's letter, that George, too, was now on Iwo Jima.

As we have seen from the earlier Basilone monologue, which, again, was developed from his letters to Phyllis, the two brothers did meet again at the dock where they discussed the impending battle. The real sequence of events regarding John's meeting with Dr. Fox and his brother George may never be known, but the bottom line is that John did have an opportunity to say his last goodbyes to George

John's brother George, following service in the Marine Corps and after living in Raritan for the rest of his life, died on October 29, 1990. Alphonse, who served in the Army in Iceland with General Patton in Europe, is deceased also. Donald, a Marine veteran of Korea, survives. The rest of the Basilone immediate family has passed.

A letter was sent to the Basilone family on March 22, 1945 from Bill Taylor, announcer on the Sunrise Serenade Program, WOR Radio, 1440 Broadway, New York City.

Dear Mr. and Mrs. Basilone,
I know there is nothing I can add to the messages of sympathy you have received since the loss of your son John.

I have a program on Sunday mornings from 5:45 to 8:00 AM over WOR. On the program of March the 11th I paid a tribute to your son, Sgt. John Basilone and the Marine Corps. I had that portion of the program recorded, a copy of which accompanies this letter. I would like you to have it with WOR's and my compliments.

The first part of the tribute consists of excerpts from a broadcast made over the entire Mutual Network by Paul Schubert, an autographed copy of the broadcast, in its entirety, is also enclosed. Mr. Schubert's broad-cast took place the night of the announcement of the landing of the Marines on Iwo Jima.

The portion starting with the words 'At this time I would like to pay tribute to one Marine who will never again march to the Marine's Hymn' was a personal tribute, of my own, to your son John. If, when you receive this record, it is cracked or broken let me know by return mail and I will have another copy made for you. If, at any time, in the future, you want another copy of the record do not hesitate to write for one, as I have the original on file.

Following burial on the island, John's body was removed to Arlington Cemetery. There, on April 20, 1948, John Basilone was peacefully laid to rest.* Eighteen other servicemen were buried with John that day, two being Marines. One of those Marines was Sgt. William Gary Walsh who was awarded the Congressional Medal of Honor postumously for heroism on Iwo Jima. He was a member of John's regiment.

Ceremonies started at 2:00 p.m., after a lengthy procession from the cemetery office. Escorting the Basilone family to the gravesite was Sergeant G. B. King from Detroit. A platoon of Marines in full-dress blue participated in the ceremonies along with the Marine Band that played "Nearer My God to Thee" and "Onward Christian Soldiers."

Conducting the Catholic religious service was Lieutenant-Commander J. J. Twiss from the Anacosta Naval Receiving Station. From St. Ann's Church in Raritan, John's dear friend, Rev. Amadeo Russo participated also.

---

* Section 12, Grave 384

EPILOGUE

Mild he lays his glory by
Born that man no more may die

Robert Leckie, *Helmet for My Pillow*

Lieutenant John T. Casey has since passed. As explained above, Chuck Tatum believes he was among the last to speak with John before his death and did not tell of John's last words. Knowing a bit about John Basilone this author will take some liberty, deservedly or not, and venture a guess about John's last words. So indulgence from the reader is begged. Surely, if Casey advises that he would not have revealed John's last words it is doubtful that John spoke only of the battle on Iwo Jima. John, who so loved his new wife and family, would have wanted them to know that. They were the most important people to him and he knew he was leaving them.

John was as courageous in death as he was in life. I believe he would have said, "Tell Lena I love her and I'm sorry I couldn't keep my word and come back to her. Tell her, 'Blood and Sand.' Tell my family to pray for me and that I love them, too. Take care of my boys."

And Lena would remember the letter.

> *"I miss you more than anything in the world darling. You know I have a new song now ('Some day I'll meet you again'). I look at your picture and sing, and it always seems like you are real in the picture and you are answering me."*

General Kuribayashi, after issuing an order to fight to the last man, left his blockhouse at the Gorge along with his staff and a few hundred men, retreating through tunnels to a place unknown. On March 21st he sent a final message to the last hold-out base at Chichi Jima advising that the enemy was approaching his position but his men would fight to the death. Although his fate is unknown, it is assumed that he committed hara-kiri shortly thereafter.

Many would fall with John Basilone that day on Iwo Jima and in the days to come as they fought to take that God-forsaken ash-soaked island of death. Tough combat continued into March, especially at Cushman's Pocket, the Gorge and the Meat Grinder. Admiral Chester Nimitz announced on the 17th that the island was "officially secured" at 6:00 P.M. on that date. But the fighting and dying continued with most Marines standing in astonishment at Nimitz's proclamation.

It would not be until the 27th that the battle of Iwo Jima was truly ended. During those final ten days 1,724 more Marines died or were wounded.

The fighting continued far after Joe Rosenthal took the immortal photograph that would bring to America a lasting poignant reminder of the sacrifices there. Total casualties to all services would be 28,686. The Marine Corps total casualties would be 25,851 including 5,931 dead and 17,272 wounded. With the inclusion of Navy dead, the total would be closer to 6800. Japanese total killed numbered approximately 20,000.

More Medals of Honor would be awarded following the fighting. Twenty-two of eighty Medals of Honor awarded to Marines in World War II went to Marines at Iwo Jima. No other Marine Corps combat action would yield more. Additionally, five more went to US Navy men. In all of military history there never had been before, nor has there been since, such a consecutive string of Marine Corps combat victories as those achieved in the Pacific campaign. From their landing on Guadalcanal to the bitter struggle at Okinawa, the Marines fought to a distance of more than 10,000 miles.

Of Guadalacanal President Franklin Roosevelt would say, "The successful defense of Henderson Field and Guadalcanal was the turning point in the Pacific War." From Japanese Admiral Tanaka, "There was no question that the U. S. defense of Guadalcanal was the doom of the Japanese war effort in the Pacific."

John Basilone's Marine Corps idol, Sergeant Major Dan Daly, would certainly have been proud. John read all that he could find about Daly. There are some startling similarities between the two Marines. First, both were unquestionably brave and both were undyingly dedicated to the Marine Corps. Secondly, both are remembered for rallying their men on when they were terrified and pinned down. Basilone screamed out the order for his men to get off the beach at Iwo Jima, and at Guadalcanal he lead the defensive center of battle with courage and inspiration. For Daly it was at Lucy le Bocage just within the Belleau Wood in France during WW I. He ordered his tired, outgunned and outnumbered men on with the cry "Come on, you sons of bitches, do you want to live forever?" Like Basilone, Daly was ever conscious of the needs of his men, and both trained their men rigorously. Each disdained the limelight that follows heroic action. Basilone surely followed Daly's role modeling as he went from one machine gun emplacement to another during that epic night on Guadalcanal before the battle began in order to gauge the preparedness of his men. Daly did the same at Belleau Wood.

The crosses at Arlington stand forever silently, as if sentinels, lasting guardians to those who fell at Iwo and at other battlefields where the gallant and courageous gave of themselves so selflessly. Marine veteran Major Shelton Scales reminds us that all of life's gifts were taken from them. "And you don't give your life for your country. You don't give it. It's taken from you, in many cases brutally."

The epitaph on the grave of Marine Pfc. Cameron on Guadalcanal read:

And when he goes to heaven
To St. Peter he will tell:
Another Marine reporting sir;
I've served my time in hell.

★   ★   ★

ABOUT JOHN BASILONE

Perhaps the best praise comes from one's peers rather than from one's superiors. A master sergeant who had served with John said the following:

> He was a neat military man, always made a favorable impression on both officers and enlisted men. He was able to solve any military problem which might confront him and he demonstrated leadership ability to a marked degree. He was a natural at inspiring the men of his section to greater effort.

Another NCO said:

> He was a rugged, aggressive, type of Marine. I suppose there are some who'd call him an uninhibited extrovert—a remark inspired by jealousy. Well, he certainly wasn't obnoxious about it in my book. Sure, he took great pride in accomplishment—but not for himself alone. His machine gun section got in on the act through John's remarks, and he didn't hesitate to tell the world about it! He maintained high morale—a resourceful, competent, and energetic leader who looked out for the men serving under him first, last, and all the time. And it paid off! Look at Lunga Ridge—at Iwo Jima.

Basilone called the men he fought with on Guadalcanal "the best damn company in the world. The record bears him out. In addition to his Medal of Honor, the men of his company hold three Navy Crosses, four Silver Stars and eleven Letters of Commendation from Admiral William "Bull" Halsey. The Honor Roll is as follows:

Medal of Honor: GySgt. John Basilone

Navy Cross: PFC's. Jack Sugarman
         Edmond J. Dorsogna
         Billie Joe Crumpton

Silver Star: Capt. Robert J. Rodgers
        1st Lt. Leonard R. Heller

PFC. Cecil H. Evans
Pvt. Sam Hirsch

Letters of Commendation: Capt. Douglas M. Smith
1st Sgt. Claud E. Cooper
GySgt. Rufus A. Stowers
Sgts. Gerard J. Golden
James P. Morgan
PFCs Ira L.Sherman
Roy M. Fowel
Pvts. Harold G. Burke
W. L. Bradshaw

Corpsmen: Alonzo F. Sink
Earl Marshall

Richard Greer and Phil Hernandez were two of John's closest friends on Guadalcanal. Both respected and admired Basilone and both fought with him during the major battle. Greer said that John was a fun-loving guy who did love his wine, women and song, but he stressed that John "was deadly serious when he came into the Marine Corps. It was when he was on liberty when he had a lot of fun. He was deadly serious, as serious a Marine as you ever saw, when he was on duty. John would borrow money, but would always pay it back." Greer allowed this writer to have a copy of a letter he sent to John on November 27, 1943. Basilone was involved in the bond tour at the time. It reads as follows:

Dear John,
Company News: Jake is acting First Sgt., Cooper has the Second Platoon, Bunky the First Platoon, and Morgan and Dawkins are assistant these days. John Anel is shipping over today, guess he's in for the count.
Smiley was busted to Chief Cook, Rocco is Staff Sgt., Dietz got a bust.
Dillard broke his hand on somebody's jaw but a few weeks before took the count from Demarah. The Mortars are still leading the Company Ball League. Packard's dog "Jockstrap" is still around. Dunc Campbell stole one of Mom's dogs and he's around too. I believe it was spare parts he took. Daugherty has a big idea how to make a million after the war, he claims $30,000 is all he needs. Some kind of service man's club or some damn thing.
John we are near the ocean and get down once in a while. As usual we wash clothes, bathe, and swim in the nearby river. There is plenty green thick growth around with the usual sprinkling of palm and hard-wood trees. A few fuzzy wuzzies pass

every day and I saw some of their women the other day. The young are black, bush headed with those pointed breast [s] and the old gals are baggy and their breasts hang down to their waist. We saw in the newspaper that you are engaged to Helen Helstowsky * and would be married soon. What's the dope on that? We thought you had a wife and kids in Manila to take care of let alone one in the States.

Ever hear from Nora? Or the gal you ran up a coconut tree about eighteen months ago? I believe Morgan dragged you out of the church in Georgia one time, boy you've had some close calls, but this time it's news and you're_____. [left blank by Greer]

How's liberty in the States, probably plenty of gals but how's about the liquor? Angel just dropped in and told me to ask you if you're still borrowing money on payday to pay up the past two weeks debts?

That's all for now and let us hear from you sometime because you know You can't believe the newpapers.

P.S. Just because Morgan and I used to do part of your letter writing don't stop writing get somebody to do it if you won't. Morgan is O.K. and said hello.

Iwo Jima veteran Marine Roy Homerding from Grand Lake, Colorado, wrote of his time of combat there in an article entitled, *Japanese Combat Flares*. John had already been killed:

By the first night on February 19, 1945, the 81mm Mortar Platoon had made it over Motoyama airstrip No. 1 and dug in on the southwest side of the strip. Heavy action , both ground and air, was in clear view of Mt. Surabachi. I saw a plane dive with napalm—he never pulled out. He hit the west side of Surabachi. I thought briefly to myself how sudden and quick death came for him as I observed it. My foxhole was shallow, and as darkness came, the contining roar of gun fire now included the screaming of bonzai charges—adrenalin was high and sleep was impossible, Japanese flares were in the air to illuminate our position and movements....As the sounds of war raged on, I thought of men I knew who were hurt or killed like John Basilone (Medal of Honor winner from Guadalcanal), whom I had become so well acquainted with in Camp Tarawa. As a Gunnery Sgt., he would get my ear to tell me how many eggs, sausages, pancakes, bacon and cof-

---

* See Chapter 26

fee I should keep coming to him in the NCO mess hall when he saw I had the duty there as a PFC. He was a great guy and I liked him a lot.

*   *   *

JOHN BASILONE THE SERGEANT.

Gunnery Sergeant is the seventh enlisted rank in the United States Marine Corp, just above Staff Sergeant and below Master Sergeant and First Sergeant. The Gunnery Sergeant is a staff Non-Commissioned Officer. Today's pay grade is E-7. The abbreviation "Gunny" is the common reference in the Corps, but use by lower ranking personnel is at the gunnery sergeant's discretion. The Marine Corps sergeant, however, is not to be addressed as "Sarge" as commonly heard in the U.S. Army.

The sergeant in all services is expected to have greater experience, leadership skills and responsibility as compared to his lower ranking personnel and he is expected to exercise that responsibility most intimately when it comes to their protection and welfare.

The sergeant is to be there on the battlefield at the gut level defining that leadership through his direction and action in combat. He is to be an example to the lower ranks most consistently and personally. In so doing he builds trust and transmits to those lower ranks the values, traditions and the very culture of the Corps.

To his superiors he thereby defines the character and level of self-confidence and competence of his men. Through his example he infuses professionalism, dedication to the cause, moral character and esprit de corps.

Gunnery Sergeant John Basilone was, and is, the epitome of all upon whom the title has been bestowed.

*   *   *

JOHN BASILONE WRITES

An article written by John Basilone follows, again the publication is unknown, but the time of writing is definitely just after his arrival at Pendleton following the bond tour, and just prior to his meeting Lena Riggi.

I'm glad to get Overseas Duty
by GySgt. John Basilone

To start with, don't get the idea that I've enjoyed any part of this war. I don't like to slog around in the South Pacific and let little monkey-faced characters shoot at me any more than the next Marine. I've got a girl back East and, thanks to the people of my home town, Raritan, N. J., I have enough money invested in war bonds to get a start in civilian life as soon as the shooting is over. It'll either be a restaurant or a farm, I haven't decided which.

But, if it's all the same to everybody. I'd much rather spend the rest of the war oveseas. I think all real Marines, who are not physically disqualified, feel about the same way.

I'd been down in the islands for a year and a half when I came home, and I was happy and excited, at first. It was good to see my parents and my nine brothers and sisters and my girl. But after that first homecoming, I ran into a lot of hippodrome. I was sent with some movie people on a bond-selling tour. Then I made the rounds of the war plants with some other decorated servicemen, and we were supposed to give those people in the plants "The Word" on how badly the equipment they were producing was needed in the combat zones.

Now, I'm not a good speech-maker, though they say I'm a fair instructor. But instructing a bunch of kids on machine guns and sounding off to a bunch of civilians in a war plant are two different things. I felt pretty embarrassed every time I spoke. There were two wounded sailors with me on this tour who were pretty good speakers, though. These two swabbies could really tell the sea stories. And, sometimes, they told those civilians such gruesome yarns that they even had me buying bonds.

There was one type of guy who annoyed me on these tours. He's the sort who button-holes you in a slop chute and asks, "What's the blue ribbon and the white stars you're wearing soldier?" (They ususally call you soldier and not Marine, especially in the Middle West.). I answered, "Why that's for good conduct." Then this guy, if he's middle-aged, always starts blowing smoke up your trousers about the first World War. If he's fairly young he starts crying on your shoulder about how he has tried and tried to get in the armed forces but he always gets turned down because of housemaid's knee or adenoids, or something.

After about six months tours and speeches, I found myself doing guard duty at Washington D.C. Navy Yard. I felt like a museum piece. It seemed ages ago since I'd left the South Pacific the previous summer. Washington was a pleasant place, but I wasn't very happy. I wanted to get back to the machine guns. I felt out of things. I've done three years duty in the Philippines and it has been my ambition ever since Pearl Harbor to be with the outfit that recaptured Manila. I kept thinking about how awful it would be if some Marines made a landing on Dewey Boulevard on the Manila warerfront and Manila John Basilone wasn't among them.

I went to see "The Man" at the Navy Yard. I said, "Sir, I want The Fleet." The man must have known what I'd been thinking , for he rushed the cadence on my transfer. Within ten days I was joining with a regiment in training at Camp Pendleton.

You don't know what a thrill it was to me to walk into one of those battleship gray barracks at Pendleton and see a long line of machine guns parked in the aisle between the bunks. I felt like kissing the heavies on their water jackets.

This regiment to which I've been assigned is mostly a veteran outfit with some of the Marines going on their third little trip to the Pacific. It's good to be with this bunch.

This writer found the below prayer among documents probably supplied by Chuck Tatum. The time of the writing is unknown. Most likely Basilone was inspired to write it shortly after the hectic time of the bond tour. His footnote: "volume" is unknown also.

★　　★　　★

PRAYER BY A
MARINE CORPS SERGEANT *

O GOD, I confess that I did not really appreciate the value of religious freedom until I was wholly certain of the righteousness of our course. Born of humble parentage I was not endowed with a spiritual expressiveness. Since my exploits I was uplifted by the power of Christ. It was He who watched over me with an unmistakable sign of divine guidance. How I ever was spared from the Great Beyond only the Lord knows. I pray each night for my comrades who paid the Supreme Sacrifice and I know that they are triumphant inhabitants of heaven—white flowers of blameless life. I now carry the riches of God in my heart—something that I shall forever be thankful for. Almighty God, I ask for your continued guidance. Please redeem and purify humanity, For thine is the power forever and ever. *Amen.*

Sergeant John Basilone
United States Marine Corps

* Written especially for this volume

★　　★　　★

LENA BASILONE

In 1948 Lena Basilone and a friend traveled to Arlington, Virginia to see John's grave. After having dinner Lena and her friend stepped out to the street to get a cab. They saw a few lined up at the curb and called out to one. They happened to choose the right cab. While riding she mentioned to the cab driver that she had been looking for the John Basilone Amerian Legion Post, but was unable to find it in the phone book. The driver, Vance Lennon, laughed and said, "That's easy, I'm a member of it." Lennon called William Waters, the Post Commander, who put wheels into motion.

Lena was made the guest of honor at the Post in Arlington. Men who had fought with John were there and his picture was prominently displayed on the wall. Stories and memories were shared with Mrs. Basilone and dinner was arranged at the Naval Gun Factory. She just happened to pick the right cab.

After the war Lena purchased a home in Lakewood, California, and remained there for fifty years until her death. She died on June 11, 1999, never having remarried. She said to this writer, "After meeting John, there was no one else for me." Her friend Barbara Garner quoted her, "Once you have the best, you can't settle for less." Lena did say, however, that it was "rough being alone all these years," and now her legs were "deteriorating." She maintained a large group of friends, was active in her church, was a volunteer at the Long Beach Veterans Hospital, was a member of the American Veterans Auxiliary and the Women's Marine Association. Said Barbara Garner further, "She was a very determined lady, loved by many...when she saw a need, she would go about fulfilling it."

Offered burial at Arlington, Lena declined saying, "I don't want to cause trouble for everyone." She was buried at the Veteran's Administration National Cemetery in Riverside, California. In November 1999, Barbara Garner sent me a letter saying, ..."Just yesterday November 11th [1999], Veteran's Day, I went to the cemetery in Riverside to honor Lena. I had not seen the marker because it wasn't completed and set until October sometime. What an honorable lady she was, it gives me peace to know she is at home with the Lord enjoying all He has promised those who believe."

Barbara Garner supplied this writer with a typed letter from Thomas Lyons, one of John's buddies. It seems to finally clear up the question of which wave John was in when he landed on Iwo Jima. Undated, but from about 1992 it is presented here, un-paragraphed, as written:

Dear Lena,
You may not remember me, But I remember you because I was with John when you met him. We were roomates at Camp Pendleton at the time, I don't remember your girl friends name. I never saw her again. You worked in twenty-four area. We were asssigned to the Twenty-Seventh Marines, after that we were so busy training for Iwo Jima we didn't get any liberty together, and I had to leave my car at home. Your name came up at a reception I attended held in the Commanding General's Quarters at MCRD in honor of Dr. Felix De Weldon who designed the Iwo Jima Memorial, he offered his services for one at Pendleton on Basilone Road. I often wonder if you keep in touch with John's family. He came from a large family, and they are all getting elderly now, George passed on about two years ago, Al last year, Mary is ill now, but they honor John every year, with a parade. They have a small museum for him in his hometown. Carlo is OK his phone mumber is 908-725-

3603 if you need it. He would be glad to hear from you. John was the best example of the Marine's Marine that I ever met, he had all the right stuff, he was quiet, shy, and yet very impressive, and very religious, handsome enough to be a movie star and we called him a Hollywood Marine in jest. He just looked like a real Marine should look. He was well liked by us all. He wanted to go where he was needed most, but he was so embarrassed by all the attention he got after getting his Congressional Medal of Honor. At the time he joined the Marine Corps it was smaller than the New York City Police Dept., and John Basilone was a standout. They called him Manila John because of his Army service and he didn't like that. After Sea School I was assigned to USS Philadelphia at Mare Island, CA. Went to machine gun school at Clamente Island, then went up to Alaska, down to South Pacific over to Cuba, then up to the north Atlantic on convoy and escort duty when the Bismark was sunk. I left the Philly at the Brooklyn Navy Yard to help form the First Marine Paratroop Bn at Lakehurst, NJ near John's home. There I met First Lt. Krulak (The Brute) who later became a General, and later his son Charles made Commandant, and Lt. Justin Duryea, later John's Commander, who lost a limb on Iwo Jima, and got a Bronze Star. After Paratroop training we went to North Carolina to form the First Marine Division. There I met Lou Diamond, and John Basilone in the machine gun and mortar school on old World War I weapons. We went to the Solomon Islands armed by the lowest bidder. Our best weapons went to Europe, our best people went to the South Pacific Islands by way of New Zealand on a Swedish troopship named John Erickson. We split up there to go the rest of the way on smaller Navy combat ships, we jumped out of Higgins Boats not planes and landed on Gavutu on August 7th then Tanambogo, Tulagi, and Florida Island, then we joined John on Guadalcanal in September. We were shelled every night by Japanese Battleships, and Cruisers as they landed reinforcememts. They killed a lot of palm trees, but when they fell they brought us fresh coconuts, and more protection because we were being bombed every day. We raided the Japanese base at Tasamboko Mission about eight miles up the coast from Henderson Field, burned their camp, blew up their ammo dump and artillery. We stole all their food and new blankets we could carry beause we didn't have any, then destroyed the rest and got out fast. We knew they had to attack us or soon starve, and about 5000 did, but they split up half attacked us on Lunga Ridge, the rest attacked across the river, and had John to contend with. I was put out of action before dawn, but all the Nips were dead, wounded or gone by then. I went to a hospital in New Zealand. Our field hospital was bombed out, John stayed on for about a month fighting off new landings of Japan's best troops. His weapons unit dug in at the mouth of the Tenaru River. In desparation the General said, "Meetum on the beach an giveum Hell."

John did, and the rest is history. When they formed the Fifth Marine Divison I was asigned to the Twenty-Seventh Marines. My roomate at Camp Joseph H. Pendleton was John. He had volunteered but was exempt from combat. We had lots of good liberty together. YOU would not even kiss him good night, but he thought you were great. We were due to ship out to Hawaii to train on the volcanic terrain like Iwo Jima, but John wanted to marry you anyway. He said you were worth it, and it may be his last chance. He knew what we were getting into, did not have to go you know. He had to volunteer. We landed on Iwo Jima at dawn February nineteenth in the third wave. John had machine guns and mortars, I had thirty-seven millimeter anti-tank guns towed by small tracked vehicles called weasels. One didn't come up on line so I went back to look for it. The driver Tom Kelly was wounded so I had to drive it, a few hundred yards it got stuck. I found the axle of the gun hung up on the horn of a kettle mine the kind usually found at sea. With some help we were able to get the gun free without blowing it up The mine field was quite extensive with more of the same, but we were lucky and dug in between them to fire on the pill boxes (our day one objective). John was leading a charge to my right. The enemy fire was withering. Artillery from Mt. Surabachi, sniper fire from wrecked planes on Motoyama #1. John's return fire took care of that, but then mortar fire began to rain down on us from the caves. I was hit in the right shoulder, not fatal just another gold star in my Purple Heart. A corpsman told me that John got a direct hit and died of a thousand cuts from shrapnel. He was still conscious and the Chaplain was with him to the end. The medical corpsman tried to bandage all his wounds, there were so many. They carried him back to the beach, gave him a shot to ease the pain, but they were unable to save him. John went into shock and passed peacefully away, but he was not forgotten. His commander wanted to recommend him for another Congressional Medal of Honor, but he already had that so he was recommended for the Navy Cross. I am glad I did not see him. That way I can remember him from better days. The longest road on Camp Pendleton from the entrance all across the base bears his name. It ends at Twenty-Four area. It is not just a street, it's a legend. A picture of John there inspires recruits who would like to quit, but are reminded that John never did. It was an honor to serve with him, one I shall never forget, I am so sorry it had to end. You did not even invite me to your wedding and I started it all. If it was not for me you might not have met him. I got to see the flag raised on Mt. Surabachi, I was evacuated to Guam after only eight days. I don't think I ever did anything above and beyond the call of duty. I just did my best, and survived, and went on to Japan, China and Korea. I tried to look you up, but you were not in the book. The WMR Association gave me your address. I would like to hear from you, if you find time. I got married too and raised four kids. Of course my son is named John too. The General said "Uncommon Valor was a common virtue on Iwo Jima."* I think he was right."

Thomas Lyons
850 State Street #320
San Diego, CA 92101

---

* Actually said by Fleet Admiral Chester Nimiz on March 17, 1945

POSTSCRIPT

I had some doubts about doing this work on John's life. So many years had gone by since the war and many of John's friends and wartime buddies had passed on. But his statue standing there in the loneliness of history nagged at me and drew me in. It was a reminder of his courage every time I passed by it. He was our hero, a Raritan Boy, like me. I saw him there and thought, someone has to tell John's story, and others have to remember him, too, and know of his sacrifice.

Although still unsure, I asked John Pacifico, the John Basilone Parade Coordinator how to get in touch with John's wife Lena. He provided the introduction over the phone and I will always remember her response after asking if she would consent to a visit from me. She said, "But it's been so long, I really don't know." I pressed, sensing that she was truly reluctant to bring those memories back, painful memories of losing him. I told her that it was a very personal thing for me as John returned to Raritan after the bond tour the week I was born. She finally agreed; we met and became great friends. I knew after that phone call, I would have to write the book. I only wish that this writing had been completed before her death. But she is finally with him.

It has been said that the strain of war turns the strong soldier into the tough battle-hardened fighter—sick with it all, fighting only to bring it all to an end—clear "the Canal," be done with it and go home. With Basilone I believe there is more to consider.

I would like to draw the reader back, back to that day in 1940, when John realized that he could not drive the laundry truck for Gaburo any longer. Something intensely transforming happened to him that day—he felt it. It comes when we know deep in our hearts that something, some event; something trapped in time is waiting for us. I believe that on that day John Basilone, even through his restlessness, knew that destiny was waiting. It was as if pre-ordained. He became a man possessed. It was beyond his comprehension, but he was awakened to it and it gave him courage to face even death.

In 1935 at a reunion of the famed Rainbow Division, for those of their comrades who had fallen in France in World War I, Douglas MacArthur so eloquently said:

> "They died unquestioningly, uncomplaining, with faith in their hearts and on their lips the hope that we would go on to victory....They have gone beyond the mists that blind us here, and become part of that beautiful thing we call the spirit of the

unknown soldier. In chambered temples of silence the dust of their dauntless valor sleeps, waiting in the Chancery of Heaven the final reckoning of Judgment Day. Only those are fit to live who are not afraid to die."

Courage—with faith—allowed John to confront his destiny. And when man comes to face his destiny, awareness follows, then inner peace comes, and that peace gives silent comfort when he is dying. So John Basilone's faith and courage carried him through it all, to Iwo Jima.

★   ★   ★

A GRATEFUL NATION REMEMBERS

The State of New Jersey honored Basilone with the naming of an 800-foot span bridge over the Raritan River on the New Jersey Turnpike. It was dedicated on November 30, 1951. At the dedication Marine Corps Lt. Gen. Franklin A. Hart said to the Basilone family: "We of the Marine Corps, in all humility, share your pride in him, share the esteem that time cannot destroy—and time, thank God, cannot destroy the spirit that makes a Basilone.

On December 21, 1945, less than a year after his death the Navy launched the *USS Basilone* (DDE 824). It was commissioned July 26, 1949 and decommissioned on November 1, 1977. Sadly, and shamefully, she was used as a target and sunk April 2, 1984.

On June 6, 1948, Phillip Orlando's eight-foot bronze statue of John Basilone was unveiled on Old York Road in Raritan at the west end of town where it still stands.

On February 25, 1950 a formal program was held on the *USS Basilone* commemorating the fifth anniversary of John's death at Iwo Jima. It was entitled

Presentation

of the

Portrait of the Late

Sgt. John Basilone

to the

U. S. S. Basilone (DDE-824)

by

Garrison No. 868

Army & Navy Union, U. S. A.

At Charleston Navy Yard

Boston, Mass

In November 1959, a delegation from Sante Moretti Post 1748 of the Veterans of Foreign Wars dedicated Basilone Square at Raymond Plaza, Newark, New Jersey.

In 1962, the Governor of New Jersey proclaimed July 25th as "John Basilone Day." On that day in 1962, the first of yearly ceremonies was held, as seventy-five young men from the Raritan, New Jersey, area took their Marine Corps enlistment oath in front of the John Basilone Statue.

On April 15, 1963, the Camp Basilone Display was dedicated at the International Photography Fair at the New York Colliseum.

In June 1966, the Basilone Memorial Field was named at Bridgewater-Raritan high School West in Bridgewater, New Jersey. The dedication service was held on Feb. 16, 1967 at the field house. At that service a color portrait of Basilone was unveiled. A rededication was held at the field on September 10, 2004.

In 1974, in Raritan, the John Basilone Memorial Museum was named. The museum is situated on the second floor of the town's library. Appropriately, the building itself had been the home of Raritan's Frelinghuysen family, a family whose roots go back to the American Revolution. They had been patriots and clergy alike who played an important part in our country's history. The home dates to 1740 and was declared a national historic site in 1974.

Much is to be seen of "Manila John" in his memorial room. Authentic ribbons that John Basilone was entitled to wear are displayed there.* Portraits of John are hung on the walls along with one of him wearing the Medal of Honor. A Marine officer presented the portrait to John upon his return in 1943.

Numerous photos adorn the room showing John with actor John Garfield and the great showman Danny Thomas. Original articles from Life and Parade Magazines and from Ed Sullivan are there, along with those of New Jersey historians Harry Kels and Joseph Monti.

---

* John's Medal of Honor is displayed at the Marine Corps Museum in Washington, D.C.

In 1981, the first of many John Basilone Memorial parades was held. Conceived by teacher JoAnn Liptak's 3rd Grade class in Raritan during that same year, the parades have been held each year to this date.

In 1981, signs were erected through the Borough of Raritan proclaiming the town: "Home of John Basilone, Congressional Medal of Honor recipient, USMC, Raritan, NJ"

On June 14,1999, three days after Lena's death and following the tireless efforts of Marine Silver Star winner Frank Turiace, a 17-mile stretch of the San Diego Freeway near Camp Pendleton was named, "Gunnery Sergeant John Basilone Memorial Freeway." A roadway entrance to Camp Pendleton in San Diego bears Basilone's name along with a base street at the Marine Corps Training Base at Quantico, Virginia.

Most recently, in 2006, the John Basilone U.S. Postal Stamp, a 1943 photo of Basilone in uniform bearing the insignia of the 5th Marine Division, was issued. Basilone appears on a sheet of stamps included with the most famous Marines of all time: Lejeune, Puller and Daly. It finally happened after retired Union, New Jersey, resident Peter Ippolito collected over 250,000 signatures to make it reality. An appeal to congress to support the Basilone stamp first failed, but Representative William Pascrell, Jr., a New Jersey Democrat, was able to convince twenty-nine of his colleagues to support a bill pressuring the Citizens' Stamp Advisory Committee to support the Basilone stamp. Jordan A. Jaffee, a member of the Marine Corps League's John Basilone Detachment, was frustrated at the lack of congressional support saying, "I can't believe that in this climate of patriotism, we can't even get recognition."

Through his efforts Marine Corps League detachments across the nation participated in a silent vigil with flags at American Legion and Veterans of Foreign Wars halls nationwide lowered to half-mast. From Pascrell and his co-signers, a bill * was introduced recommending to the Postmaster General that a commemorative stamp be issued honoring Basilone. Consequently, Senators Corzine, Torricelli, Kennedy and N.J. State Senator Leonard Connors co-sponsored resolutions to create the stamp. Similar resolutions were passed in Philadelphia and New York City.

Artist Charles Waterhouse, a retired Marine Colonel was at Iwo Jima also. "When John's outfit went right, my outfit went left toward Mt. Surabachi." He didn't know Basilone personally, but he remembered seeing him on base with his men. "We'd yell, 'Hey, Manila John!'" Waterhouse was so inspired by Basilone that while recuperating from wounds received on Iwo Jima, he drew a five-part cartoon strip depicting Basilone's combat action on Guadalcanal, titling it, "The

---

*107th Congress, 1st Session, H. CON. RES. 4

Fighting Marine, John Basilone." The strip includes John's landing on Iwo Jima and his death there. After the war no one was interested in anything related to the war so the cartoon was never published.

Says Waterhouse, "Inside a couple hours everybody knew he died. They got John Basilone on the airstrip. Everybody knew."

In the cartoon Waterhouse featured a popular John Basilone expression, "I'll se ya in the funnies." He would often say those words to his family in his letters to them.

On one of the walls at the John Basilone Museum hangs one of Waterhouse's paintings of John. Thus inspired by Basilone, the artist has produced artwork for various other military publications and became the Marine Corps' Artist in Residence having returned to the Marine Corps by request.

★ ★ ★

JOHN BASILONE STATUE*

In the mid-1940's Philip Orlando created several Basilone faces destroying them all as he struggled with how he should do John's eyes. Should he seek to show the "Invincible John" or should he allow the childlike fun-loving character of John to be more evident? Should a field view of John be developed within a combat setting or should the view be more formal in nature? Finally, it would be the Basilone following combat after that horrific night on Guadalcanal. Veteran Marine Michael Santoro visited Orlando as work progressed on the casting. Santoro would tell the *Plainfield Courier News*:

> I saw the original plaster cast and he asked me how authentic it was. I thought it was very authentic. A lot of (Marine) brass wanted him in some kind of uniform, a more formal uniform. But the portrayal was exactly the way we operated in the Pacific, most of the time with no shirts. It was hot and the uniforms were raggedy. I told him I thought the original statue was just exactly the way it should be. That's what he eventually carried out.

The entire monument is twelve feet high with the eight-foot statue sitting on a six-inch base. Basilone's Medal of Honor Citation is etched in a plate set into the stone mount.

---

* John's statue stands at the west end of Main Street, at the end of town, in Raritan, New Jersey, out of view of the traveling public. Businessman Ed Danberry, another tireless "Basilone Watcher" suggests moving the statue, placing it at the south end of First Avenue fronting the new Basilone Memorial Bridge that crosses the Raritan River. How very appropriate.

John and Phil had been grade school friends. Only Philip Orlando could have captured the essence of John Basilone in the great bronze statue. Only Philip Orlando could know John and only Philip Orlando would be *driven* to do the project. Having rented a second floor loft above a bank in Plainfield, New Jersey, just for the project, Orlando, with his family there with him, took on the work with loving devotion and a desire to present the spirit of John Basilone. He called both on memory and those who knew John, including John's family, to examine the hero's features and to offer their opinion and acceptance of his work as it progressed.

The boyhood comradery would yield true knowledge of John's being, and it is only boyhood's bonding that can bring insightful perspective and real knowing. Philip Orlando, another Raritan Boy, was, ironically, also the son of a tailor. He was an Army Bronze Star recipient having served in North Africa. Even in the field he sought out good clay, and there in the tundra would sculpt form and face of the soldier in the field to the amazement of his buddies and officers alike. So he truly knew the soldier.

His children played near him in a sandbox and with small tools they pretended to be daddy as they scraped and shaved the little pieces of clay he had given to them. Orlando allowed them to scratch their names into the statue's base, not concerned, for he knew he would be covering the area over with Palm fronds.

When it was completed, the critics loved it. *Monumental News* would say of it: "...a sophisticated work....done by a sculptor qualified by training to express himself with unfaltering skill and technique." The form and composition, they said, achieved "an arresting emotional appeal." The critic went on, saying that the work was not "a petrified effigy," but rather "a descriptive portrait...the work of an artist who really feels." Lastly, he said that to produce Orlando's rendition the artist had to be more than "a born genius...the formula is study, work and more study; these and a soul attuned to the nobler emotions of men."

Orlando's formal training consisted of study at the Leonardo Di Vinci Art School under the eminent Attilio Piccirilli. Later at the Art Student's League in New York City he won the coveted Earl Winthrop Award and following that he won three successive competitions at the Beaux Arts Institute becoming an assistant to American National Academy Sculptor Max Kalish.

25 years after cancer attacked Philip Orlando, he died in 1986 leaving a large collection to his wife. She donated the original thirty-four inch working model of the Basilone statue to the Basilone Museum in Raritan.

HISTORY OF THE BROWNING 30-CALIBER MACHINE GUN*
By Charles Chuck Tatum

Gunnery Sergeant John Basilone U.S.M.C., Medal of Honor was awarded to him for his actions on Guadalcanal, his Navy Cross for heroic deeds on Iwo Jima. It has left a legacy of valor unparalleled in the history of the United States Marine Corps. History has recorded his deeds on the battlefield of World War II, but his fame overshadowed one of his other contributions to warfare. John Basilone was also the inventor of the Basilone Bail.**

Sergeant Basilone was an expert on the Browning machine gun, caliber .30, M1919A4 Light Machine Gun (LMG).*** He lived and breathed machine guns, he trained marines on how to use it and how to fight with it. He fought with it [Model 1917] on Guadalcanal and Iwo Jima [Model 1919] to defeat his country's enemies.

The Browning 30-Caliber machine gun was invented by John Moses Browning (1855 to 1926) in 1900. He filed for a patent one year later, but it wasn't until 1910 that he produced a prototype. The United States War Department showed little if any interest in his new weapon.

This was a new type of automatic weapon, for Browning believed that his short-recoil design for a machine gun was superior to his earlier designs. His first machine gun known as the Colt M1895 was gas operated, a feature Browning considered one of its faults in addition to its weight and lack of mobility.

In 1917 with the clouds of war filling the skies over Europe the U.S. War Department woke up to the fact that it didn't have a good light machine gun in its arsenal. This opened the door for Browning to demonstrate his new weapon. No decision was forthcoming at this time. In April of 1917 the United States

---

* Reprinted with permisson.

** The Basilone Bail was essentially a square loop of heavy gage wire that was inserted into two of the cooling holes on the gun's perforated barrel jacket. This allowed carrying and firing the gun independent of the tripod with the left hand holding the bail so that the gunner could avoid being burned by the barrel.

*** While in the US Army Basilone was trained on the water-cooled Model 1917A1. When training with the Marines he began to use the later Model 1919A4. The Model 1919A4 air-cooled gun, along with the Basilone Bail, gave him the mobility that was to be so crucial to him at Iwo Jima. To clear up some confusion: When Basilone spoke of the "heavies" he was referring to the heavier water-cooled gun that he used on Guadalcanal. It must be remembered that the heavier water-cooled gun was primarily a defensive weapon as used, and as required for, the defense of Henderson Field. The lighter air-cooled version was used offensively at Iwo Jima. However, the Browning guns in both configurations were known as Browning Light Machine Guns (LMG) since, by definition, they utilized ammunition of .30 caliber (7.62mm). Heavy machine guns used .50 caliber (12.7mm) ammunition.

went to war and in May of the same year Browning was asked to demonstrate his design again. The test must have been successful because the War Department ordered 45,000 guns, and the Browning M1917 entered the conflict. The M1917 was water-cooled. Its use in World War I showed up some flaws. To correct these faults selected parts were made of steel instead of bronze and the newer weapon received a newly designed bottom plate and an improved water-cooled system. The new weapon was designated M1917A1. The need for a reliable machine gun on airplanes set the design parameters for an air-cooled version known as the M1918, and the later M1919 with a heavier barrel was used in tanks and armored vehicles.

It was in the 1920's that the War Department discovered how good Browning's machine gun was for groundwork, so the M1919A4 was issued. The M1919A4 tripod-mounted model was soon to supplement, and later largely replace, the M1917A1 water-cooled version. The gun was manufactured by a number of firms including Remington Arms, Winchester Arms, Westinghouse and Colt Patent Firearms.

If "necessity is the mother of invention" improvisation has to be the father. I don't know if "inventor" is the right word to ascribe to Basilone for his modification to the Browning LMG, perhaps "originator" would be more correct.

In its 1919A4 form it had served the Marines well in training and peacetime field situations, but some of its shortcomings became apparent when the 1st Marine Division invaded Guadalcanal in August of 1942. America was up off the canvas fighting back, and the LMG was ideal for a Marine rifle company's major source of firepower in the jungles of the Solomon Islands. It [the later M1919A4] was small and relatively light (gun-35.75 lbs., tripod-14 lbs.), could be carried anywhere a Marine could go and could be put into or taken out of action in a minimum of time.

★   ★   ★

CITATION FOR NAVY CROSS
JOHN BASILONE

"For extraordinary heroism while serving as a leader of a machine-gun section of Company C, 1st Battalion, 27th Marines, 5th Marine Division, in action against enemy Japanese forces on Iwo Jima in the Volcano Islands, 19 February 1945."

"Shrewdly gauging the tactical situation shortly after landing when his company's advance was held up by the concentrated fire of a heavily fortified blockhouse, Gunnery Sgt. Basilone boldly defied the smashing bambardment of heavy caliber fire to work his way around the flank and up to a position directly on top of the blockhouse and then, attacking with grenades and demolitions, single-handedly destroyed the entire hostile strong point and its defending garrison."

" Consistently daring and aggressive as he fought his way over the battletorn beach and up the sloping, gun-studded terraces toward Airfield Number One, he repeatedly exposed himself to the blasting fury of exploding shells and later in the day coolly proceeded to the aid of a friendly tank which had been trapped in an enemy mine field under intense mortar and artillery barrages, skillfully guiding the heavy vehicle over the hazardous terrain to safety, despite the overwhelming volume of hostile fire."

"In the forefront of the assault at all times, he pushed forward with dauntless courage and iron determination until, moving upon the edge of the airfield, he fell, instantly killed by a bursting mortar shell."

"Stout-hearted and indomitable, Gunnery Sgt. Basilone, by his intrepid initiative, outstanding professional skill and valiant spirit of self-sacrifice in the face of fanatic opposition, contributed materially to the advance of his company during the earlier critical period of the assault, and his unwavering devotion to duty throughout the bitter conflict was an inspiration to his comrades and reflects the highest credit upon Gunnery Sgt. Basilone and the United States Naval Service."

"He gallantly gave his life in the service of his country."

★　　★　　★

DECORATIONS AND CITATIONS, JOHN BASILONE

Congressional Medal of Honor
October 24-25, 1942, Guadalcanal

Navy Cross
February 19, 1945, Iwo Jima, Posthumous

Purple Heart
February 19, 1945, Iwo Jima, Posthumous

Presidential Unit Citation
1942 Guadalcanal
1945, Iwo Jima, Posthumous

American Defense Service Medal
1941, Culebra, Cuba

Asiatic-Pacific Campaign Medal with Two Bronze Stars
1942-1943 Guadalcanal
1945, Iwo Jima, Posthumous

World War II Victory Medal
1941-1945, Posthumous

American Campaign Medal
1945, Posthumous

New Jersey Distinguished Service Award
1951, Posthumous

★　　　★　　　★

1ST DIVISION, UNITED STATES MARINE CORPS
Motto of the 1st Division: No Better Friend, No Worse Enemy

The 1st Marine Division, one of three active duty divisions in the Marine Corps, was activated aboard the battleship *Texas* on February 1, 1941 and is the oldest, largest and most decorated with nine Presidential Unit Citations. The division boasts an active duty combat-ready force of 22,000 Marines and Sailors. Nicknamed the "Old Breed" it is under command of the I Marine Expeditionary Force (I MEF) and is headquartered at the Marine Corps Base Camp Pendleton, California.

The 1st Division is comprised of the 1st, 5th, 7th (Basilone) and 11th Marine Regiments, 1st and 3rd Light Armored Reconnaissance Battalions, 1st Tank Battalion, and 3rd Assault Amphibian Battalion. Division regiments were in existence as early as March 8, 1911 when the 1st Marines was formed at Guantanamo Bay, Cuba. The 1st participated in actions at Haiti in 1915, the Dominican Republic in 1916 and, in World War I, in the Caribbean. The 5th Marines, formed in Vera Cruz, Mexico on July 13, 1914, served in Santo Domingo in 1925 and in World War I, taking part in fifteen well known major engagements; those were Belleau Wood, Chateau and St. Mihiel.

7th Marines was activated on August 11, 1917 in Philadelphia. The 7th was placed in Cuba for the duration of World War I, then was disbanded with no reactivation until 1941. The 11th Marines was formed in January 1918 at Quantico, Virginia as a light artillery regiment, but its action in World War I was as an infantry unit. The 11th was in and out of activation twice between the world wars but was formed up again to fight in Nicaragua as an infantry unit. In 1941 it was reactivated once more as an artillery unit when it was placed within the Marine 1st Division.

1st Division battles include those of Guadalcanal, Peleliu and Okinawa in World War II, and Inchon and the Chosin Reservoir in Korea. Combat continued for the division in Vietnam, Operation Desert Storm and, to the present day, in Operation Iraqi Freedom (Operation Vigilant Resolve and Operation Phantom Fury).

Guadalcanal, the first major Pacific battle, saw the 1st Division fighting, for the first time, as a division.

BIBLIOGRAPHY

Clark, Johnnie M., *Gunner's Glory,* New York: Bantam Books, 2004

Cutter, Phyllis Basilone, *The John Basilone Story,* Somerville, New Jersey: Somerset Messenger Gazette, 1962

Davis, Burke, *Marine, The Life of Chesty Puller,* New York: Bantam Books, 1964

Frank, Richard B., *Guadalcanal,* New York: Penguin Group, 1992

Griffith, Samuel B. II, *The Battle for Guadalcanal,* Chicago: University of Illinois Press, 2000

Hammel, Eric, *Guadalcanal, Starvation Island,* Pacifica, California: Pacifica Press, 1987

Hoyt, Edwin P., *Closing the Circle, War in the Pacific: 1945,* New York: Van Nostrand Reinhold Co., Inc.,1982

Keegan, John, *The Second World War,* New York: Penguin Group, 1990

Leckie, Robert, *Challenge for the Pacific,* New York: Doubleday and Co., 1965

Leckie, Robert, *Helmet For My Pillow,* New York: Bantam Books, 1992

Leckie, Robert, *Strong Men Armed,* New York: Random House, 1962

Lord, Walter, *Lonely Vigil, Coast Watchers of the Solomons,* New York: Viking Press, 1977

MacArthur, Douglas, *Reminiscences,* New York: Crest Books, Fawcet World Library, 1964

Manchester, William, *American Caesar,* New York: Dell Publishing, 1978

McMillan, George, *The Old Breed: A History of the First Marine Division in World War II,* Nashville, Tennessee: The Battery Press, 1949

Newcomb, Richard F., *Iwo Jima*, New York: Bantam Books, 1988

Owens, William J., *Green Hell, The Battle for Guadalcanal*, Central Point, Oregon: Hellgate Press, 1999

Prosner, Jim, *I'm, Staying With My Boys, The Heroic Life of Sgt. John Basilone, USMC*,
South Carolina: Light Bearer Communications, 2004

Richter, Don, *Where the Sun Stood Still, the Story of Sir Jacob Vouza and the Guadalcanal Campaign*, Agoura Hills, California: TAWE Press, 1992

Ross, Bill D., *Iwo Jima, Legacy of Valor*, New York: Vanguard Press, 1985

Shaw, Henry I. Jr., *First Offensive: The Marine Campaign for Guadalcanal*, Washington, DC: U.S. History and Museums Division, 1992

Stokesbury, James L., *A Short History of World War II*, New York: Morrow Quill Paperbacks, 1972

Tatum, Charles W., *Iwo Jima, Red Blood Black Sand, Pacific Apocalypse*, Stockton,
California: Charles W. Tatum Publishing, 1995

Tregaskis, Richard, *Guadalcanal Diary*, New York: Random House, 1943

Wheeler, Richard, *Iwo*, New York: Kensington Publishing Corp., 1980

Whyte, Wiliam H., *A Time of War*, New York: Fordham University Press, 2000

Mother's Day Greeting by Western Union

```
NAK56 FT=GI GOVERNORSISLAND NY MAY 8
MRS BAISLONE=
       113 FIRST AVE RARITAN NJ=

ALL MY LOVE GOES TO YOU MOTHER DEAR ON THIS MOTHERS DAY=
     JOHNNY.
          1244P
```

Christmas Dinner
December 25, 1938

MERRY CHRISTMAS AND HAPPY NEW YEAR

Company "D"
Thirty First Infantry
Manila, P. I.

ROSTER

COMPANY "D", THIRTY FIRST INFANTRY
POST OF MANILA - MANILA, P.I.

COMPANY COMMANDER
Captain James R. Simpson

LIEUTENANTS
1st Lieut. Paul J. Bryer   2nd Lieut. Walter C. Hyzer

FIRST SERGEANT
William J. Solenay (act'g)

SUPPLY SERGEANT   **MESS SERGEANT**
Herbert L. Crowley   Robert W. Podvin

COMPANY CLERK   **COMPANY MECHANIC**
R. H. Morgan   Wilton J. Swenson

COOKS

James Baker   Don D. Clark   John J. Cook Jr.   James D. Johnson

SERGEANTS

Leonard O. Erickson   William M. Hannah   John J. Lally   Jesse F. Price

CORPORALS

Howard C. Barnes   Joseph A. Miller   Morris Shaffer   Robert B. Sizemore
Joseph H. Devlin   Bart J. Sockle

PRIVATES FIRST CLASS

John Basilone   Evlyn Dempsey   Patrick F. Helm   Robert R. Powell
Delmar D. Bennett   Walter H. Doores   Clarence P. Lofing   Frederick W. Rabe
James L. Crunk   James Drozda   William H. Marshall   Clarence C. Tarr
Nathan B. Deaton   James A. Hunt   Richard E. Olson   Walter L. Temple

PRIVATES

Alfred F. Anderson   Jim Cornett   William T. Harrison   Sebastian J. Nys
Olaf Bakken   Cecil R. Cottingham   Herman W. Hislope   Antonio F. Ottaviano
John R. Bell   Paul Dashkovitz   Uino L. Hudson   Samuel Samples
Scott Brogan   Herbert L. Dickson   George W. King   Walter T. Wenner
Frank M. Brown Jr.   Harold F. Duncan   Franklin L. Kline   Donald E. West
Otis L. Brown   Edmund Forsythe   Elliott Martin   Milton M. Wexler
Floyd W. Cardinal   Eugene D. Freeman   Lester J. Meiss   Walter A. Willis
Elmer C. Casper   Sebastian Gibilisco   William R. Miller   John Witzman
Paul L. Clark   Melvin E. Harris   James L. Moore   Russell A. Wyatt
Clarence E. Copeland

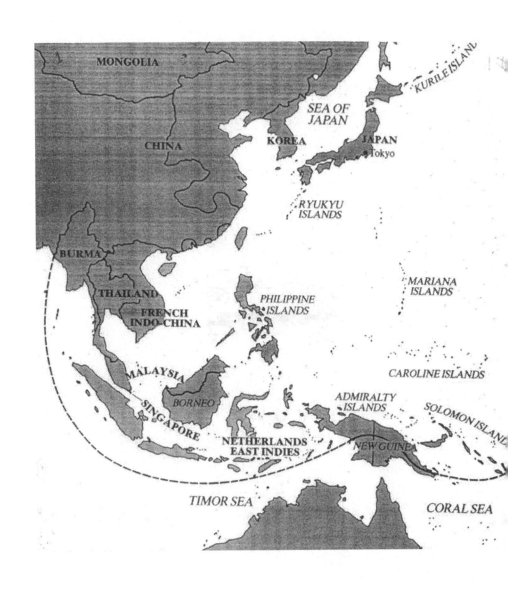

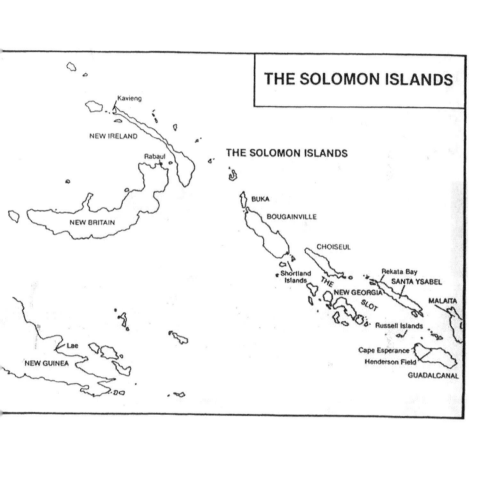

THE SOLOMON ISLANDS

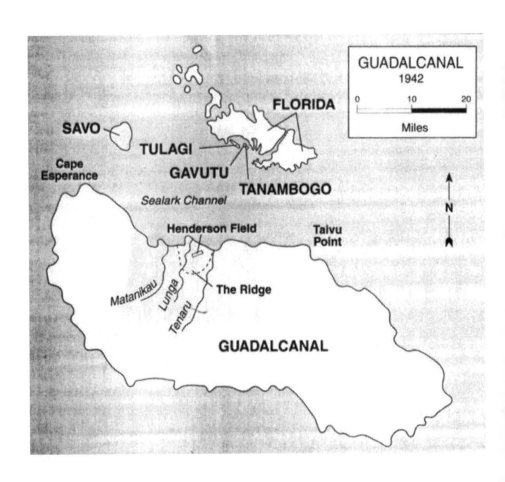

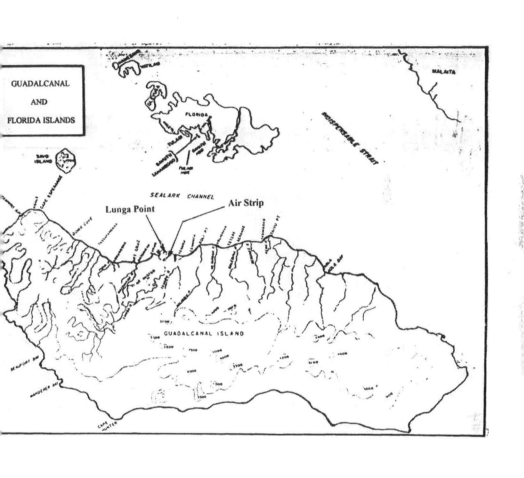

GUADALCANAL
AND
FLORIDA ISLANDS

MALAITA

FLORIDA

SEALARK CHANNEL

Lunga Point   Air Strip

GUADALCANAL ISLAND

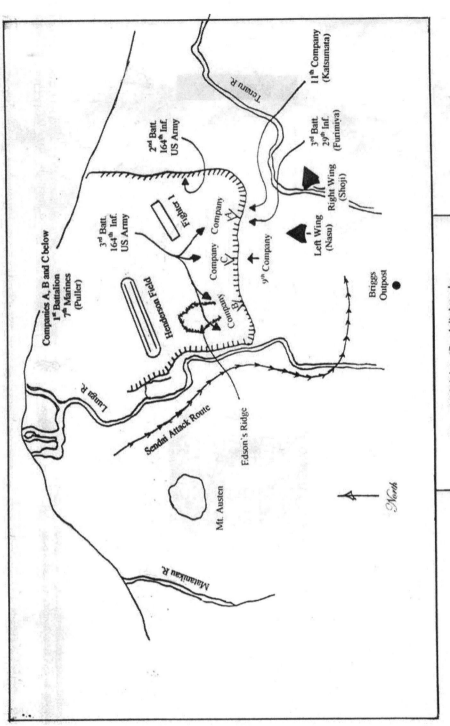

Second Division (Sendai) Attacks
Night of October 24-25

Basilone commands machine gunners in Company C

Guadalcanal

Left: Carrying wounded.
Below: During a lull in the
fighting, a Marine machine
gunner takes a break. .30
caliber light machine gun in
position. Sub-machine gun
at his knee.

Department of Defense (USMC) Photo 13628

Guadalcanal
Howitzer Crew

At top: Presentation of Medal of Honor. Basilone is fourth from left. General Vandegrift is first with his aide behind.

Below: John at a press conference, New York City.

At top: On the bond tour with actress Virginia Gray
Below: John as a baby in 1917, seated, with brothers and sisters

At top: John, fourth from left, at home after Guadalcanal.
Below: John, bottom left, with buddies, probably at Hilo.

John, at left, with buddies

At top: John with his priest friends. Unknown location. Below: John doing a re-enactment.

John drove a truck for Gaburo's Laundry before joining the Army.

Showing his Medal of Honor to his buddies.

Rebuilding a machine gun while blindfolded

John, at left, with Ed Sullivan, right, on CBS radio.

Dora Basilone

John with his family after receiving the Medal of Honor

John and actress Virginia Albritton following the Basilone Day Parade

John's medal is examined by one of his nephews

The crowd at the Basilone Day ceremonies

The town dignitaries greet John on his first trip home.
Every county sent delegates to the celebration.

Basilone Day Parade.
John's buddy, Pfc. Stephen Helstowski, Pittsfield, Mass., up front.
Basilone said of Helstowski: "He prayed in the same foxhole with me on Guadalcanal."
Female Marines marched beside the car.

Courtesy Somerset Messenger Gazette

At top: John reaching out to friends on Basilone Day.
Below: At St. Ann's Church, Raritan, prior to the parade.

Father
Paul
Bradley

At top: John and Lena and wedding party with Fr. Paul Bradley
Below: Lena, bottom row, second from left, with fellow female Marines

John's brother Carlo, daughter Carolyn, and wife Ann, 1942

Cutting the cake

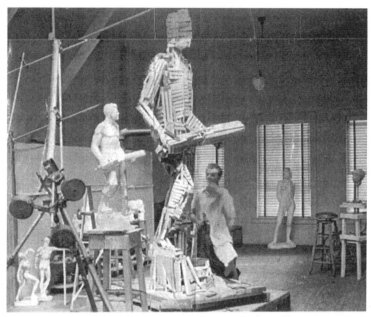

Sculptor Phil Orlando at work on Basilone statue in his studio in Plainfield, NJ.

John Basilone statue as it stands today

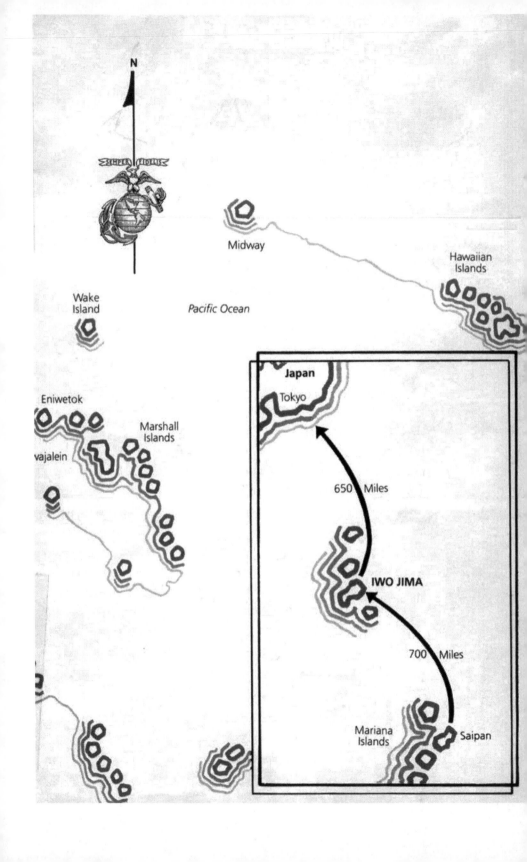

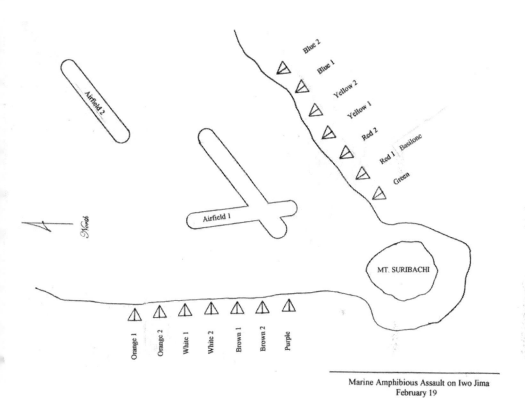

Marine Amphibious Assault on Iwo Jima
February 19

Marine amphibious assault on Iwo Jima, Feb. 19, 1945

LOUIS R. LOWERY

Early Fifth Division wave under heavy fire in quagmire of sand on Red Beach 1

At top: H-Hour plus forty minutes. 27th Regiment jumps off to cross island at base of Suribachi.
Below: H-Hour plus twenty minutes. 4th Division pinned down on Yellow Beach 1.

Hero's grave. March, 1945. Marine Sargeant Francis Halota of Lackawana, New York, smoothes earth about the cross marking the temporary burial place of Marine Gunnery Sergeant John Basilone (Fifth Division Cemetery, Iwo Jima). On April 20, 1948, Basilone's body was laid to rest at Arlington National Cemetery.

John Basilone's grave at Arlington

Destroyer USS Basilone

Lena Basilone christens the USS Basilone

After presenting orchids to the ladies of the Basilone family, Commander Mark E. Dennett welcomes the family aboard the USS Basilone.

Presentation of the colors, USS Basilone.
Lena Basilone just to the left of the gun.

Author with Lena Basilone at her home in Lakewood, CA.

Browning .30 caliber machine gun, model mM1919A4

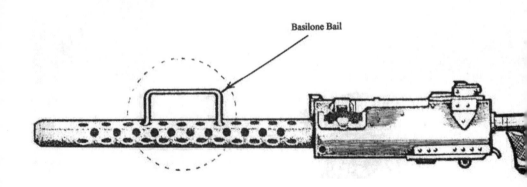

Model 1919A4 machine gun with Basilone Bail attached

1st Division patch

OATH AND CERTIFICATE OF ENLISTMENT
THE UNITED STATES OF AMERICA

STATE OF **New York**

CITY, TOWN, OR MILITARY POST **NYPE Brooklyn** ss:

I, * **John** (None) **Basilone** **6873706 RAR**
(First name) (Middle name) (Last name) (serial number)

a citizen of the United States born in **Buffalo** **New York**
(City, town, or county) (State or country)

on **Nov. 4, 1916**, and now aged **22** years and **10** months, by occupation a **Truck driver**
(Month, day, and year)

having last served in the **Regular Army**
(Regular Army or Regular Army Reserve)

for **3 yrs and 7 months**, such service terminating by honorable discharge on
(Years and months)

September 7, 1939, as **Private**, character **Excellent**
(Month, day, and year) (Grade)

from **Infantry, Unassigned**, at **O.D.&R. Depot, Brooklyn, N.Y.**
(Organization or arm or service)

and whose home address is **113 1st Avenue, Raritan, New Jersey**
(Street and number, city or town, and State)

do hereby acknowledge to have voluntarily _____ enlisted this † **7th** day of **September** , 19 **39**

as a **Private First Class, Infantry**, in the Regular Army Reserve, for
(Grade and arm or service)

a period of 4 years under the conditions prescribed by law unless sooner discharged by proper authority, and subject to active duty immediately upon the declaration of an emergency by the President of the United States; and do also agree to accept from the United States such bounty, pay, rations, and clothing as are or may be established by law. And I do solemnly swear (or affirm) that I will bear true faith and allegiance to the United States of America; that I will serve them honorably and faithfully against all their enemies whatsoever, and that I will obey the orders of the President of the United States, and the orders of the officers appointed over me, according to the Rules and Articles of War.

(Signature) ‡ _____ *John Basilone*

I CERTIFY that the above oath was subscribed and duly sworn to before me this † **7th** day of **September** , A. D. 19 **39**

I further certify that this soldier was minutely inspected by me previous to his subscription to the oath; that I found him entirely sober and in full possession of all his mental faculties; that to the best of my judgment and belief he fulfills all legal requirements, and that in enlisting him into the service of the United States I have strictly observed the regulations which govern the recruiting service. I further certify that the above oath, as filled in, was read to the applicant before his subscription thereto.

_____ *Harry W. Benson*, **Harry W. Benson, Major, Cavalry**, Recruiting Officer.
(Signature) (Name typed) (Grade and organization) (Summary Court)

* Carefully compare with name at top of page 1.
† The dates in the oath and certificate must be the same.
‡ The signature must be identical with that subscribed to Declaration of Applicant.

NEAREST RELATIVE AND PERSON TO BE NOTIFIED IN CASE OF EMERGENCY

Nearest relative **Dora Basilone**
(Other than wife or minor child) (Name in full)

Relationship **Mother** Address **113 1st Avenue** **Raritan,** **N.J.**
(Number and street or rural route; if none, so state) (City, town, or post office) (State or country)

Person to be notified in case of emergency **Salvatore Basilone**
(Name in full)

Relationship **Father** Address **113 1st Avenue** **Raritan,** **N.J.**
(If friend, so state) (Number and street or rural route; if none, so state) (City, town, or post office) (State or country)

PRIOR SERVICE

Co D 16 Inf., from **Feb. 5** , 19 **36** to **May 10** , 19 **37**
(Organization or arm or service)

Discharged as **Pvt.** ; **Ex** ; by reason of **Conv. of Govt.**
(Grade) (Character)

Inf. Unasgd, from **May 11** , 19 **37** to **Sept. 7** , 19 **39**
(Organization or arm or service)

Discharged as **Pvt.** ; **Ex** ; by reason of **Conv. of Govt.**
(Grade) (Character)

_____ , from , 19 , to , 19
(Organization or arm or service)

Discharged as _____ ; ; by reason of
(Grade) (Character)

FINGERPRINTS
(Right hand)

1. THUMB	2. INDEX	3. MIDDLE	4. RING	5. LITTLE

(2)

5-16158

ENLISTMENT RECORD
REGULAR ARMY RESERVE

Basilone   John   (None)   6873706 RAR   White

(Last name)   113 1st Avenue   (Middle name)   (serial number)   Sept 1939   New Jers

Home address .... N.Y.P.E. Brooklyn, N.Y. .... (City, town, or post office) .... (County) ... 39 (State) .. Pvt 1c

* Enlisted at ...., on the .... 7th .... day of .... September .... 19...... (In the grade

* by   Harry W. Benson, Major, Cavalry   Infantry   to serve 4 ye

     for .... (Arm or service) ....

Last enlisted service in the Regular Army or Regular Army Reserve:

Inf., Unasgd   September 7, 1939   Private

(Company, regiment, and arm or service) ..... Date of discharge .... (In the grade of)

* Care will be taken to make place and date of enlistment and name of enlisting officer the same as in oath.

DECLARATION OF APPLICANT

I,   John Basilone , desiring to ...... enlist in the Regular Army Reserve of
United States for the term of 4 years under the conditions prescribed by law, do declare that I am a citizen of the United Sta
of the legal age to enlist (or reenlist) and believe myself to be physically qualified to perform the duties of an able-bodied soldier;
I do further declare that I am of good habits and character in all respects and have never been discharged from the service of
United States or any other service on account of disability or through sentence of either a civil or military court, nor discharged f
any service, civil or military, except with good character and under honorable conditions, and for the reasons given by me to
recruiting officer prior to this enlistment or reenlistment. I am not now a member of the Army, Navy, Marine Corps, Natio
Guard, or Coast Guard in an active, inactive, reserve, or retired status.

Given at ... N.Y.P.E., Brooklyn, N.Y. ... this ... 7th ... day of ... September ... 19 ... 39

Signature   *Harry W. Benson*   Major, Cavalry   *Basilone*

    (First name)   (Middle name)   (Last name)

Witness: .... (To be witnessed by recruiting officer)   (Grade and organization)

PHYSICAL EXAMINATION AT PLACE OF ENLISTMENT
(MADE BY AN AUTHORIZED MEDICAL EXAMINER)
(Applicant stripped. See Instruction 6)

Eyes ... Brown ... Hair ... D. Brown ... Complexion ... Ruddy ... Height ... 68 ... inches. Weight ... 150 ... pou

Girth of chest (at nipples): At expiration ... 36 ... inches. At inspiration ... 39 ... inc

General examination (physique, skin, head, chest, abdomen, extremities, etc.) ... Normal

General surgical conditions (including hernia, hemorrhoids, varicose veins, and state of abdominal wall and viscera) ... Normal

Organs of locomotion (including bones, joints, muscles, and tendons) ... Normal

Genito-urinary system ... Normal

Vision: Right eye 20/20   Left eye 20/20   Eye conditions ... Normal

Hearing: Right ear 20/20   Left ear 20/20   Ear, nose, and throat conditions ... Normal

Teeth: Upper 8 7 6 5 4 3 2 1   1 2 3 4 5 6 7 8   (Strike out those that are missing; circle those that
Lower 8 7 6 5 4 3 2 1   1 2 3 4 5 6 7 8   be restored)

Mouth and gums ... Normal

Cardio-vascular system (including functioning of kidneys) ... Normal

Lungs ... Normal

Neuro-psychiatric examination ... Normal

‡ Remarks ... None

†I CERTIFY that I have carefully examined the applicant and have correctly recorded the results of the examination; and tha
the best of my judgment and belief, *he is mentally and physically qualified for service in the Army of the United States,

Place ... NYPE., BKLYN., N.Y.   Signature: *Chas P Ward*   CHAS. P. WARD,
                                CAPTAIN, M.C.

Date ... September 6, 1939   Name typed or stamped: .... , Medical Cor
                                           (Grade)

*Strike out clause not applicable.   †Strike out word not applicable.   ‡See Instruction 7.

W. D., A. G. O. Form No. 181—January 20, 1939.   (1)   3—10820

Honorable Discharge

from

The Army of the United States

HEADQUARTERS FORT JAY, N.Y.
May 11, 1937.

Reenlisted by me this 11th day
of May, 1937, to serve three (3)
years.

EDWARD J. M. GLAVIN,
1st Lt. 16th Infantry,
Asst. Retg. Officer.

TO ALL WHOM IT MAY CONCERN:

This is to Certify, That* *John Basilone*
† 6873706 Pvt Co D 16th Inf atchd to Serv Co 16th Inf

THE ARMY OF THE UNITED STATES, as a TESTIMONIAL OF HONEST
AND FAITHFUL SERVICE, is hereby HONORABLY DISCHARGED from the
military service of the UNITED STATES by reason of † Section X-615-360
"Convnof Govt"

Said *John Basilone* was born
in *Buffalo* in the State of *New York*
When enlisted he was 19 ¾ years of age and by occupation a *Truck Driver*
He had *Brown* eyes, *Brown* hair, *Ruddy* complexion, and
was *5* feet *8* inches in height.

Given under my hand at *Fort Jay New York* this
10th day of *May*, one thousand nine hundred and *Thirty Seven*

C R Boyd

Major 16th Infantry

, company, regiment, and arm of service; as "1620302"; "Corporal, Company A, 1st Infantry"; "Sergeant, Quartermaster Corps."
n of service, give number, date, and source of order or full description of authority therefor.
3—2164

O: 55

RECRUITING OFFICE
NEW YORK
PORT OF EMBARKATION
BROOKLYN, N.Y.
Date SEP 7 1939
This soldier enlisted by
me this date to serve a
period of four (4) years
in the REGULAR ARMY
RESERVE.

Harry W. Benson, Major, Car.
Recruiting Officer

11 July, 1940.

Reenl. by me this date

E.E. SULLIVAN,
Lt-Comdr. (MC), USN,
Asst. USMC Rect'g.Of

Honorable Discharge

from

The Army of the United States

TO ALL WHOM IT MAY CONCERN:

This is to Certify, That* *John Basilone*

† *6893706, Private Inf. Unasgd.*

THE ARMY OF THE UNITED STATES, as a TESTIMONIAL OF HONEST AND FAITHFUL SERVICE, is hereby HONORABLY DISCHARGED from the military service of the UNITED STATES by reason of ‡ *Conv of Gov*
par 10 (b) AR 615-210

Said *John Basilone* was born in *Buffalo*, in the State of *N.Y.*

When enlisted he was *20 6/12* years of age and by occupation a *Truck-driver*

He had *Brown* eyes, *Black* hair, *Dark* complexion, and was *5* feet *8 1/2* inches in height.

Given under my hand at *Q.M.R. Depot Bklyn N.Y.* this *7th* day of *September* one thousand nine hundred and *Thirty nine*,

George Chase Lewis

Colonel Infantry
Commanding.

and arm or service; as "1620302"; "Corporal, Company A, 1st Infantry"; "Sergeant, Quartermaster Corps."
er, date, and source of order or full description of authority therefor.

W.D.,

Honorable Discharge

from the

Regular Army Reserve

TO ALL WHOM IT MAY CONCERN:

This is to Certify, That * _____ John Basilone _____

_____ 6873706, R.A.R., Pvt.lcl, Infantry _____

THE REGULAR ARMY RESERVE, as a TESTIMONIAL OF HONEST AND FAITHFUL SERVICE, is hereby HONORABLY DISCHARGED from the military service of the UNITED STATES by reason of ‡ enlistment in the United States Marine Corps

Said _____ John Basilone _____ was born in _____ Buffalo _____, in the State of _____ New York _____ When enlisted he was 22 10/12 years of age and by occupation a _____ Truck driver _____ He had _____ Brown _____ eyes, Dark brown _____ hair, Ruddy _____ complexion, and was _____ 5 _____ feet _____ 8 _____ inches in height.

Given under my hand at Hq. 3rd Corps Area, Baltimore, Maryland, this 10th day of _____ July _____, one thousand nine hundred and _____ forty,

By command of Major General PARSONS:

C. C. B. Warden

Captain, (Inf) A.G.D.,
Assistant Adjutant General

Adjutant General.

* Insert name; as, "John J. Doe."
† Insert Army serial number, grade, and arm or service; as "1620302 RAR"; "Private, Infantry"; "Private, Quartermaster Corps."
‡ If discharged prior to expiration of service, give number, date, and source of order or full description of authority therefor.

W.D., A. G. O. Form No. 185
    July 1, 1938

United States Marine Corps

First Battalion, Seventh Marines
First Marine Division, Fleet Marine Force
Marine Barracks, Parris Island, S. C.

15 May, 1941

JOHN BASILONE

by the direction of the Major General Commandant, is hereby appointed a

CORPORAL

in the UNITED STATES MARINE CORPS, and he is therefore carefully and diligently to discharge the duties of that position by doing and performing all manner of things thereunto belonging. I do strictly charge and require all Non-commissioned Officers and others under his command to be obedient to his orders, and he is to observe and follow such orders and directions from time to time as he shall receive from his Commanding Officer or other superior officers set over him, according to the rules and discipline of the Navy.

TEMPORARY WARRANT

Auth: MGC 1tr to CG 2165-15/5-1 over AV-wrk dated 14 May, 1941

Lieutenant Colonel, U. S. M. C.,
First Battalion
Commanding 7th Marines

No. -1-
LOWEST NUMBER OF SAME
DATE TAKES RANK.

(ORIGINAL)

4—6851 U. S. GOVERNMENT PRINTING OFFICE

N. M. C. 1150—A&I

United States Marine Corps

First Battalion, Seventh Marines,
First Marine Division, Fleet Marine Force,
Marine Barracks, New River, N. C.

January 23, 1942.

JOHN BASILONE (287506)

by the direction of the Major General Commandant, is hereby appointed a

SERGEANT

in the UNITED STATES MARINE CORPS, and he is therefore carefully and diligently to discharge the duties of that position by doing and performing all manner of things thereunto belonging. I do strictly charge and require all Non-commissioned Officers and others under his command to be obedient to his orders, and he is to observe and follow such orders and directions from time to time as he shall receive from his Commanding Officer or other superior officers set over him, according to the rules and discipline of the Navy.

TEMPORARY WARRANT

Auth: MGC ltr 2165-15/5-1 over AV-ehk, dated 21Jan42.

L. B. PULLER,

MAJOR U. S. M. C.,
FIRST BATTALION,
Commanding SEVENTH MARINES.

No. -1-
LOWEST NUMBER OF SAME
DATE TAKES RANK.

(ORIGINAL)

4—8951 U. S. GOVERNMENT PRINTING OFFICE

237508

BASILONE

John

BORN: 4 November 1916

AT: Buffalo, N. Y.

NEXT OF KIN: Salvatore Basilone – Father

113 First Ave., Raritan, N. J.

enlistment extended ~~two~~ yrs *7-9* JUL 1 3 1940

ENLISTED: 11 July 1940

AT: Baltimore, Md.

5 Feb 36-10 May 37 Army-EXCELLENT
11 May 37- 7 Sep 39 ARMY-EXCELLENT
8 Sep 39-10 Jul 40 USAR-INACTIVE

MB, Quantico, Va. CO. D, 1st 5th MAR FMF

Appointment

...ST CLASS SEP 1

ABOARD "McCawley SEP 2 8 1940

Guantanamo Bay, Cuba ASHORE OCT 2 1940

Jd CO. D, 1st BN. 7TH MARINES, FMF. JAN 1 1941

Jd CO. D, 1st BN. 1st Marines FMF MAR 1 1941

AT Parris Is., S.C. APR 1 9 1941 Via "Geo. F. Elliott"

Temporary warrant
CORPORAL MAY 15 1941

Furlo MAY / 3 1941 to MAY 3 1 1941 to JUN 1 1941

Jd CO. D, 1st BN. 7TH MARINES, FMF. MAY 2 9 1941

ABOARD "HARRY LEE" JUN 7 1941 to JUL 2 3 1941

ABOARD "FULLER" JUL 2 4 1941 to AUG 1 3 1941

AT MB. New River, N. C. SEP 3 0 1941

Temporary Warrant
SERGEANT - LINE JAN 2 3 1942

Furlo NOV 1 9 1941 to NOV 2 6 1941

In the Field MAY 8 1942

...OON SGT. LINE NOV 2 1942

over

TEMPORARY
PLATOON SGT.   LINE   JUN - 1 1943

Hd. & Sup't Co., 2nd Prot. Co.   27 1943
                    Via Rochambeau

Jd. 3/4 BD. MB. Nyd. Wash. D. C.   AUG 3/ 1943

2d Guard Co. MBNYd. Wash. D. C.   DEC 29 1943

TEMPORARY
GUNNERY SGT.   / LINE   MAR - 8 1944

Jd. Hd.&Ser.Co. 27 3/4 Gunners FMF   JAN 17 194:

Jo. Hq.Co.   1st Bn. 27 Mar, FMF   JAN 26 1944

In The Field   AUG 12 1944
                 Via Baxter

Killed in action   FEB 1 9 1945

Buried in grave #1, Row 3, Plot
1, 5th Mar. Div. Cemetery, Iwo
Jima, V. I.

m. J. M.

ADDRESS GIVEN ON DISCHARGE:

Printed and bound by PG in the USA